THE GUN CULTURE AND ITS ENEMIES

Edited by
William R. Tonso

FIRST EDITION

The Second Amendment Foundation is a non-profit educational foundation dedicated to promoting a better understanding about our constitutional heritage to privately own and possess firearms. For more information about activities, write to Second Amendment Foundation, James Madison Building, 12500 N.E. Tenth Place, Bellevue, Washington 98005. Telephone 206-454-7012.

This book is distributed by Merril Press, P.O. Box 1682, Bellevue, Washington 98009. Additional copies of this book may be ordered from Merril Press at $9.95 each.

Library of Congress Cataloging-in-Publication Data.

The Gun Culture and its Enemies/edited by William R. Tonso.
p.
Includes bibliographical references.
1. Gun control -- United States. 2 Firearms ownership --
United States. 3. Fireams -- Law and legislation -- United States.
I. Tonso, William R. II. Second Amendment Foundation.
HV7436,G87 1989
363.3′ 3′ 0973 -- dc20   89-13434
ISBN 0-936783-05-2: $9.95   CIP
Printed in United States of America

THE GUN CULTURE AND ITS ENEMIES

Edited by
William R. Tonso

Published by
Second Amendment Foundation

Distributed By **MERRIL PRESS**
Bellevue, Washington

To my parents, Eva and Joe Tonso, my wife, Beverley,
and my fellow contributors to this book.

TABLE OF CONTENTS

INTRODUCTION

The objectives of *The Gun Culture and Its Enemies* are to provide insight into what has been called the American "gun culture," and also to provide insight into the nature, dimensions, and various manifestations of that culture's conflict with what has been called the "adversary culture." Scholarly investigations of these phenomena have barely begun: hence the rationale for this book.

Outside of the gun-hobbyist and outdoor publications, almost everything written about the widespread civilian possession of firearms in the United States deals with the related issues of gun crime and gun control. Until the mid-1970s, scholarly treatments of American firearms ownership generally followed the journalistic lead unquestioningly; consequently, this scholarly work tended to take too much for granted and to be anti-gun and pro gun control. Since that time, however, a number of scholarly books and articles have appeared that not only question the existence of a clear-cut link between the widespread civilian possession of guns and the high levels of violent crime in the United States, but also to question the desirability and utility of extreme forms of gun control. While the main focus of these works that challenge the intellectual (defined broadly) community's conventional wisdom on guns has still been on crime and control, some of them, such as *Under the Gun: Weapons, Crime and Violence in America,* by James D. Wright, Peter H. Rossi, and Kathleen Daly, touch on broader cultural phenomena that have shaped the gun controversy in this country, and in doing so they have relativized this controversy. The same holds true for many of the chapters in *Firearms and Violence: Issues of Public Policy* edited by Don B. Kates, Jr. Only two books concentrate primarily on shedding light on the American attachment to firearms, however, and only a handful of book chapters and scholarly and popular articles have explored the various manifestations of the conflict between those who cherish this attachment and those, many of whom are to be found in media and academic circles, who reject it.

My own *Gun and Society: The Social and Existential Roots of the American Attachment to Firearms,* a phenomenologically-oriented, cross-cultural, social-historical work that rarely gets "up close and personal" is one of the two aforementioned books. The other book is *Gun People,* by Patrick Carr, with photographs by George W. Gardener, and it presents over sixty full-page photographs of individual American gun users, each accompanied by a one-page commentary expressing that user's feelings concerning guns — "up close and personal," but brief and not analytical apart from the editor's introduction. The last chapter of *The Gun in America: The Origins of a National Dilemma,* by Lee Kennett and James LaVerne Anderson, introduced the culture-conflict aspect of the gun issue to the scholarly world, and Chapter IV of *Magnum Force Lobby: The National Rifle Association Fights Gun Control,* by Edward F. Leddy, describes the ideological groundings of this conflict. However, while complementing the gun-culture works mentioned above, *The Gun Culture and Its Enemies* goes beyond any works yet published in examining the everyday overall impact culture conflict has had on the debate over gun control and on the media treatment of that debate.

The Gun Culture and Its Enemies is a collection of papers that in their original forms have been presented at the national meetings of the Popular Culture and American Culture Association from 1986 through 1988. All of these papers illuminate some aspect or other of the traditional gun culture or its conflict with critics of traditional American culture in general, some of whom have come to be seen as subscribing to an adversary culture. As can be seen from their biographical sketches, all of the authors of these papers-turned-chapters have academic or legal credentials, but it should be noted that almost all of us also have insider knowledge of the world of guns. Though this collection is not intended to be a pro-gun or anti-control polemic, its contributors all know and appreciate the gun culture, and criticisms of the conventional media and scholarly treatments of this culture surface in a number of our offerings. Nevertheless, we all hope that anyone, layman, professional, or scholar, even remotely interested in the gun issue specifically, or in the various manifestations of the broader cultural conflict between what have been called bedrock (small-town and rural) America and cosmopolitan (urban, upper-middle class) America find something of value in this book. Two of the book's chapters are rare indeed, incidentally, because they have been written by a Canadian and explore the Canadian extensions of the gun culture.

The Gun Culture and Its Enemies is divided into two parts containing seven chapters each. Part I's chapters focus on various aspects of the gun culture itself, while Part II's chapters focus on various aspects of this culture's conflicts with its enemies. Written informally with magazine publication rather than scholarly presentation in mind (footnotes have been added), Chapter 1 is mine and serves as something of an extended introduction. Through this autobiographical piece I have attempted to explain my own practical, recreational, and symbolic enthusiasms for firearms by introducing the reader to the people, places, and times, the popular culture, historical events, and various concerns that fostered my acquisition of these enthusiasms. I hope that this chapter will help the reader to understand why I was so impressed by the following Popular Culture and American Culture presentations that I felt the need to bring them together under one cover in book form.

What happens when the police stand on one side of a political fence and you and yours stand on the other side? Sociologist and social activist John Salter, a product of the gun culture of the American Southwest, gives a very vivid and personal account of what can happen under these conditions in Chapter 2, "Social Justice Community Organizing and the Necessity of Protective Firearms." Salter's is another rather informal piece, and through it he tells the seldom-told story of the part that guns (legally or otherwise possessed) played in the peaceful efforts by blacks to acquire their civil rights in the rural and small-town South and the urban North.

Can carrying firearms for personal protection be justified in the modern urban world? New York parole-officer-turned-sociologist Edward Leddy, a product of the non-gun culture of the urban Northeast, thinks so for reasons that he puts forth in

Chapter 3, "The Ownership and Carrying of Personal Firearms and Reduction of Crime Victimization." Even when the police are dedicated and not political enemies of the sort with which Salter often had to contend, they cannot be everywhere at once.

What happens when the surviving strains of the American dissenting and libertarian traditions come into conflict with our changing, modern, bureaucratic society? The rules and regulations of this bureaucratic society are simply, and often enough in a principled fashion, violated, as historian Roy Wortman describes in Chapter 4, "Aspects of Survival Hunting: Resistance and Defiance as Assertion and Autonomy," his analysis of a principled poacher's how-to handbook.

Since the principled poacher Wortman puts into sociohistorical context hunts to put food on his table, as many legal hunters still do in North America, Chapter 4 along with Chapters 2 and 3 of this book deal with the practical or tool use of guns, though there is certainly a playful side to poaching, an activity that neither Wortman nor I endorse. But the last three chapters of Part I focus on the recreational and symbolic aspects of gun ownership and use. Sociologist Barbara Stenross, who is not a gun-culture product, attempted to penetrate the gun world through in-depth interviews with 43 "recreationists," and her findings are reported in Chapter 5, "The Meaning of Guns: Hunters, Shooters, and Gun Collectors." Sociologist A.D. Olmsted, on the other hand, is not only a gun-culture product but a Western Canadian gun-culture product; consequently, his Chapter 6, "Gun Ownership as Serious Leisure," complements the Stenross chapter and also gives the United States reader an occasional enticing glimpse of the world of guns north of the border. Chapter 7, "Gun Collecting in Western Canada: The Influence of Popular Culture and History," is also by Olmsted, and in it he goes beyond the glimpse of the Canadian gun culture he provides in the previous chapter to present a fascinating insider's perspective on part of that culture and how it has been affected by the historical and popular-cultural West south of the Canadian border.

Are gun enthusiasts compensating for their sexual inadequacies, as the more Freudian-inclined among the anti-gunners often claim? This is the question addressed by law-professor-turned-civil-liberties-attorney Don B. Kates, Jr. and psychology graduate student Nicole Varzos in Chapter 8, "Aspects of the Priapic Theory of Gun Ownership," the first chapter of Part II of this book. And Kates and Varzos essentially conclude that even Freud would have problems accepting this explanation for the interest in guns. Of course, one could just as well ask the questions, "Who benefits and how do they benefit from marking off as pariahs those, gun enthusiasts or otherwise, with whom they disagree, and how do pariah groups respond to their negative labels?" And these are the questions criminologist F. Frederick Hawley explores in Chapter 9, "Culture Conflict and the Ideology of Pariah Groups: The *Weltanschauung* of Gun Owners, Southerners and Cockfighters." Among other things, Hawley's chapter touches on the role that elites play in establishing societal moral boundaries that they expect non-elites to accept. In Chapter 10, "The New Class and the California Handgun Initiative: Elitist

Developed Law as Gun Control," sociologist Brendan F.J. Furnish focuses on the role that a particular new elite of "university-oriented Americans" played in the 1982 attempt to freeze the number of handguns in California.

The last four chapters of *The Gun Culture and Its Enemies* deal in one way or another with various media treatments of guns, gun owners, and/or gun controls. How do the fictional entertainment media of television and films distort the nature of firearms and their uses, and what impact do such distortions have on public perceptions of guns and their place in our culture? Sociologist and gun enthusiast Richard Hummel presents several examples of such distortions and makes an initial attempt at trying to determine their public impact in Chapter 11, "Firearms' Stereotypes in American T.V. and Films: 'Truth' and Consequences."

In Chapter 12, "Popular and Media Images of Firearms in American Culture," communications and media specialist Eugene H. Balof explores regional cultural differences concerning the acceptance of guns and gun ownership, and how these differences are reflected in the ways that outdoor, hunting, and gun publications on the one hand, and the national general media on the other hand, treat guns and gun ownership. In this chapter, Balof touches on the subject of anti-gun media bias on the part of the general media which he sees in terms of "sins of omission rather than commission." But each of the last two chapters deal specifically with the issue of anti-gun bias on the part of the general media, and though they grapple with this complex issue in different ways, they both question whether the sins of these media are primarily of the omission variety. In Chapter 13, "Media Bias in Coverage of Gun Control: The Press Evaluates the Popular Culture," David B. Kopel, who has served as an assistant district attorney in New York City and is not a gun-culture product, analyzes the different treatment that two public-opinion polls reporting similar findings, one sponsored by a pro-gun-control organization and the other sponsored by the National Rifle Association, received in newspapers large and small across the country. And in Chapter 14, "The Media and Gun Control: A Case Study of World-View Pushing," a much revised version of my original and quite skeletal Popular Culture and American Culture paper, I examine how the newspapers of the small Midwestern city in which I live and work treated the "assault-weapon" issue for the first six months after it arrived on the national scene in early 1989.

Had it not been for the existence of the Popular Culture and American Culture Associations, several of the pieces that have been brought together in this book might not have been written, or if they had been written might not have come to the attention of anyone interested in bringing them together under one cover. Had it not been for the interest in this project exhibited by Joseph P. Tartaro, the executive editor of *Gun Week* and the president of the Second Amendment Foundation, and the assistance that he and SAF's founder, Alan Gottlieb, gave me, it probably would have taken a much longer time to make this book available to the public. I wish to express my appreciation to these individuals and organizations.

Had it not been for the very special group of men and women who provided me with what I (and I hope, readers) consider to be an excellent collection of gun-issue papers, this book could not have been done. Had it not been for my wife Beverley's support and patience and her proofreading skills, my own writing efforts would have been sorely handicapped. Had it not been for the world my parents, Eva and Joe Tonso, provided me as I was growing up, I doubt that I would have the all-consuming interest in the gun, ethnic, and other socio-cultural phenomena and their interrelationships that prompted me to bring these readings together. To everyone that I have mentioned in this paragraph, I dedicate this book.

Part I THE GUN CULTURE
Chapter I

A VIEW FROM INSIDE THE GUN CULTURE

by

William R. Tonso

One day at the beginning of April, 1986, I was having lunch in the University of Evansville cafeteria with several professorial colleagues when one of them, a political scientist, asked me about the reform of the Gun Control Act of 1968 (GCA 68) then being pushed to a House vote by a discharge petition. During the discussion that followed, I mentioned that the imprecise wording of GCA 68 had allowed (perhaps encouraged) the Bureau of Alcohol, Tobacco, and Firearms (BATF) charged with enforcing that act to run up impressive arrest records by entrapping legitimate gun collectors who had had no intention of violating the law.

At that point, the philosopher sitting directly across the table from me looked me straight in the eyes and asked me why anyone would want to collect guns. I responded with a "You've got to be kidding!" smile, though I suspected strongly that he wasn't kidding, a suspicion he quickly confirmed by telling me that he wasn't kidding. I then nodded toward a fellow sociologist sitting to the philosopher's right whom I knew to be collector of cut glass and asked, "Why does anyone collect anything? Cut glass, for example." But the philosopher couldn't be dismissed so easily. He replied that people seldom killed each other with cut-glass objects.

Now, I'm sure that many readers will feel that the philosopher put me in my place right and proper. How could anyone be silly enough to suggest that collecting something as inoffensive as cut glass has anything in common with collecting killing instruments? I suspect, however, that like my friend the philosopher those readers who feel this way about guns either have had little personal experience with them and know only as much about guns as can be picked up through media coverage of their harmful uses, or that the personal experiences they have had with guns have been negative, involving the accidental or criminal victimization of themselves or those close to them.

I really don't find it difficult to understand why such people readily associate guns exclusively with violent crime, the ravages of terrorism and war, tragic accidents, and/or what some of them consider to be the cruelties of the hunt. Nor do I find it difficult to understand why they are inclined to see guns rather than those who do harm with them as culprits. But millions of ordinary people in the United States and elsewhere have had very rewarding and socially legitimate experiences with guns that more than compensate for the harmful gun uses of which they are aware and may have even experienced themselves. These people are likely to associate guns with wholesome recreation and security from and heroic defense against crime and political oppression. Being aware of positive as well as negative uses to which guns are put regularly, gun enthusiasts are likely to attach blame for the harm done with guns to those who misuse guns rather than to guns themselves. Therefore, while the cliche, "Guns don't kill people; people kill people!" may seem ridiculously simplistic to those who consider guns to be troublesome unto themselves, it is an accurate description of reality as experienced by ordinary gun enthusiasts.

To most gun collectors and other gun enthusiasts, therefore, guns aren't simply killing instruments as they are to the philosopher and to many other Americans, particularly those in certain intellectual, media, and other circles whose members like to think of themselves as being enlightened and progressive. Consequently, the interest in guns wherever it is found is seldom as mysterious, sinister, or psychiatrically suspect as it is assumed to be in circles where ignorance of the gun world prevails. People acquire positive, or for that matter, negative feelings toward guns the same way that they acquire positive or negative feelings toward cut glass or anything else; through their experiences in the world around them as they associate with other people who purposely or inadvertently help them to acquire their feelings.

Why am I so sure that I know so much about this subject? Because I've studied this interest and related phenomena quite closely for over two decades, and more importantly, because I've spent the half-century plus of my life around people who are interested in guns, and I'm interested in them myself. So, if like my friend the philosopher you find it difficult to understand why anyone would want to collect guns, let me see if I can help you to acquire an understanding of what makes people like me tick by introducing you to the people, places, and times, the popular culture, historical events, and various concerns that turned me, the gun enthusiast I know best, on to guns. While I'm not trying to convert anyone, if nothing else, what follows may help people like you to understand why people like me stubbornly oppose the gun controls that you may consider to be so reasonable and necessary.

Though somewhat roundabout, perhaps the best way to begin is to introduce you to my family and the America to which they came just after the turn of the century. During this period, all of my grandparents and my father came from the foothills of the Alps, the Piedmont region of northern Italy, to my home town of Herrin in the coal fields of the southern tip of Illinois. The Martoglios, my mother's side of the family, got to the United States first in the person of her father. After a few years in Illinois, he returned to his small home town near Turin to marry my grandmother, and then he came back to settle in Herrin and work in the mines. My mother, the third of three children, was born in Herrin in 1910.

The Tonsos came from another small town near Turin, where my father, an only child, was born in 1906. In 1910, he came to Herrin with his mother and an uncle who was returning to the Illinois mines where my paternal grandfather was still working. But shortly after the Tonsos were reunited in Herrin, the miners went on strike and the family packed up and moved to the small coal-mining community of Gibson, located near Gallup in what was then still New Mexico Territory. My grandfather's brother-in-law (a future mayor of Glendale, California) had already established himself in Gibson as the owner of a small mine and three saloons. In 1916 or '17 (my father isn't sure which) he and his parents moved back to Herrin.

Now the New Mexico of the period 1910-17 had much of the frontier left about it, but my father doesn't remember Gibson as a particularly wild community, apart from the occasional saloon brawls that could be expected in mining towns. The violent labor war that rocked Colorado for thirty years and lead to the Ludlow massacre in 1914 apparently didn't overflow into New Mexico enough to make an impression on him. However, he does remember when Mexican raiders allegedly lead by the bandit/revolutionary, Pancho Villa, crossed the new state's southern border to attack Columbus in 1916. But Columbus was over 200 miles from Gibson. The excitement would be much closer when my father and his family moved east of the Mississippi. Herrin is located in Williamson County "Bloody Williamson."

Williamson county acquired its wild reputation as the result of a feud, known locally as the "Bloody Vendetta," that was fought there from 1868 to 1876, but events during the 1920s seemed to reaffirm the appropriateness of the county's nickname and made it known all across the country.[1] The bloodiest of these events involved the massacre of 20 unarmed strikebreakers and mine guards at a strip mine just south of Herrin in 1922. Striking miners had agreed to let "scabs" strip coal if no attempt was made to load it or transport it from the mine. When the mine owner had coal loaded and transported in violation of this agreement, the angry miners laid siege to the mine, two of them being killed and a third fatally wounded during the ensuing battle. When the besieged scabs and guards finally surrendered with the promise of safe conduct out of the area, the miners (allegedly with the blessing of mine-union czar John L. Lewis) simply executed 20 of them. No one was ever punished for these killings. Earlier labor conflicts in the area had resulted in bloodshed, but nothing comparable to what came to be known nationally as the "Herrin Massacre."

Shamed by the negative publicity that the massacre had brought to their county and concerned about the ways that the coming of the mines had transformed the economy, ethnic composition, mores, and so forth, of the area, many Protestant residents of Williamson and its adjacent mining counties mounted a campaign to enforce Prohibition and "clean up" the area. In 1923 the Ku Klux Klan made its

---

[1] The best history of this area done to date is Paul Angle's *Bloody Williamson: A Chapter in American Lawlessness* (New York: Alfred A. Knopf, 1952), but though less polished, local author Gary DeNeal's *A Knight of Another Sort: Prohibition Days and Charlie Birger* (Danville, Illinois: The Interstate Printers & Publishers, Inc., 1981), is also very interesting and informative. In my opinion, Donald Bain's *War in Illinois* (Englewood Cliffs, New Jersey: Prentice-Hall, Inc., 1978) lacks local flavor. The sociological study done by Herman R. Lantz with the assistance of J.S. McCrary, *People of Coal Town* (Carbondale, Illinois: Southern Illinois University Press, 1958), also provides very interesting insights into this area, though some scholars think that this study is of a Pennsylvania coal town. Coal Town is actually Zeigler, Franklin County, Illinois, which is located only a few miles north of Herrin, but the identification problem came about as a result of the sociological tradition of not using the true names or specifying the locations of small communities studied.

appearance, and with the support of a number of Protestant ministers, set out to conduct this campaign through quasi-legal liquor raids and mass arrests of suspected bootleggers. Of course, most of the southern- and eastern-European immigrants who came to work in the mines saw nothing wrong with alcoholic beverages, and many of them continued to make wine and home brew for their own use, thereby confirming their troublesomeness in the eyes of the Klansmen and attracting the Klansmen's unwanted attention. My father's house was raided once and my mother's was almost raided, possibly by mistake.

As might be expected, the Klan's Prohibition-enforcing activities produced a reaction from those opposed to the Klan and/or Prohibition, and the clash between the two factions resulted in 18 killings in street gunfights in less than two and a half years, 16 of those killings resulting from three major battles. One of these casualties was S. Glenn Young, a colorful ex-revenuer who regularly wore a pair of pearl-handled Colt .45 automatics and led Klan raids. Young once literally took over the county and his Klansmen even shot up the Herrin Hospital in an attempt to capture anti-Klansmen being treated there. Ora Thomas, the deputy sheriff who shot Young and was himself killed in the same fight, had been a bootlegger. Once Klan influence faded, competing factions developed within the bootlegging camp, and the shooting continued into the late '20s. In fact, although Southern Illinois calmed down considerably after this period, the last shooting associated with these gang wars occurred in 1950.

Of course the great majority of Williamson County and other area residents were bystanders with regard to these violent events, their prime concern being to keep themselves and those dear to them out of harm's way. I've heard stories many times from family members and friends concerning how they avoided passing through the uptown area when they could hear shooting coming from that direction. But even those on the sidelines kept and sometimes carried guns. Both of my grandfathers, a great uncle (who came to the States after World War I, during which he had served in the Italian army and had been captured by the Germans), and a number of their friends all owned shotguns that they used for hunting. But my grandfathers, great uncle, and several of their friends also kept handguns in their homes. And once my father started to work at the largest hotel in town back in the '20s, a hotel he was to manage for most of the forty years he worked there, he often carried a pistol to work with him.

My gun-keeping and -packing relatives never brandished their guns, nor did they engage in macho posturing with them. They seem to have considered gun possession to be prudent at a time when no one knew when they might be drawn further into the labor, Klan, or gang conflicts raging around them than they cared to be drawn, and when the law was a sometime thing — sometimes in the Klan camp, sometimes in the anti-Klan camp. My father's hotel job brought him into contact with a number of the central figures on the various sides of the Klan and gang wars. Glenn Young, the Klan's raider who established himself as dictator of the county for a few days in 1924, was staying at the hotel at the time that he came out second best in his gun duel with Deputy Thomas in a Herrin cigar store in 1925. Approximately two years before that, Young had raided my paternal grandparent's house and ordered my father, a teenager, to throw out the home brew that had been hidden under the house. While all of my close male relatives have owned guns at some time during their lives, only my father could be considered a gun enthusiast in that his appreciation for guns goes beyond the utilitarian to aesthetic, historical, and other considerations. To a great extent, his appreciation for guns is probably related to his appreciation for practically anything mechanical, but it also came about as a result of his contacts with guns and with people who owned guns and now and again wanted to sell them for needed cash. If the price was right, my father bought the gun, and a small but interesting collection gradually took shape — an interesting collection to my father and me, at least.

I was born in 1933, and among my very earliest memories are those of my father cleaning his pistols. And some of the very most special and significant recurring events of my childhood were the shooting expeditions on which my father and mother started taking me almost as soon as I could walk out beyond Herrin's eastern city limits. We would walk three blocks south to the Illinois Central track and then follow it east about three-quarters of a mile or so to the Number Seven Mine area, with its two-segment mine pond divided by the track trestle. The area around the mine was of open fields, some cultivated, and patches of woods, some swampy, crisscrossed by railroad tracks that provided many embankments against which tin cans and other targets could be placed. The best embankment, providing the safest shooting, was a mile or so beyond Number Seven on the way to Jeffrey mine where the sunken track of the Chicago, Burlington, and Quincy was spanned by the massive steel twin bridges of the Illinois Central and the Missouri Pacific, and a gracefully arched, old-style automobile bridge constructed of heavy timber.

Our shooting expeditions generally, but not always, took place between the time that we finished our main Sunday meal, about 1:15, and 3:00 P.M. when my father had to start back to work. He worked seven days a week, starting out from home at about 7:00 A.M. and getting home around 7:30 P.M., a half hour or so earlier on Sundays and holidays, but he also came home for a two and a half hour lunch break. I still find it amazing how much home remodeling and yard work was accomplished after meals during these breaks, but now and then time would be taken off from the chores and we would go shooting. As I got older, my mother stopped going with us so that my father and I could have more time to ourselves — after all, I was around her much more than I was around him due to his long working hours. Not until I was a junior in high school was I allowed to go shooting by myself or with friends my own age. Though I welcomed this independence as a sign of growing up, I now consider those family expeditions, which sometimes included visiting relatives, to be especially memorable.

Once allowed to go shooting by myself, I headed for Number Seven any time I had the urge and the time to do so. Sometimes I took a camera along to record familiar sights as well as the changing of the seasons as they were reflected in the flora of the fields and woods. As anyone familiar with mining areas might suspect, my old "stomping ground" was neither pristine wilderness nor pure arcadia, yet such industrial encroachment in the form of the mine and railroads as existed at the time made an area that was to me a combination of the Wild West and Africa especially intriguing. This was a place to ponder growing up and the world around me, and I just liked to roam around and absorb it. Though I always took my .22 rifle or one of my handguns (all gifts from my folks) with me, and they were necessary parts of the experience, sometimes I wouldn't fire a shot on the walks I took by myself.

Whether with my parents or by myself, walking out beyond the edge of town almost always meant taking a gun along. For the most part, this was done to take advantage of plinking opportunities that might develop with the discovery of tin cans or other suitable targets. But there was also an underlying concern with self-protection, since drunks could be encountered along the tracks occasionally, and there was always the possibility that they could be troublesome.

I've mentioned nothing about hunting because I've never really been a hunter. The great majority of the shots fired on our expeditions were fired at inanimate objects, though now and then turtles on logs, snakes, and birds would draw our fire —something that as confirmed animal lovers, neither my father nor I would consider doing now. I've even been a contributor, along with my wife and in her name, to Defenders of Wildlife, hardly a pro-hunting organization. Yet my feelings about hunting are ambivalent, and I can understand why some people, including relatives and friends of mine, find the activity so fascinating. Along with the other kids in the neighborhood, I used to shoot sparrows, blackbirds, and starlings with a BB gun, and I'll have to say that this junior-hunter experience was enough to make me aware of the satisfaction associated with hunting — satisfaction that has much to do with being outdoors and with displaying stalking and marksmanship skills to one's self and to others, and little to do with the destruction of the creatures being hunted. Yet since a successful hunt results in the destruction of a creature, I won't hunt anymore unless my survival or that of those important to me is at stake. Since I'm not a vegetarian, however, I can hardly condemn hunters who eat what they shoot. In fact, shooting sparrows and other birds with a BB gun didn't trouble me as much when my friends and I bagged enough of them to make it worthwhile to take them to my maternal grandmother so that she could stew them up with tomato sauce, onions, and other tasty ingredients to be eaten with an Italian cornmeal-mush dish known as "polenta." Don't look for white meat on sparrows, but they can be tasty if fixed properly.

After World War II, a relative of ours (one of his brothers married my mother's sister, and his sister married the uncle who escorted my father and his mother to the States from Italy) established himself as one of the better gunsmiths in the area. His shop, located on the far west side of town, drew customers not only from Southern Illinois, but from Kentucky across the Ohio and Missouri across the Mississippi. I used to enjoy visiting the shop, though about the only time that I did so was when my aunt, uncle (the gunsmith's brother) and cousins came down from Detroit for summer vacation, always a big summer event for me, and we would all visit on the west side. The Ferrero brothers (sometimes a third brother would also be visiting from Michigan) and their uncle, all avid hunters and fishermen, and any customers in the shop at the time would swap hunting and fishing stories, and there were usually interesting guns to examine — some real relics.

As can be seen, I grew up with guns and people who knew guns. Some other "gun people" were part of the picture more because they and the guns they owned were out there to be talked about than because I interacted with them often. There was the friend of my parents from the days of their youth who would come down from Chicago (300 miles to the north) to visit his folks, a nice fellow whom I still associate with several interesting handguns he owned, including a Colt .38 revolver that was one of three specially made for one of the local gang leaders of the 1920s. And there is the friend of my father's who, as I remember it, was a member of the National Rifle Association before my father joined back in the 1940s — gun control wasn't an issue at that time. After reading the *American Rifleman,* the NRA's official magazine, this gentleman would give it to my father who would bring it home for the two of us to read. I came to await anxiously the arrival of the *Rifleman* every month, and as an NRA member myself since 1955, I still look forward to that monthly event.

As the years passed, my gun people contacts expanded — my teammates on the Southern Illinois University-Carbondale Air Force Reserve Officer Training Corps target-shooting team, friends in the Air Force (one of whom was an avid hunter from North Carolina), and fellow gun-club members in Montana, Illinois, and Indiana. One of my Illinois gun-club friends, a collector of military firearms, owned and allowed me to fire a Gatling gun and a couple of antitank guns. But these later gun-enthusiast friends of mine have contributed very little to the enthusiasm for guns that I acquired at home from contact with the family members and friends I've mentioned, and from others I've yet to mention. I never met these "other" gun people in person. In fact, it would have been impossible for me to meet most of them, because they were either fictional or historical characters. Yet they made impressions on me.

The popular-cultural heroes I knew as a kid were basically good guys who fought and defeated unadulterated bad guys in a world that tended to be morally black and white even in its more sophisticated depictions of the time. And aside from super heroes of the "Superman" variety, the pop heroes of the period used their personal weapons as well as their wits and strength to right wrongs. Prince Valiant had his jeweled "Singing Sword," the Lone Ranger his fancy sixguns and silver bullets, Flash Gordon and Buck Rogers their "ray guns," and the Phantom his pair of .45 automatics, all weapons that could get the job done in the hands of a master while producing no more damage than that job required — sometimes no more than a hand stung by having had a gun shot out of it. Dick Tracy didn't even use his submachine gun as a weapon of wholesale extermination, as current movie heroes tend to do. I was fascinated by these newspaper comic-strip heroes. For that matter, as an avid popular culturist, I'm still fascinated by them and by the comic strips in general.

On most Sunday afternoons after my father went back to work and my mother had cleaned up after dinner, she and I would go to the matinee at the larger of the two movie houses in town. While I had friends, I had started going to the movies with my mother on Sundays when I was very small, saw nothing strange about it, and continued to do so most of the way, if not all of the way, through my grade school years. Consequently, while my friends saw "B" westerns and other "B" movies at the Saturday matinees, I saw, along with many "women's movies" that I could have done without, the "A" westerns and other "A" adventure movies featuring big name Hollywood stars. So it was that many of my early contacts with various legendary gun people came to me via Hollywood's none too accurate but quite colorful and romanticized depictions of them — Errol Flynn's General Custer, Tyrone Power and Henry Fonda's Jesse and Frank James, Robert Taylor's Billy the Kid, and Joel McCrea's Buffalo Bill, to name a few of my favorites. I became a lifelong Custer and Little Big Horn buff after seeing Flynn's "They Died With Their Boots On" back about 1941, and "Garry Owen," the 7th Cavalry's marching song, remains one of my favorite tunes to this day.

With World War II came the war-movie heroics, plus the newsreel and magazine and newspaper pictorial coverages of real Allied good guys at war with real Axis bad guys. General George S. Patton quickly became my favorite WW II personage; I coveted his ivory-handled handguns. Thus the popular culture and contemporary events of my youth complemented and reinforced an interest in guns that I'd acquired from my own contacts with guns and with people who owned and used them. And my own familiarity with guns linked me more closely to the popular-cultural depictions of people and events as well as to things that were actually happening on the world stage at the time. While my friends had only seen them on the silver screen and in the comics, before I graduated from grade school I had fired a Colt frontier-style sixshooter, a Winchester lever-action rifle, a Government Model .45, a German Luger, and other western- war- or spy-movie mainstays, some of which were in my father's collection, others of which belonged to friends of his. In fact, I had even fired a gun that was rather new to our military at the time, an M1 carbine that my Navy-officer uncle, bending the rules a bit, brought home with him on leave for us to try out. That was a big thrill for me, because I had found the little carbine aesthetically appealing since I had first seen a photograph of one in the early '40s.

Until the late 1950s, when gun control started to become a national issue again (I wasn't aware at the time of the previous push for controls that had faded as WW II approached), it hadn't crossed my mind that being interested in guns needed any explaining. I had already been to college and I was just finishing my Air Force active duty at the time, and though I had known people who didn't like guns, I hadn't known anyone who made enough of an issue about not liking them to make an impression on me. In fact, many people I knew seemed to appreciate my knowledge of guns, and to envy my modest marksmanship skills and my possession of a few quality rifles and handguns. And I found shooting to be an enjoyable pastime and demanding sport, and guns to be what I would now call symbolically appealing. They could also be used to fend off evil, then still an easily recognized and absolute condition, as far as I was concerned. In my world everything pointed to the utility of guns for purposes of self, community, and national defense, and I identified myself with the good guys and assumed that I would always be accepted as one of them —though that assumption was already starting to be undermined along with my civics-books view of the world.

Back during the war I never doubted that Germany and Japan deserved to be wiped off of the face of the earth, but the fact that Italy was also our enemy gave me pause. I thought of myself as an American, and as a blond, blue-eyed, 6'1" stringbean by the time I was a sophomore in high school, I didn't look like what many people think Italians should look like. But I was also conscious that my people had come from Italy, and I was in close and continuous contact with them and others who had come from there. When someone asked me what I was, referring to my ethnicity, without hesitation I answered, "Italian." Fortunately, for my peace of mind, less-formidable Italy didn't receive the villain treatment that Germany and Japan got during the war, and I could root wholeheartedly for the Allied good guys against the Axis bad guys (who became our good friends shortly after the war) and conveniently overlook Italy's halfhearted involvement in the conflict.

But as I came into contact with more people who knew nothing about my Italian background, I eventually acquired some sense of my minority status through occasional unguarded comments from people who weren't aware that tall, blue-eyed blonds could be of Italian descent. Such incidents generally provided learning experiences for those individuals who in my presence had expressed negative feelings toward Italians. But I also learned. The stories about the Klan activities of the 1920s that I'd heard so often from family members and friends started to make sense to me, and gradually I became aware that my American good-guy status was more tentative than I'd assumed. Very much more tentative, in fact, because I was not only an Italian-American, but a nonreligious Italian-American. All of my grandparents and several of their Piedmontese friends not only dropped out of Catholicism but out of religion altogether when they came to this country. Consequently, I grew up in a circle of freethinkers and was a freethinker myself. So after World War II the ready association of atheism with a political-economic system that I myself opposed — communism and the widespread campaign against communism (which often emphasized its godlessness as that system's most hateful and destructive feature) further impressed upon me my minority status and the tentative nature of my acceptance as a loyal American good guy. Even as an anti-communist, I could be suspect because of my nonbelief.

Now I find it rather ironic and somewhat amusing, as well as intimidating, that many "enlightened" people who righteously condemn ethnic and religious "prejudices" readily display similar "prejudice" toward another category of people to which I belong — gun enthusiasts. Consider the way that we are regularly depicted in newspaper political cartoons and editorials and elsewhere in the general media, particularly those of us who oppose gun controls.[2] And consider the atrocities committed against quite a few ordinary gun collectors and dealers by BATF —though you won't find much about them in the "watchdog" media.[3]

Although I've never attempted to keep them secret, since none of my various "minority" affiliations are marked off by anything as obvious as skin color, I've seldom experienced overt discrimination due to any of them. Nevertheless, the few experiences I have had, those had by members of my family, conversations overheard, media commentaries, and social histories read have made me well aware that people who share either my ethnic origins, or my lack of religion, or my interest in guns have been, or still are, resented by significant numbers of my fellow citizens. That these fellow citizens have often been able to use various official agencies of social control, the media, the schools, and other means to try to impose their views on those of us who reject them has caused me some concern. At the intellectual level, this concern was at least partially responsible for my becoming in my thirties a very relativistic, nonjudgmental sociologist fascinated by our collective efforts to make sense of the world around us, and by the understandable conflicts often generated through our contacts with others who have made different sense of the world than we have. At the political level, this concern has made it impossible for me to accept the police, various other agents of social control, and government in general as neutral, and has caused me to conclude that only the sociopolitically naive can assume that these agencies will always be on their side if they do their part by living decent lives. Second Amendment author James Madison and his fellow Founding Fathers seem to have reached a similar conclusion over 200 years ago, and I have no use for current politicians, intellectuals, and others who seem incapable of appreciating the profound lack of trust in government reflected in that amendment. No, I'm neither anarchist nor survivalist.

Though I'm an extreme relativist sociologically, my own values are still firmly in place, and the private citizen side of me would react violently and without apology toward those who might threaten me and mine or inoffensive others, even though the sociological side of me would find their behavior understandable. As far as I'm concerned, to understand others in some relativistic, analytical sense is not necessarily to condone what they do. Consequently, there have been a few times in my life when I've felt uncomfortable because I didn't have a gun with me, and a few times when I've felt more comfortable because I did have a gun with me. But while practical concerns such as defense against governmental or free-lance oppression and criminal victimization that have grown out of my considerations of the world around

---

[2] Several of the chapters in Part II of this volume, particularly Chapters 8 and 14, examine anti-gunner perspectives on pro-gunners.

[3] See David T. Hardy, "On Turning Citizens Into Criminals," *Law & Liberty*, Vol. 4, No. 4 (Winter, 1979), and Joseph Goulden, "The Fat Man and the Gun Collector," *Washingtonian Magazine* (December, 1979).

me and the experiences of my family explain part of my interest in guns, there are other sides to that interest.

As should be clear by now, I've been a recreational shooter since I was a small child; consequently, it should come as no surprise that I enjoy shooting. To me the thrill of hitting a small and distant target is akin to the thrills experienced in other sports involving the precise placement of projectiles — swishing a basketball through a hoop 20 or so feet away, bowling a strike, or even (less precisely) hitting a ball over a fence, or at least over the heads of the outfielders. Such accomplishments involve sort of an extension of self, an affecting of something at a distance that only those possessing the required skills can regularly do. Doing it, therefore, produces an immediate sense of satisfaction from the awareness that others knowing of the difficulties involved will be impressed. But unlike making baskets or bowling strikes, being able to hit that at which one is shooting is a skill that has practical and what many people would consider to be legitimate applications — defending oneself and others, and hunting for food. I enjoy shooting for these reasons, but there is still more to my interest in guns, and that "more" brings me back to the subject of collecting.

It seems that people who aren't interested in guns tend to assume that a gun is a gun is a gun. Not so! Guns are very specialized, and even those designed for one type of target shooting may be next to useless for another type of target shooting. Consequently, an individual with several different shooting interests may need a number of guns. But I have more guns than my shooting interests require, and I have them for reasons that are essentially symbolic. I have them because they link me symbolically to the people, places, and times, the popular culture, historical events, and other concerns that have been and still are important to me, and that I have tried to introduce to you, the reader, in the preceding pages. The guns that my parents have given me, my father's guns that he no longer uses, guns inherited from family members and close friends are sacred to me — they link me to people for whom I care, important people in my life. The guns I've grown up with link me to my past, to places like Number Seven, to the wild, fascinating, and instructive history of my home area, to the far simpler world of the late '30s through the middle '50s. Even guns that I have not grown up with link me to historical reactions against oppression, to clashes of interest, and to causes that people cared about enough to fight for. They also link me to the gentlemanly, principled, and highly romanticized gun-toting Hollywood heroes of my youth, who along with my gentlemanly, principled, gun-owning male relatives, provided me with role models when I needed them. Though I currently belong to a gun club, I'm not doing as much shooting as I would like to be doing. But used or not, my collection is something to hold on to, something locked away for safekeeping, something not likely to be surrendered easily simply because those of you who fear guns eventually succeed in outlawing the possession of types that I now own legally.

While the combination of experiences and concerns that have fostered my interest in guns is uniquely mine, the practical, recreational, and symbolic attachments to guns, as I've demonstrated elsewhere in a less personal, more scholarly, and much longer fashion, aren't unique to me or even to Americans.[4] Guns aren't just killing instruments to the great majority of us who are interested in them. Did I explain all of this to my philosopher friend? No. Realizing that the world-view gap between us was far too wide to bridge in the few minutes remaining in a lunch break with others only minimally interested in the subject of guns, I answered his questions concerning collector motivation by muttering something about the aesthetic and historical appeals of guns and let the discussion run its course. But the philosopher's question continued to nag at me, because I know that many other Americans (as well as foreigners who observe us) are capable of asking it. You have just read the answer that I would like to have given him, and that I would give the others if I had the time to do so.

[4]. See William R. Tonso, *Gun and Society: The Social and Existential Roots of the American Attachment to Firearms* (Washington, D.C.: University Press of America, 1982).

Chapter 2

SOCIAL JUSTICE COMMUNITY ORGANIZING AND THE NECESSITY FOR PROTECTIVE FIREARMS

by
John R. Salter, Jr.

Community organizing for social justice purposes is, by its very nature, controversial — frequently drawing violent attacks from adversaries and hostility or cold indifference from law enforcement and other governmental agencies. This paper will discuss the necessity of personal firearms protection in the organizing context, citing a number of representative, first hand examples.

In the mid-1960s, as a full-time grassroots civil rights organizer for the radical Southern Conference Educational Fund, I was directing a large-scale and ultimately quite successful community organizing project in the extremely recalcitrant, poverty-stricken, and intractably segregated northeastern North Carolina black-belt. The multi-county setting was Klan-ridden and night-time terrorism was common: cross-burnings, armed motorcades, arson, shootings. Local law enforcement was almost completely dominated by the United Klans of America in some of the counties and at least strongly Klan-influenced in others. Halifax County, in which our project started and where our central base existed in the town of Enfield, was the toughest. (Klan dues were paid and collected in the Enfield police station!) Thoroughly hated by the segregationists, I was — as I had been for several years in the hard-core South — on several death lists and received many death threats. And, as I had for years, I carried a .38 Special Smith & Wesson, generally in my attache case.

Late one fall night in 1964, I left a Halifax County civil rights rally at Weldon and drove back toward Enfield, twenty-odd miles away. Normally, because of the terroristic atmosphere, we traveled two or three vehicles together at night but, on this occasion, I was the only person heading to Enfield. At this late hour, the road was almost always deserted; two miles out of Weldon, however, a large white car came up behind me — showing no inclination to pass. In the bright moonlight I could see several persons there-in, and knew these were Klansmen. Although there was no question but that they were quite open to shooting at me, I was not surprised that they did not. Months before, we had diffused word on the local grapevines that we, and certainly myself, were armed. They knew full well that I was capable of returning fire

Previously published in *Against the Current*, July August, 1988.

— and willing indeed to do so. Hence they settled for futile efforts to force me into a high speed chase situation — "revving" their motor practically bumper-to-bumper with mine. But I continued to drive sedately, mile after mile. When I finally stopped in Enfield, with my revolver in my hand, they drove past me, obviously frustrated and cursing. But that was the evening. Not long thereafter, a local civil rights stalwart, Mrs. Alice Evans of Enfield, opened fire with her double-barreled 12 gauge, sprinkling several KKKers with birdshot as they endeavored to burn a cross in her driveway one night and, simultaneously, approaching her house with buckets of gasoline. When we arrived, having heard the nearby shots, Mrs. Evans had matters well in hand. The Klansmen were gone — to a hospital, we later learned. We gave the cross to the Smithsonian. These are two instances in a flow of time which includes many direct personal examples.

A half-breed Indian, I grew up in the West, principally in Northern Arizona —and in a hunting family. I had my first rifle when I was seven years old and, by the time I was eighteen, had had sixty-seven different firearms. In my very early twenties, as I was embarking on my principal life-long career — that of a social justice organizer —I was strongly influenced by old-time Wobblies (members of the Industrial Workers of the World) and by organizers of the always radical and militant International Union of Mine, Mill and Smelter Workers (Mine-Mill). Committed to tactical nonviolence, these men were also, in the quasi-frontier traditions of our section, very much committed to the use of firearms for personal protection in the face of attacks by company thugs. In the latter 1950s, as I became deeply involved on behalf of controversial labor unionism in the rough-and-tumble Southwest, I frequently and routinely traveled in an armed fashion. And this was certainly my approach in such murderous crucibles as Mississippi and eastern North Carolina and other Deep South citadels in the 1960s and South/Southwest Side Chicago in the 70s. I am convinced that I'm alive today because I traveled with firearms — and that this fact was generally known.

Direct Firearms Protection

There is no question but that the known existence of pervasive firearms ownership in Southern Black communities prevented much (though not all) massively violent racist retaliation.[1] This was certainly true in the northeastern North Carolina black-belt and it was true across the South generally. In a few instances, this involved formally organized Black self-defense groups — e.g., the Louisiana-based Deacons for Defense. Mostly, though, it was characterized by innumerable ad-hoc and individual examples.

[1] A well known example of racist retaliation against armed Blacks was Robert F. Williams situation in Klan-ridden Monroe, N.C. In the late 1950s, Williams, a Black, organized self-defense groups in conjunction with the local NAACP and with an NRA charter. This kept the Klan at arm's length but, in 1961, the KKK, encouraged by some elements in state government and with the Federals openly hostile to Williams because his growing pro-Cuban sympathies, attacked the Black neighborhoods. Blacks resisted, some were arrested, and Williams fled the country. Even so, the armed nature of Monroe's Blacks, which had held the KKK off for years, prevented many Black injuries during that climactic night. See Robert F. Williams and Mark Schleiffer, editor, *Negroes with Guns* (Chicago: Third World Press, 1973).

Beginning in 1961, I taught for several years at Tougaloo College, a private Black school on the outskirts of Jackson, Mississippi — right in the heart of the blood-dimmed, Closed Society; and I served as Advisor to the Jackson Youth Council of the NAACP and chief organizer and strategy committee chair of the Jackson Movement, which developed in 1962 and 1963 into the most massive grassroots upheaval in Mississippi's history and one of the major efforts in the United States of the 1960s.[2] Along with many others, I was often beaten and arrested in Mississippi but, as the primary civil rights organizer in the Jackson area, was a very special target. During the Christmas season of 1962, soon after we had begun active and open Jackson Movement development, night-riders attacked my home on the Tougaloo campus, firing shots into our house — with one bullet passing just above the crib in which my infant daughter, Maria, slept. If anything, local law officials were strongly supportive of the night-riders; the U.S. Justice Department and the FBI had no interest in enforcing the Constitution in cases such as ours. Those of us on campus at that point then began standing an organized, armed guard at several strategic locations — letting this be known to the news media. The attacks ceased for a long time; when they resumed, the guard resumed, and the vigilante moves against Tougaloo subsided.

In North Carolina, in February, 1965, I had become so much a target that even the far from friendly FBI and Justice Department became somewhat concerned. An agent came to our home at Raleigh and, indicating an informer in a United Klans "klavern" had reported a conspiracy to bomb our house, concluded by saying the Federal government could do nothing about it. Local law enforcement was not reliable. Fortunately, we lived in the middle of a heavily armed Black community — with our neighbors, obviously supportive of my civil rights work in North Carolina and across the South, very protective, especially when I was away in the field for long periods of time. We immediately apprised them of the FBI warning, barricaded our windows, and fed our "preparedness" to several grapevines. We were not surprised when the bombing effort never materialized.

Years later, in Chicago in the summer of 1970, I was Southside Director of the Chicago Commons Association (a private social service organization), coordinating a very large-scale grassroots community organizing project involving mostly Black, Puerto Rican, and Chicano people in racially changing sections of the turbulent South/Southwest Side. White racial attitudes and frequent practices exemplified a racism often more violent and sanguinary than the Deep South of the previous decade. The Richard Daley machine was openly antagonistic to us and the Chicago police in some of the local districts (not in all districts) were frequently in league with the racists. Again, as the prime organizer and the project director, I was a special target. Police harassment and death threats were common, increasing in direct

2 For a full account of the Jackson Movement of 1962-63, see John R. Salter, Jr., *Jackson, Mississippi: An American Chronicle of Struggle and Schism*, (Melbourne, Florida: Robert E. Krieger Publishing Company, 1987).

proportion to the growing power and militancy of our grassroots organizations. One afternoon, while I was at work, men with knives in their hands came to my home; their intent was quite clear but a vigilant next door neighbor with a revolver frightened them away. In three days time, I performed more "home improvement" services than the total of anything before or since: barring and boarding windows, chaining doors, changing locks. But my basic reliance lay in my several firearms — and when death threats came over the telephone, I now began telling the callers, somewhat to the discomfiture of my gentle wife, that I had a ticket for them, a pass to permanent eternity via my Marlin .444. No men returned to my home and the death threats tapered off.

Firearms as a Force to Compel Responsible and Egalitarian Law Enforcement

In the late fall of 1964, in response to the increasing successes of our northeastern North Carolina black-belt project, the United Klans of America scheduled a large-scale, state-wide rally in Halifax County — very close to a Black residential area. Not surprisingly, posters advertising the affair were conspiciously displayed in, among other places, most law enforcement offices in the county. We knew the Justice Department and the FBI would be no help and, early on, we petitioned the state government for state police. This request was not even acknowledged and, with the approval of our local grassroots leaders, I went to Governor Terry Sanford's office at Raleigh. He declined to meet with me directly but did send in his chief aide. To this person I was blunt in a cold and angry fashion, telling him that either the state send a large contingent of police into Halifax County a day before the Klan rally — and to remain through the affair and at least a day afterward — or our people, armed to the hilt, would have no hesitation about utilizing armed self-defense in the event of Klan violence. Visibly shaken, the aide left me and conferred with Sanford. He returned quickly to promise the state police. The day before the rally, many state police cars rolled into Halifax County and remained there for two days after the event. For our part, we actively and successfully encouraged tactical nonviolence but, of course, we and our constituency continued to keep arms handy. There was no violence except a brutal fight among several Klansmen. For months afterward the United Klans continued to hold rallies near Black neighborhoods in Halifax County and we continued the same effective formula — pressuring the state (next under Governor Dan K. Moore), with our people armed and watchful. Eventually, the Klan rallies ceased in northeastern North Carolina and the local Klans faded.

In the South/Southwest Side of Chicago, the known armed nature of grassroots people deterred both conventional criminal elements and white racist gangs. In our far-flung community organizational project (almost 300 multi-issue block clubs and related groups organized by the summer of 1973), a setting where honest police were tired and overworked and the others downright hostile, we set up public citizen "watch-dog" patrols. Although generally non-armed, these had — regardless of

22.

police attitudes one way or the other — primary backup from a network of armed citizenry in the neighborhoods with which the patrols maintained close and consistent communication through citizens' band radios, volunteer dispatchers, and telephone linkups. The effects of this well known campaign in reducing crime and deterring white racial violence were consistently substantial. Before long, frightened politicians forced into effect increasingly responsible and egalitarian law enforcement practices. But the patrols and the vigilance of armed neighborhoods continued.

*　　*　　*　　*　　*　　*　　*

I am not taking the position that there would have been no fatalities in social justice organizing, and that none will occur, if organizers and constituents were and are armed. A close friend and colleague, Medgar W. Evers, was shot to death in front of his home one night in June, 1963, in the Jackson Movement campaign. But the heavily armed — and known to be heavily armed — Medgar lived for nine effective years after he became Mississippi NAACP field secretary, about nine years longer than most friends and enemies felt he would. A few days after his death, I was seriously injured and almost killed in a rigged auto wreck. But I had survived to that point, weathered the injuries, and have survived pretty effectively ever since. And all of our community organizational campaigns over the years have been essentially quite successful.[3] I am stating categorically that the number of fatalities would have been, and will be, much smaller if organizers and their grassroots groups were and are sensibly armed for self-defense. And the success of the campaigns and the projects themselves have and will be greatly enhanced.

[3] All of my papers covering more than thirty years of grassroots organizing are held in the national Social Action Collection, State Historical Society of Wisconsin, Madison; and at the Mississippi State Department of Archives and History, Jackson. These two essentially parallel collections include considerable materials relating to other community organizational campaigns in which I've been substantially involved. Several of these (some recent) have included protective firearms dimensions.

Chapter 3

THE OWNERSHIP AND CARRYING OF PERSONAL FIREARMS AND REDUCTION OF CRIME VICTIMIZATION

by
Edward F. Leddy

Introduction

It is widely accepted that the ownership and carrying of pistols and revolvers by anyone except the police and those whom they choose to permit is a cause of violent crime. We know this without having to prove it, because it is so obviously reasonable to assume so. Indeed, until recently, in academic circles one would be accused of being radical or at least slightly eccentric to assert that this might not be true. Most of the governments of both Eastern and Western Europe have justified their laws and policies on this belief. Yet there is another side to the issue.

History

It is not generally realized that control of firearms is largely a twentieth century phenomenon. In the nineteenth century and earlier, people, except political and religious dissidents, legally owned and carried guns as a matter of course in most countries. Being armed was considered normal. Except for concealed weapons, there was little challenge to it. People simply accepted it as necessary and even desirable.

In 1889 British ambassadors were ordered to report on firearms laws in the countries of Europe. Nowhere was possession of guns prohibited. As to carrying guns:

In Montenegro, Norway and Sweden, Denmark, Serbia and Switzerland there were no restrictions on the carrying of arms and in Hungary restrictions were placed only on convicted persons and the insane. Concealed firearms were prohibited in the Duchy of Coburg, Hesse, Saxony and Wurttemberg as they were in France ... In the Duchy of Baden and in Germany the carrying of firearms at public meetings was prohibited and in the Netherlands the carrying of firearms on roads or in public places was forbidden with some exceptions.In Bulgaria, Belgium, Greece, Italy, Portugal, and Spain a permit was required to carry any type of firearm whilst the same restrictions with some exemptions applied to Austria, Rumania, Russia, and Turkey. It was clear from some of the reports that many of these laws were not well enforced.[1]

[1] Colin Greenwood, *Firearms Control* (London: Routledge & Kegan Paul Ltd. 1972) p. 20.

As for Great Britain itself:

England entered the twentieth century with no controls over the purchasing or keeping of any types of firearm...Anyone, be he convicted criminal, lunatic, drunkard or child could legally acquire any type of firearm and the presence of pistols or revolvers in households all over the country was fairly widespread...The right of the Englishman to keep arms for his own defense was still completely accepted and all attempts at placing this under restraint had failed.[2]

In the United States, a few trail towns in the West required cowboys to check their guns before getting drunk. Most western states prohibited carrying concealed weapons by 1850. In the urban east there were few places where even this restriction existed. In the state of New Jersey until 1927, the only gun law was a prohibition on dueling.

Strict gun control was a fixture of the pre-Civil War (1860-65) Slave Codes in the South. This restriction was a result of the fear of slave uprisings. After the war, laws were passed to continue this control over the freedmen. Blacks initially were not allowed to possess guns in many southern states. Civil rights legislation made an obvious refusal impossible but laws were written restricting pistols to the "Army pistol" (the most expensive) The effect was similar to the poll tax. It discriminated against blacks and poor whites.

Traditional Attitudes

The traditional attitude toward weapons ownership and carrying in most nations was that each person was considered responsible both for his own protection and for the defense of the state. Citizens could and were encouraged to possess arms equivalent to those of the armies of the day. They could be called up as part of the militia to use them in the national defense. In many lands, citizens, up to the late 19th century, were required to own swords, bows and later guns and to practice with them.

The United States was not unusual in that regard. Most Americans today are unaware that they are legally members of the militia of "their state and of the United States" and can be called to military duty in an emergency. This was required by the "Militia Act of 1789." This act originally applied only to men but in the 1970s it was amended to include women. State Governments enforced militia laws with inspections and fines at the yearly "militia muster" when all men were required to present their guns and ammunition for inspections.[3]

THE DENIAL OF FIREARMS OWNERSHIP AND CARRYING

It is only beginning in the second decade of this century that the ordinary citizen

[2] Ibid., 25.

[3] James B. Wisker, *The Citizen Solider and United States Military Policy* (New York:North River Press, 1979), pp. 3-11

was denied gun ownership and use in many nations. This came about by different routes in different countries.

Great Britain

The current British firearms laws did not originate as an effort to prevent crime. Instead they were primarily designed to attempt to suppress anarchists and other revolutionaries after the famed "Sidney Street Siege" (December 16, 1910) in which three police were killed and four wounded. The police had to call on the army for assistance. The "Blackwell Committee" commented on what it saw as the two great sources of danger to the British Empire: "Savage or semi-civilized tribesmen" and "The anarchist or intellectual malcontent of the great cities." Both needed to be disarmed.[4]

The suppression of the Irish Republican Army was also a crucial influence since the IRA was preparing the revolution which was soon to produce Irish Independence:
... the committee made reference to the Peace Preservation (Ireland) Act 1881, under which the carrying of firearms could be and had been proscribed ... The committee concluded that the control of firearms was essential in Ireland ... The problems of Ireland obviously weighed heavily on the committee.[5]

The fear of anarchist attacks declined over time. The IRA succeeded in its effort to free Ireland by force of arms. The firearms laws remained after their original causes had departed. The rationale of crime prevention developed in combination with political concerns. Indeed it appears in some instances to have been a smokescreen for them. In Britain, for example, gun crime actually increased after the passage of the firearms laws but not because of increased anarchy or revolutionary activity.

United States

In the U.S.A., in the early twentieth century, dominant corporations were challenged by the developing labor union movement. Employers replied by systematic violence and intimidation. Unions fought back with guns and other weapons. The influential corporate leaders supported laws requiring gun permits because they could put pressure on the police to issue permits to company police and deny them to union organizers. The Supreme Court of the state of North Carolina, in 1921, stated:
... great corporations, under the guise of detective agents or police forces, terrorize their employees by armed force. If the people are forbidden to carry the only arms within their means, among them pistols, they will be completely at the mercy of these plutocratic organizations.[6]

[4] Ibid., 25.

[5] Ibid.

[6] North Carolina Supreme Court opinion in "State vs. Kerner" quoted in Stephen P. Halbrook *That Every Man Be Armed* (Albuquerque, New Mexico: University of New Mexico Press, 1984), p.182

Germany

In Germany, guns were available relatively freely under the Kaiser and the Weimar Republic. When Hitler assumed power in 1933, the Nazis reoriented the enforcement of laws, restricting gun ownership essentially to their supporters. By a process of discretionary permit issuance and cancellation, Storm Troopers and officers in the Hitler Youth were effectively exempted from the gun law. The Jews and other proscribed groups were denied the right to have guns. A Jewish survivor of the death camps told the writer "When the Gestapo came to our home, we had no guns. I will never make that mistake again." Current West German gun laws are oriented toward prevention of terrorism not crime.

Colonies

Colonies, ie. almost all of Africa, Asia, Australia and the Americas, generally followed the rules of their mother countries at least for white men. Often they did not allow the natives to have guns or restricted them to outdated single shot flintlock types. Most of these nations, after independence, basically continued the colonial laws in this area without the discrimination against natives.

European and European influenced gun laws originated out of the desire to protect society, not from criminals but from anarchists, private armies and revolutionaries. In some of these countries a rationalization later developed that the gun laws were designed to prevent crime and protect the citizens by keeping dangerous weapons out of the hands of criminals. After a time, this was often thought to have been the reason for the laws.

Jefferson, Hamilton, Marx and Lenin

Since gun laws are so frequently the product of political conflict rather than crime, we should discuss their purpose as seen by some political theorists. It is interesting that the great intellectual leaders of both the American and Russian revolutions agree on the need for the people to be armed to defend their rights.

Thomas Jefferson wrote describing the thought behind the right to bear arms contained in the second amendment to the American Constitution:

> What country can preserve its liberties if its rulers are not warned from time to time that its people preserve the right to resistance. Let them take arms...the tree of liberty must be refreshed from time to time with the blood of patriots and tyrants.[7]

James Madison in The Federalist Papers speaks of "the advantage of being armed, which the Americans possess over the people of almost any other nation."[8]

Alexander Hamilton spelled the idea out even more clearly in his defense of the proposed U.S. constitution. Replying to accusations that the military power granted to the federal government would lead to tyranny, he points to the armed citizen as a counterweight:

[7] Letter from Thomas Jefferson to William Steven Smith, Nov. 13, 1787, reprinted in Roy G. Weatherup, "Standing Armies and Armed Citizens," *Hastings Constitutional Law Quarterly*, (Fall 1975), p. 981.

[8] Alexander Hamilton, James Madison and John Jay, *The Federalist Papers*, (New York: Mentor Books, 1961), p. 299.

... that army [the regular army] can never be formidable to the liberties of the people while there is a large body of citizens, little if at all inferior to them in discipline and the use of arms, who stand ready to defend their own rights and those of their fellow citizens. This appears to me the only substitute that can be devised for a standing army and the best possible security against it, if it should exist.[9]

The private ownership of guns was seen by the designers of the American constitution as a positive good. It served to protect liberty against potential oppression by the new government. Those who supported the proposed consitiution regarded private gun ownership as a rebuttal to the charge that the new government could be oppressive. This could not happen because the people "properly" armed and equipped" could protect their own rights. The system was designed to give the people the weapons to rebel against a tryant.

The faith of the American revolutionaries in an armed population to keep power in the hands of the people was shared by the founders of communism. Karl Marx in his "History of the Paris Commune" points out the crucial importance of the armed people as distinguished from the government controlled military forces. He emphasizes that: "The first decree of the [Paris] Commune therefore was the suppression of the standing army, and the substitution for it of the armed people."[10]

V.I. Lenin stressed the need for arming the people to preserve the gains of the revolution and prevent seizure or abuse of power against the wishes of the people by those classes who desire to control society and government:

The proletariat, however, if it wants to preserve the gains of the present revolution and to proceed further to win peace, bread and freedom, must 'destroy,' to use Marx's word, this 'ready made' state machinery and must replace it by another one, merging the police, the army, and the bureaucracy with the universally armed people ... the proletariat must organize and arm all the poorest and most exploited sections of the population.[11]

The American revolutionaries stressed arming everyone almost without exception. The Russians wanted to arm only the proletariat, the vangard of which they regarded as the people. Both agree on the importance of the armed people.

After the revolution, Stalin established strict restrictions designed to suppress counterrevolutionaries and centralize power in the hands of the Communist Party rather than the general population. They included restrictions on gun ownership which essentially prevent almost all Russians from owning a rifle or pistol. These restrictions appear to directly defy the advice of Lenin and allow those in power to control the people by military force as Lenin had feared. However, the advice of Marx and Lenin is followed to the extent that firearms training is a part of the education of every Soviet school child.

[9] Ibid., 185.

[10] Karl Marx, *Capital and Other Writings* (New York: Modern Library, 1932), p. 403.

[11] Vladimir I. Lenin, *Letters From Afar* (New York: International Publishers, 1932), p. 28.

Friedrich and Brzezinski in their description of the six necessities for the maintenance of dictatorship list: "... near complete monopoly of the effective use of all weapons of armed combat."[12]

Will the Armed People Abuse Their Power?

People are invariably convinced of their own intelligence and purity of motive. Therefore, the intent of using the armed people as a counterweight to prevent dictatorship probably seems highly theoretical to government officials.

Personal Protection

The possible risks inherent in the use of widespread gun ownership as a device to reduce crime and victimization are probably of more concern to most people. In this discussion we will focus on the use of pistols as a protection for potential victims. This is a highly unconventional idea in many places. In New York City, where I grew up, it is considered radical. There is a widespread belief instead that reduction in civilian gun ownership would reduce crime and that personal gun ownership and carrying should be discouraged or forbidden. In New York City this belief has been carried to the point that few gun licenses are issued and most of these go to retiring police.

In recent years, there has been considerable research on the effects on gun ownership and use restrictions to determine if they in fact reduce crime. The books of Don B. Kates Jr., and James D. Wright et al in the U.S.A. and Colin Greenwood of Cambridge University in England have been the most influential. Almost all have reached conclusions similar to those which Wright et al state in their section on policy implications:

... the criminally abused fraction of a percentage would be the last firearms touched by any sort of gun control program ... laws are obeyed only by the law abiding! If we were to outlaw, say the ownership of handguns, millions of law abiding handgun owners would no doubt turn theirs in — most of them people who would never even contemplate, much less commit a criminally violent act. But would we expect a person who owns a handgun for illicit reasons to turn his in? ... It is assuredly not in the interest of progressive causes that we be foolish about such things.[13]

Analysis of American crime statistics taken from the Federal Bureau of Investigation's Uniform Crime Report, when broken down into categories of severity of firearms restrictions by state, show that there are clear differences in some crimes and none in others. It is important to note that the differences are usually in favor of the states which have the least restrictions:

The most restrictive states record the highest ratio of street robbery to commercial robbery (2.5 compared to 2.2 for the moderate grouping and 1.6 for the 'carry' states) and the highest levels of street robbery (140 per 100,000

12 Carl J. Friedrich and Zbigniew K.Brzezinski, *Totalitarian Dictatorship and Autocracy* (New York: Frederick A. Praeger 1968). p. 22.

13 James D. Wright, Peter Rossi and Kathleen Daly. *Under The Gun* (New York: Aldine Publishing Co. 1983), p. 320-21.

compared to 66.0 and 52.5). They also recorded the highest level of commercial robbery, simply not by the same margin (65.5 compared to 30.2 for the moderate and 32.5 for the 'carry' group). And relatively speaking, assault was more likely to occur in the 'carry' and moderate states, with ratios of assault to robbery of about 1.7 compared to 1.1 for the restrictive states, but the assault rate was higher in the restrictive states and there was no difference in gun use in the assault.

Other rates and ratios fail to indicate that the laws 'work' even with the expected mixed blessings. There was no particular difference in firearms use in robbery or assault, with the former ranging from 35.7% to 37.4% for the various groups, and the latter ranging from 20.1% to 22.2%. There were no significant differences in handgun involvement in homicide, ranging from 43.6% in the 'carry' states, and 42.7% in the moderate states to 45.2% in the restrictive group, with homicide (and handgun homicide) rates similarly unimpressive for the most to the least restrictive: 8.9 (4.0) per 100,000 for the most restrictive group, 6.5 (2.8) for the moderately restrictive group and 5.9 for the least restrictive. In terms of saving the lives of robbery victims, the percentage of robberies ending in fatalities (based on robberies and robbery related homicides) was slightly lower in the restrictive states, but the overall robbery-homicide rate was almost twice as high — 1.9 per 100,000 in the restrictive states compared to about 1.0 for the other two groupings.[14]

The Honest Citizen and Guns as Protection
Historically, keeping the peace and suppressing rebellion were considered the duty of the state in most of Europe. There was little effort made in the past to track down criminals or to protect individuals. People were expected to protect themselves. Until the early decades of this century, the average citizen was permitted and often encouraged to own and carry guns freely. Travelers routinely went armed and in groups.

   . . . the Common Law right to keep arms and the tradition of owning arms for protection, was built up [in England] during a period when there was no effective police when the individual was compelled to see to his own protection.[15]

Police Protection
Prohibiting the private ownership and carrying of guns is often justified by the assertion that the modern state is now able to provide all the protection a person can

---

[14] Paul H. Blackman, "Carrying Handguns For Personal Protection: Issues of Research and Public Policy." Paper presented at the American Society of Criminology 13-16 November 1985, p.36.

[15] Greenwood, 246.

reasonably need. Armed self protection is derided as vigilantism. However, as we all know, crime rates have risen in the last twenty years to the point that it is four times more likely that we shall be the victims of violence today than in 1963.[16] Accordingly, this claim rings rather hollow. The ability of the state to protect us from personal violence is limited by resources, legal restraints, and personnel shortages. Most of all, the state is usually unable to know that we need protection from attack until it is too late. By the time that the police can be notified and then arrive at the scene the violent criminal has ample opportunity to do you serious harm. I once waited twenty minutes for the New York City Police to respond to an "officer needs assistance" call which has their highest priority. On the other hand a gun provides immediate protection. Even where the police are prompt and efficient, the gun is speedier.

Handgun Ownership

In the United States, the people living in forty four of the fifty states can legally own and purchase pistols without obtaining a police permit for ownership. Laws do prohibit possession of handguns by felons, and other undesirables. There has been much more research on the issue of handgun ownership than on carrying. There are extensive studies in this area which I will not touch on here except to note that it has not been established that crime is increased by widespread gun ownership. I wish to address the specific problem of legal gun carrying as a crime preventive program.

LICENSING SYSTEMS

Carry Licensing

Carrying concealed weapons is much more regulated than ownership, requiring permits in most states. I find this rather odd because it would seem that if one has a gun there is little practical obstacle to prevent putting it on and carrying it. I found in many years of gun carrying when I was a Parole Officer that people do not notice. However, there are many more laws regulating carrying than ownership. Many people who own pistols cannot legally carry them. Yet it is generally accepted that there is a need for *some* people to carry guns for protection. In almost all states procedures are established to license selected people to legally carry concealed weapons.

There are essentially two different types of concealed weapons licensing, discretionary and mandatory. Both are in use in different areas of the United States. Both require a license to carry concealed weapons. The difference is in the manner in which the decision to issue is made.

Discretionary Licensing

A discretionary carry licensing law allows the permit issuing authority, usually the police, to reject applications without providing clear and reasonable guidelines or

---

[16] Federal Bureau of Investigation *Crime in the United States*, Washington D.C. 1963 to 1986 as compiled in Edward F. Leddy, *Magnum Force Lobby* (University Press of America: Lanham, Maryland, 1987) pp. 187-190.

process of appeal. The guidelines are such vague phrases as "good character, public safety, reasonable cause, or need." Terms which can mean anything depending on the wishes of the issuing agent. The license applicant is regarded as a supplicant begging a privilege. Accordingly it is easy to deny licenses and the issuer has strong incentives to do so. Routine and unjustified refusal of licenses is a perennial complaint in many jurisdictions where discretionary permit laws exist.

Why Refuse?

The issuer may want to deny licenses for several reasons having nothing to do with the suitability of the applicant or his/her reason for going armed. In other nations, use of the gun laws for political control has been frequent. A government which does not have the support of its people may wisely fear to let them be armed. As Jefferson, Lenin, and others assert, the armed people can overthrow a tyrannical government.

In America, some, though not most, police accept the conventional wisdom that guns cause crime and simply want to reduce the total number of guns. Perhaps more important, when an issuer gives a license he may fear criticism if any trouble should follow. Studies show that licensed civilians commit only a trivial amount of crime, but an official may justly feel that a thousand correct decisions will be ignored while he will be criticized for one mistake. Carol Ruth Silver, civil rights activist attorney, and former chief counsel of the San Francisco Sheriff's Dept. wrote:

> Police bureaucrats—all of whom carry a gun twenty four hours a day for their own protection incidentally, work on the principle that if they give a threatened woman a gun permit and she misuses it there will be an immense clamor in the newspapers. Whereas if they deny the permit and something happens to her, no one will pay attention to her complaints(even if she is still alive to make them).[17]

Position and influence have often been strong factors in police decision making. There is little question that race, wealth, and political power have all been important.

If anybody in our society does not need handguns for self defense it is the mayors, the Sulzburgers, the Lindsays and the Brotherses, the Nelson, David, Winthrop and John Rockefellers, and all the other millionaires, socialites and celebrities who have New York City permits to carry concealed weapons while ordinary citizens can't even get permits to own them...not only does a handgun prohibition not affect them first it never gets around to them at all.[18]

Where the issuer is not restrained by the provisions of the law or subject to review, issuers can and have exercised their own prejudices and fears. The propensity of southern American police for denying licenses to blacks is well documented by civil rights groups. Other nonracial prejudices also have been manifested. Here are a few random samples, thousands of additional routine examples of arbitrary refusals can be documented.

One British police official said that he routinely denied all applications regardless

[17] Carol Ruth Silver and Don B. Kates Jr. "Handgun Ownership and the Independence of Women in a Violent, Sexist Society" reprinted in *Restricting Handguns: The Liberal Skeptics Speak Out* (Hastings on Hudson, New York: North River Press, 1979), pp. 138-69.

[18] pp. 138-69.

33.

of the suitability of the person because he didn't feel that anyone needed a gun and because guns might be stolen. Thus an official was enabled to, in effect, administer his own personal law. He was not alone. St. Louis sheriff Martin Tozer routinely denied all applications from citizens who did not register to vote (for him?) and from all women unless their husbands consented in writing. He justified this as an effort to prevent spouse crimes — a sexist effort since he didn't require husbands to get letters from their wives.[19] A head of the New York City Police Department pistol license bureau refused to allow gun purchase even to other law enforcement officers who were not members of his own department. Federal Agents stationed in New York had to sue to overturn his decision so that they could buy guns.

Of course it is not necessarily true that a discretionary system must be unfair, this depends entirely on the people administering it. But the record of discretionary licensing systems is not one to inspire confidence that the typical applicant will be licensed unless there is good reason not to do so. The issue is left to the personal whims of the issuer and the issuer is also under some pressure to deny licenses to protect himself. To reform this situation and provide fairness, it is not necessary to advocate uncontrolled gun carrying. There is the alternative of mandatory licensing.

Mandatory Licensing

In a mandatory system, the law establishes clear and specific criteria as to the qualifications for a license. When an applicant fills the criteria, a license must be issued. The majority of applications are approved. If a license is to be denied, it must be for clearly defined causes, such as a history of violence, crime, alcoholism, mental disturbance, or drug abuse. Denial may be appealed to a state license review board or to the courts. The applicant is regarded as a citizen exercising a right which may only be denied for good cause. It has been suggested that the state use gun licensing as a positive crime control tool to establish an auxiliary to the police.

The American Experience With Citizen Gun Use

Perhaps we will ultimately decide to alter the administration of these laws to permit more law-abiding citizens to carry weapons. The only alternative in many crime-ridden cities is an enormous increase of police, and most city administrators are unwilling or unable to bear the expense. If the licensing laws were administered with intelligence and a bit of courage, they could be used to create a volunteer, armed police auxiliary that would be very effective in deterring crime...Each citizen who obtained such a permit and carried a weapon with him would be in effect a law enforcement auxiliary...

Does all this sound far fetched to you? Well, it isn't, because that's how most cities and towns in the United States administer their concealed weapons laws.[20]

Experimentation With Gun Laws

Because of its diverse laws, the U.S.A. can be regarded as a "vast sociological laboratory." In some parts of the nation, guns are almost banned by strict regulations. In others gun possession in the home or business is not restricted except that persons with records of crime or insanity, minors, and certain other categories may not have

[19] Stephen Darst, "A Violent Majority" *Harper's*, April 1976, pp. 28-35

[20] George Hunter, *How To Defend Yourself, Your Family and Your Home* (New York: David McKay Company, 1967), pp. 136-7

guns. Carrying concealed weapons is regulated by both mandatory and discretionary permit systems.

One can compare the results of different gun law strategies because of the variety of laws. These, in effect, have been informal experiments in the use of guns by civilians. While they have not been formal controlled experiments, the results have been so dramatic that the relatively small experimental errors which may have occurred are probably of no real significance.

In Detroit, Michigan, grocery robberies declined 90% after a firearms training program for grocers was instituted by a grocers association.

Highland Park, Michigan, police trained storekeepers to shoot producing a dramatic decrease in store robberies from 80 in the previous four months to none in the subsequent four month period.

In New Orleans, Louisiana, pharmacy robberies dropped from three per week to three in six months.

In Kennesaw, Georgia all households have been required by law to keep a firearm since 1982. Serious crime dropped 74.4% in the year after the passage of the law and has remained low.

On the other hand the town of Morton Grove, Illinois adopted a ban on handguns. Rates of armed crime increased dramatically in comparison with neighboring communities.

Nearby Oak Park, Illinois passed a similar law in 1984. Burglary rose 35% in the following year.

How Many People Carry Guns?

According to a 1985 NBC News survey, about one in twenty (7,500,000) Americans carry a firearm for self defense. If the fears of anti-gun advocates were of substance this would produce millions of gun murders instead of the total of about five thousand actually committed in the U.S.A. Crimes of any kind committed by citizens having gun licenses are so rare that the police do not even bother to keep statistics. Few murders are committed by people without prior criminal records. Of course people with criminal histories should not be licensed.

What If Everyone Carried a Gun?

Opponents of allowing citizens to be armed often present this "what if?" argument. They imply that the removal of the discretionary restrictions that they believe in would result in catastrophe. Gun carrying would become universal and we would re-enter "the wild west" with everyone going armed. Aside from its historical inaccuracy, this is pure speculation. Where gun licensing is mandatory no such thing has happened. Instead researchers have found that when a mandatory permit system is implemented, only three to eight percent (four percent is the most frequent) of the population apply for a license. These are largely individuals who are in real danger from crime. Many of these people only carry guns on dangerous occasions, e.g. when they are carrying large sums of money or traveling in bad neighborhoods. Some others apply because they wish the convenience of a carry license to transport guns for sport without legal concerns. Far from becoming universal, gun carrying increases by only a few percentage points. The main difference is that many people without criminal records who were carrying illegally regularize their activity.

The 4% figure, however, would project nationwide to a potential carrying population of 8-10 million, [out of 225,000,000] a figure higher than that for those who carry regularly now, but lower than that for those who carry handguns for protection some of the time. With regard to most of the population, widespread issuance of permits to carry to those who wish them, or allowing concealed carrying without a permit, would result in legalizing the technically unlawful activities of a few million Americans and in causing an additional percentage or two of the population to carry protective handguns.[21]

The writer lived for six years in Laramie, Wyoming where gun carrying openly is legal. I never saw anyone carry except during "Jubilee Days" when we were asked to dress "Western."

Doesn't Gun Use Require Long Training?

This question is often asked by police and others who have gone through elaborate weapons training courses. I am a certified police firearms instructor and have conducted such police training courses. It is true that the arms training of a police officer should be elaborate. We must remember, however, that the police officer is required to know how to shoot at long distances, against multiple targets, at night, reload under fire, use pistols, shotguns, and tear gas.

The citizen seeking armed protection only needs to learn firearms safety, the law on self defense, and how to hit a criminal at room distance or less. This is a much easier task and the necessary skills can be acquired by both men and women in about fifteen hours of training. There is a social gain in a mandatory carry permit system in that classes can be conducted to teach licensed gun carriers safe and legal conduct. The current situation in many discretionary states encourages people to carry guns without training in safety or law. Mandatory licensing should reduce the chance of accidents and unintentional law violations.

Women and Guns

The protection of women is a particularly difficult issue in victimology since women are more easily victimized than men. This has caused many women to resort to firearms. In the U.S.A. 35 to 40% of pistol owners are women. This works out to 12 to 15 million women.

In Orlando, Florida, after a series of rapes, the police trained 6000 women in firearms use. The rape rate dropped from 35.91 per 100,000 population to 4.18 in Orlando while equivalent metropolitan areas either remained the same or

---

[21] Blackman, 36.

experienced an increase. Aggravated assault declined by 25%. The burglary rate declined 24%. This seems consistent since burglars might expect to confront an armed female victim.[22]

The Criminal's View

In 1985, The United States Department of Justice conducted a study of criminal behavior. Convicted criminals were asked a series of questions on their behavior. Thirty four percent reported that they had been scared off, shot at, wounded or captured by an armed victim. Forty percent reported that they had decided not to commit a crime because they thought the victim was armed:

> The first example in the sequence asked the sample to agree or disagree that 'a criminal is not going to mess around with a victim he knows is armed with a gun.' About three-fifths (56%) agreed. Another item read, 'A smart criminal always tries to find out if a potential victim is armed.' More than four-fifths agreed with that. Yet another item read, 'Most criminals are more worried about meeting an armed victim than they are about running into the police.' About three-fifths (57%) also agreed with that.[23]

The actual frequency of gun use for self protection varies widely depending on the local laws. (In the United States most gun laws are made by the fifty states. They differ widely in severity, from almost complete prohibition to easy availability.) Accordingly one can compare the results of different levels of control:

> Use of guns in defense of person and property is most common where 'controls' on guns are fewest and having needed but not had, a gun for self defense is most common in big cities where 'controls' on gun ownership are generally most stringent.[24]

Rates of those crimes which are deterrable by guns vary with the strictness of gun laws. Robbery (theft by violence) is highest in those states with the lowest gun ownership. It is lowest where private citizens own many guns. This seems reasonable since robbery tends to be a crime committed by repeat offenders. As one Wyoming police official said "Where citizens have no guns, robbers commit long strings of crimes before the police catch them. Here a storekeeper shoots them on the second or third robbery." This prevents future crimes and thus protects many who are unaware that they would otherwise have become victims.

Fourteen percent of the gun owning households in the U.S. (about 14,000,000 people) report that they have used a gun for protection of person or property exclusive of military or police work. In 60% of these cases, the gun was not fired and was used only as a threat. In only 9% of the instances was anyone injured or killed. Only 31% of instances were reported to the police. Accordingly officials tend to be

[22] Kleck and Bordua "The Factual Foundation for Certain Key Assumptions of Gun Control" *Law and Policy Quarterly* 5(1983),? 271-99.

[23] United States Department of Justice. *The Armed Criminal in America* (Washington D.C.: Government Printing Office, 1985) p. 27.

[24] Attitudes of the American Electorate Toward Gun Control (Santa Ana, California: Decision Making Information, 1978) p. 44.

unaware of the extent of citizen self defense. Armed citizens in the U.S. protect themselves from criminals at least 380,000 times a year:[25]

Given the data on private citizens' use of firearms against criminals and evidence on the slight risks of legal punishment associated with most crimes, it is a perfectly plausible hypothesis that private gun ownership currently exerts as much or more deterrent effect on criminals as do the activities of the criminal justice system. The gun owning citizenry is certainly more omnipresent than the police, and the potential severity of private justice is at least as severe as more formal legal justice, given the frequency of citizen shootings of criminals and the de facto near abolition of capital punishment by the federal judiciary.[26]

While the value to the potential victim of a gun for self protection may be admitted, officials might well be concerned about the danger that citizens would misuse their weapons injuring innocent people, committing crimes, and violating the laws on use of deadly force. Recent research in the United States indicates that this problem is more theoretical than real. A comparison was made between errors made by the police and those made by private citizens:

. . . police were successful in shooting or driving off criminals 68% of the time, private citizens were successful in 83% of their encounters. While 11% of the individuals involved in police shootings were later found to be innocents misidentified as criminals, only 2% of those in civilian shootings were so misidentified.

Private citizens encounter and kill about three times as many criminals each year as do law enforcement officials.[27]

It appears, from the writer's experience, that citizens commit fewer errors in the use of force than the police because the police often enter dangerous situations with little information. They arrive on a crime scene often not knowing who is the victim and who is the criminal. In contrast, the citizen almost always uses a weapon in response to attack. Thus the citizen can generally be sure of the criminal's identity.

The reason that few crimes are committed by licensed citizens is that criminals tend to commit crimes and acquire criminal records early in their lives. In a properly operating mandatory system, criminals cannot get licenses and seldom seek them. The chance that a citizen without any record will commit a crime is small. Giving him a gun license does not change this.

Domestic Disputes

Another objection is that most murders are committed by otherwise normal people who become angry and commit murder on an emotional impulse. They want to strike out at the enemy and grab the nearest weapon. This argument is often used to

[25] Ibid.

[26] Kleck and Bordua, 271-99.

[27] David Conover, "To Keep and Bear Arms" The American Rifleman (September 1985), pp. 40-74.

support those gun laws which are designed to disarm all citizens, not just criminals and other undesirables:

Murder is usually committed in a moment of rage. Guns are quick and easy to use. They are also deadly accurate, and they are all too often readily accessible...Because handguns are available people use them.[28]

In reality the so called spontaneous killing is rarely spontaneous. In the majority of actual family cases there have been calls to the police on previous occasions by the victim because of assaults by the perpetrator. It is clear that the typical pattern of a family killing involves a series of fights in which the victim suffers injuries which draw police or emergency room attention. It is clearly not the case that an average person kills in a once in a lifetime fit of rage. Rather, a person who has a history of repeated violence moves from assault to murder:

That the average murderer is not the average citizen can be seen by looking at his pre-murder history. Most citizens do not have even one violent felony on their records. But studies from New York, Chicago, Detroit and Washington (where over one-fifth of homicides are committed) find the average murderer has several, and that often all of them were against the person he eventually murdered. Note that these criminal record figures actually minimize the average murderer's true violent history because only in highly unusual circumstances do the police arrest for domestic violence which does not result in homicide. In other words, for every time the average murderer was actually arrested and convicted of a violent felony, he probably committed three or four that didn't result in any criminal record. No, the average murderer is not the average citizen.[29]

Criminalization of the Victim

In New York City, which has had extremely strict gun laws for eighty years there is widespread disregard for the law on the part of honest citizens. A perennial news story in that city is the honest citizen who is attacked by criminals, wards them off with a gun and is then arrested for violation of the gun law. The internationally reported Bernard Goetz case is only a recent example:

In the City of New York alone, about 6% of the population admits to owning a firearm for protection. This figure represents about 450,000 gun owners in the Big Apple or seven times the number of citizens granted permits to legally own, carry or transport their personal firearms. In other words, about 85% of those people honest enough to admit owning a gun are technical criminals under the laws of New York. But these New Yorkers have made the choice. They would rather be 'criminals' under a bad law than bodies in a police morgue.[30]

According to a 1985 survey by NBC News, about one American in twenty (7,500,000) carries a gun for self protection. (If such carrying was legal everywhere

[28] Edward M. Kennedy," The Need For Gun Control Legislation," Current History,(July/August 1976), pp. 26-31.

[29] Don B. Kates(ed.) and Mark K. Benenson, "Handgun Prohibition and Homicide: A Plausible Theory Meets the Intractable Facts," reprinted in Restricting Handguns: The Liberal Skeptics Speak Out (North River Press, 1979). p. 104.

[30] Conover, 73.

under a mandatory permit system the figure would probably rise to 8,800,000.) In many areas this carrying is illegal. This brings up the consideration that the vast majority of these "law breakers" are ordinary citizens without any record of criminal behavior. They are merely seeking to protect themselves from the violent criminals who prey on them. Discretionary licensing systems which refuse to grant licenses to these people are being disregarded. Instead they follow the old police maxim "It is better to be tried by twelve than carried by six."

Judge David J. Shields of Chicago, who tries many such illegal gun carrying cases wrote:

> Probably the most striking experience that one takes away from Gun Court is awareness of the kinds of people who appear there as defendants. For most it is their first arrest; many are old people. Shopkeepers, persons who have been victims of violent crimes and others who carry their guns because of a sincere belief in their need for protection — these constitute the greatest part of the call.[31]

It seems poor public policy to create a category of "criminals" who have no intention of committing a crime. This wastes police and court manpower to no community benefit. If rigidly enforced it would overload the corrections system. At least as important, it exposes noncriminals to the punishments designed to suppress real crime. To ruin these peoples' lives by criminal records, fines and imprisonment would appear to be cruel and serves no valid social purpose.

Advocates attempt to justify it by claiming that criminals can be stopped by the law and that others must be stopped from carrying in order to get at them. Sometimes they deny that there is any category of victims. Mayor Edward Kotch of New York claims "Good guys don't carry guns." This is obviously not true, but is an effort to justify a policy by denying its effects on the innocent.

Rather it would be advantageous and certainly more humane to separate the well intentioned innocent seeking only protection from the true criminals intent on harming others. This could be done by creating a fair carry licensing system. One which does not force citizens into the position where they feel that they have to choose between abiding by the law or preserving their lives and property.

A mandatory system appears to be the best solution. In such a system, the dangerous person or criminal can be screened out and not licensed. The citizen needing protection can feel assured that a license will be issued. Accordingly there

[31] David J. Shields, "Two Judges Look At Gun Control," *Chicago Bar Record* (January-February 1976), p. 180.

could be no valid excuse for unlicensed carrying. One could then be sure that the unlicensed gun carrier is really intent on crime rather than protection and he can be punished accordingly. This would certainly result in a high level of compliance by the innocent, increased conviction rates for the criminal, and more respect for the law.

A Modest Proposal

The National Rifle Association of America has proposed and a number of American states have adopted a model law regulating carrying concealed weapons. This law contains the following principles.

1. A permit to carry concealed weapons is required.
2. A character investigation is conducted. The person must supply identifying information.
3. It is presumed that the person has a right to a license unless there is cause for denial. The license must be issued unless there is a record of past violent crimes, pending charges, narcotic use, alien or fugitive status. Commitment to a mental institution or drug/alcohol treatment center is also cause for denial unless a physician certifies that there is no danger to the public.
4. As in other American laws, there is a presumption of innocent intent. If the person is found suitable, to carry a gun, evaluation of his or her reason for going armed is not considered the business of the state.[32]

The most significant elements of this law are, the refusal to allow police to arbitrarily deny licenses and restriction of their inquiry to clearly defined considerations of personal suitability. These are important limitations because they are designed to prevent personal prejudices from affecting the decision and to prevent social standing, race, wealth or other extraneous factors from being considered.

Conclusion

Experience indicates that the ownership and carrying of guns by potential victims reduces victimization both for the individual and for other potential victims. The deterrence of such crimes as robbery, assault, rape, and home invasion (illegal entry into occupied dwellings) is clear and dramatic. The hazards of citizen use have been greatly exaggerated because of theoretical fears not actual evidence. Therefore a revision of firearms laws in the direction of the mandatory model appears both prudent and desirable from the viewpoint of potential victims. This would benefit those who do not choose to carry guns as well as those who do so, since, when many people are armed, the criminal cannot be sure that any potential victim is unarmed. This measure would both provide protection to the potential victim and pose a significant threat to the violent criminal.

[32] Copies of the full text may be obtained by writing NRA-Institute For Legislative Action, 1600 Rhode Island Ave., Washington, D.C. 20036, U.S.A.

Chapter 4

Aspects of Survival Hunting: Resistance and Defiance as Assertion and Autonomy

A Review Esay of
Ragnor Benson, *Survival Poaching*
Boulder: Paladin Press, 1980

by
Roy Wortman

"I am a poacher. For the last forty years I have poached game with impunity and ease, to the point where it is now a big game. During the course of these forty years, I have developed many quick and easy methods of collecting deer, bear, game birds, furbearers, fish, and reptiles. In poacher's jargon, this is known as 'reducing to possession.' " Benson's innocuous and seemingly routine description may in fact cover the deeper reasons for this "how to" treatise. On the surface Survival Poaching is not a political tract, nor does it in any way have any direct connection with the so-called "survival movement" of the paramilitary underground right. Linkage is not apparently suggested to covert and hidden agendas of rightist "survivalism." The work for the most part is apolitical, yet it is simultaneously an American document in that it does connect with an earlier historical tradition. This earlier tradition cannot be connected with the equivalent of the current survivalist movement: on the contrary, the earlier heritage, goes back to the tradition of social banditry in Western Europe and to the Dissenting and Libertarian heritage in the British North American colonies and in the United States.

In its deeper meaning, then, this book is a document that is consonant with the historical dynamic and development of American attitudes toward authority. It is a heritage that is devoid of the current "left" versus "right" analysis, which may be specious when applied to the historical context of the Libertarian and Dissenting traditions. Survival Poaching has links not only with the defiant resistance to excessive authority but as well connects to a more immediate resistance to the bureaucratic and regulatory state. While most of the book is devoted to the specifics of technique, weapons, traps, urban survival, and methods of evasion and escape, the core of Benson's themes are best seen in his attitudes about why he developed his approach to hunting. Placed within the broader conceptual and analytical framework of American attitudes on excessive authority, Benson adds to the litany of grass-roots anger about the machinery of the state intruding into an individual's life. This is not to say that Benson is an avowed anti-statist. He cares for himself and his

Previously published in *Cynegeticus*, January, 1987

family while apparently giving more than lip service to conservation of natural resources. "In the final analysis, this book will give you the tools needed to bypass the jerk anti-hunter, environmentalist, preservationist, land-poster, and college educated game warden, all of whom make this book so necessary."

Benson's blunt honesty, devoid of any sophistry, addresses the question of "why poach?" The immediate answer is one of necessity. He has the perception to recognize deeper currents in socio-economic forces "that are contributing mightily to the necessity for poaching . . ." Yet he leaves this theme as is, without further amplification.

It is not Benson's task to serve as the historian, sociologist, or economist. He devotes only one brief paragraph to this matter, assuming that the rest is taken for granted by the reader and by this current generation of Americans. So, too, he is aware that many poachers, although they already know why they poach, "may not be able to verbalize their feelings well." On the other hand, "those who scorn the poacher are, in many cases, the same ones who created the necessity for poaching in the first place." In this regard Benson hits the raw nerve which has been touched by environmentalists, managers, and bureaucrats who misconstrue the way of life and the cultural attitudes of countless Americans. This is not to say that Benson's willful breaking of the law of game management and conservation is to be condoned anymore than his suggestions on the violation of firearms laws are to be encouraged or admired. His section on silencers, while practical for the effective poacher, is in blatant disregard of federal and state statutes, to cite but one example.

The incident which illuminated the world of defiance and resistance for Benson is most revealing. Like others, a negative encounter with but one representative of authority deeply marked Benson. He and his family were fishing in Michigan, he asleep in his boat with a drop line in one hand, and his wife and children on the bank with willow cane and line rigs. None had caught a fish. "About noon the local game warden came roaring up in his big power boat and demanded to see our licenses . . . I had forgotten all about the necessity of buying one in Michigan." Benson told the warden he didn't have a license but that he was willing to go into town to purchase one, and that, with primitive equipment for fishing rigs, there was no possibility of catching fish, anyway. "All of this mattered not one twiddle to The Law. The fine was $40.00, payable now, and that was that." The social bandit and outlaw was created in the course of a few minutes. States Benson, "I don't know how the bastard knew it, but $40.00 was all the cash I had in the world. For thirty minutes we talked, then argued, pleaded, then begged. But my pleas were all futile." Benson regarded himself as a law-abiding person, but after surrendering his cash to the warden, his vacation was over. The die was cast for the poacher: "It was the last time I was ever arrested for a game violation but, more important, my philosophy about poaching changed dramatically." We note that Benson, who poaches to provide for his family, "is not talking about hurting or destroying our natural resources. That would be counter-productive to my way of life as a poacher. My reference is to legislation that purposely and maliciously prevents people from using our natural resources."

Against this view, the historian must examine the opposite side of the issue: regulation for successful management of game and fish populations, the management of public resources in the public domain for the benefit of all, and the use of state power through the regulation of bag limit, harvest, and season is a compelling argument, within reason. Yet apparently for some, in the delicate balance of state power and individual needs and perceived rights coupled with resentments, an equally compelling argument might be made on the part of the poacher for deliberately violating the law. In the tradition of those who violated the king's game in France and England, those who willingly acted in defiance of royal authority, and those who asserted their natural rights as "freeborn men" acted within the tradition of the Tree of Liberty, the Dissenting republican and libertarian heritage deeply rooted in the concept of rights, privileges, and immunities in the Anglo-American political tradition. Over time this permeated to the popular element in political culture which linked "the people" to popular sovereignty. Benson may be out of his historical time frame — perhaps the 1770s would be more his element. Still, it would not be interpolating too much to state that Benson's legacy does fit within this tradition. He candidly recognizes this, recalling its English heritage as an "honorable calling, worthy of anyone with a 'quick mind and a stout leg.'" Whether or not Benson has read the history of social banditry and defiance of excessive royal prerogatives is a moot point in assessing a work of popular American culture. As historians we cannot ascribe hidden intellectual motivations to that which is a document of American culture as well as a "how-to" book. Yet the fact is that Benson has a recognition of a state of equity, and in one paragraph writes of Robin Hood "not for robbing from the rich and keeping thirty percent," but for violation of the King's game laws. In his own way, Benson suggests a visceral form of distributive justice, not on a mass or communal level, but for the individual and his or her family. Yet unlike past historical organized community movements in rural protest, we will never have an idea of how many people Benson purports to speak for; the underground and illegal nature of poaching makes this an impossibility.

Encroachment of game habitat in Europe accelerated, notes Benson, as populations increased. He all too briefly mentions the laws passed allowing "privileged individuals to control large chunks of real estate for their own use. By the early 1800s there was little private property a common citizen could own or use, let alone hunt on." Only to an extent is Benson correct: Notwithstanding even citizenship in France through the Declaration of the Rights of Man and Citizen, and in England through the various acts enfranchising the middle classes, industrial workers and agricultural workers, the fact remained that citizenship in and of itself did not constitute a birthright for the ordinary or common man or woman to hunt. While Benson does not consider this, it must be noted for the sake of historical accuracy. The English dissenting heritage — the radical Whig tradition which feared the concentration of power in any individual or politically constituted body — seems to have the echoes, historically, of pragmatism and defiance in Benson's motives. In point of fact there was convergence between this political heritage and a religious tradition of low-church Protestantism which provided a powerful ideological impetus, when coupled with the availability of land and expectations in British North America and the United States. The Dissenting Libertarian heritage feared hierarchy and centralized authority in the seventeenth and eighteenth centuries, and Benson's implied and overt fear of bureaucratic, impersonal agencies seems consistent with this tradition. That the natural rights heritage of dissent, the more radical spectrum of Lockean thought, allowed for anything else but resistance to perceived illegitimate authority cannot be ignored in the interpretation of the collective political past of the United States and, for that matter, even in examining this one individual poacher.

Benson's views are part of a broader trend, as many Americans perceive that their natural rights, and their access to nature's bounty are threatened. If poaching is Benson's statement of social protest in a mass society, it has roots: perhaps the most pronounced, without stretching the realm of historical thought too far, is the protest stemming from reaction to intrusion on deeply-rooted patterns of behavior that have been especially pronounced in the nineteenth century. Indeed, as Robert C. McMath has stated "modernization" and "mass society" are explanations in which "Inexorable forces disrupt familiar patterns of community life," and the resultant reaction is an anachronistic, backward-looking protest movement or a "forward-looking" "businesslike" movement, at least in some interpretations of past rural protest.[1] But to understand the protest movements of rural America is to go beyond "modernization." One must look to deeply-established and internalized belief systems and cultural values, as McMath reminds us.

Unlike organized rural protest movements of the nineteenth century, poaching in the United States today is not an organized institutional activity of either a voluntary self-interest group or a primary identification group. While there are segments of poaching which may be connected to those organizations which preach "survivalism," it is important to note that the only organization involved in poaching is, in some instances, the kinship-related organization in which families and only families concentrate on their activities of extra-legal hunting. Still, there are parallels in the spirit of the poacher and the spirit of the more organized protest movements of the mid and late nineteenth century in the United States which developed their culture of both resistance and rebellion as well as their concept of play and food gathering. Both came from rural areas. Both felt the overshadowing of social and economic forces as American society was transformed by market forces and social dynamics from a rural to an urban society in which community was supplanted by a larger, more organized bureaucratically structured society which had ramifications in all aspects of American life, rural and urban, public and private sector, countryside and city, and

1 Robert C. McMath, "Sandy Land and Hogs in Timber: (Agri)cultural Origin of the Farmers Alliance in Texas," in Steven Hahn and Jonathan Prude (eds.) *The Countryside in the Age of Capitalist Transformation: Essays in the Social History of Rural America.* (Chapel Hill: University of North Carolina Press, 1985).

in economic and political structure and activity.

Within a broader framework it would be proper to place the resentment of Benson within the scope of the modern, bureaucratic society. As Samuel P. Hayes noted about the nature of bureaucracy in the progressive era, "while the agents of science and technology have professed to themselves and to the world at large that they were neutral instruments rather than goal-makers, they, in fact, were deeply preoccupied with shaping and ordering the lives of men." To extend upon historical arguments made for rural America and the regulation of rural life by the more impersonal bureaucratic forces of social order and regulation, the concepts of organization, management for efficiency, and regulation, as Gary Danbom so aptly put it, clearly placed the values of industrial efficiency over the older, more traditional values of the religiously-motivated and republican-oriented pre-modern—that is, pre-industrial — person.[2]

Let the rhetoric of the Texas small farmers, as cited by McMath, echo in particular the deeply-felt resentments of their time on enclosure and on the increasing expansion of larger, more commercial-oriented market-oriented farming and ranching: In West Texas, a group of farmers stated, "We don't care to be made serfs of yet like poor Ireland and the majority of England." Upland Georgians noted in the 1880s, "The woods . . . were put here by our creator for a benefit to his people and I don't think it right to deprive a large majority to please a minority." Still, in the same rhetorical vein, another farmer declared that "The citizens of this county have and always have had the legal, moral, and Bible right to let their stock . . . run at large. We all knew this when we purchased this land." Commercial farming overshadowed the small self-sufficient farmer, and for the case of poaching — and here we exclude the market-hunter poacher who is in the business solely for profit — the transitions from past to present made inexorable changes which gnawed at the right to self-sufficiency, coupled with the state growth through invested legal and administrative powers, to regulate in the public good. Wildlife procreation and conservation, land use, and the public good all came into play in the management of hunting, as the United States made its quest for order and efficiency. That Robert Wiebe's concept of "the search for order" is applicable here is without doubt accurate in the bureaucratization and regulation of social order. This neither justifies nor apologizes for the poacher; it does, however, try to explain the frustration and anger of some of those who poach. Old patterns of rural self-sustenance were being rapidly replaced with new ways of ordering the complexity of life for both the public and the administrative state sphere. In the process those of the stubborn individualistic temperament asserted themselves not as outlaws — although they have been seen as such and many doubtless are —but as people who are deliberately disobedient of civil authority as a matter of principle and as a matter even of moral obligation and duty. This theme is implicit in Benson, and it is within this framework rather than the "how-to" framework of weaponry and technique that "survival poaching," at least when placed in historical analysis, needs to be seen.

[2] Gary Danbom, *The Resisted Revolution: Urban America and the Industrialization of Agriculture, 1900-1930.* (Ames: Iowa University Press, 1979).

Chapter 5

THE MEANINGS OF GUNS: HUNTERS, SHOOTERS, AND GUN COLLECTORS*

by
Barbara Stenross

We live in a culture replete with man-made objects. Some sociologists have begun to explore the meanings of these possessions.[1] They have found that even utilitarian objects can function symbolically as "status symbols" (Goffman, 1951) or "markers of the self" (Goffman, 1971: 41 44).[2] Through our belongings, we reveal the groups we identify with, the values we hold, and hence, the kind of persons we are, or wish to be.

Research by Tonso suggests that guns have symbolic as well as practical meaning for their owners.[3] Guns are present in half the households in the United States.[4] In many of these households, owners use guns in much the same way that others use locks and burglar alarms — as talismans that give them a feeling of control within their domiciles or about their person.[5] These people presumably don't "like guns,"

*This research was supported in part by a grant from the Faculty Research Council of the University of North Carolina at Chapel Hill. A version of this paper was presented at the Annual Meetings of the Popular Culture Association, Montreal, Quebec, March, 1987. I thank Jeanne Brooks for research assistance and Sherryl Kleinman, Don B. Kates, Jr., Michael Charles Russell, A.D. Olmsted, Gary Kleck, William R. Tonso, James White, and James D. Wright for comments on earlier drafts.

[1] Kai T. Erikson, *Everything in Its Path* (New York: Simon and Schuster, 1976); M. Csikszentmihaly; and E. Rochberg Halton, *The Meaning of Things: Domestic Symbols and Self* (Cambridge: Cambridge University Press, 1981); and Chandra Mukerji *From Graven Images: Patterns of Modern Materialism* (New York: Columbia University Press, 1983).

[2] Erving Goffman, "Symbols of Class Status," *British Journal of Sociology* Vol. 2 (1951), 294-304, and *Relations in Public* (New York: Harper and Row, 1971), pp. 41-44.

[3] William R. Tonso, *Gun and Society: The Social and Existential Roots of the American Attachment to Firearms* (Washington, D.C.: University Press of America, 1982).

[4] James D. Wright, Peter H. Rossi, and Kathleen Daly, *Under the Gun: Weapons, Crime and Violence in America* (New York: Aldine, 1983).

[5] See Kates and Varzos in Chapter 8 of this volume, and James DeFronzo "Fear of Crime and Handgun Ownership," *Criminology* Vol. 17 (1979), 331-339.

but feel "forced" to have them because they live in a violent society. Yet other people own and use guns "voluntarily," for recreation. Tonso argues that recreational gun owners can use guns to make status claims. The most obvious example is the gun collector, who participates in a status community based on the kind and condition of guns he owns.[6] But Tonso also notes that guns can contribute to self-esteem and status in other ways.

In-depth interviews with 43 gun recreationists revealed the varied meanings guns have for gun collectors, competitive shooters, and hunters. In popular imagery, hunters are the prototypical gun enthusiasts. Yet many hunters do not consider themselves to be "gun people." They are outdoorsmen who regard and use their guns as tools. In contrast, gun collectors, who are strongly attached to guns, value guns as artifacts, curios or *objets d'art*. Finally, competitive shooters identify themselves as athletes. They treat their guns as sports equipment.

Since gun hobbyists use guns voluntarily and take guns seriously, it is not surprising that they disidentify themselves from the negative images of guns shared by many in the wider society. Gun enthusiasts are as moralistic about gun ownership and use as their anti-gun opponents.

Research Setting and Method

To learn how gun enthusiasts view themselves and their guns, I conducted in-depth interviews with 43 hunters, shooters and gun collectors residing in central and eastern North Carolina. Gun owners are often wary of discussing their interest in guns with academics and other outsiders. To obtain interviews, then, I relied mainly on the method of snowball sampling. I gained the trust of two gun enthusiasts who then introduced me to others. In addition, I advertised for respondents in two local newspapers and interviewed the proprietors of 7 local gunshops and sporting goods stores. Among those contacted, there were no refusals to participate.

The gun recreationists varied in age from the early twenties to the early seventies and worked in a variety of occupations, but with a concentration in professional and technical fields (e.g., engineer, physician, welder, dental technician, attorney). The hunters were more diverse in their occupational and class backgrounds than the collectors and competitive shooters, whose avocations often require a larger financial investment. All of the respondents were white; only two were female (one hunter, one shooter). Categorizing respondents by the leisure interest that was most important to them, I interviewed 14 gun collectors, 17 competitive shooters, and 12 hunters.

I used a grounded theory approach to discover the meaning of hunting, shooting, and gun collecting to the respondents.[7] In interviews that lasted about 90 minutes, I

---

[6] Tonso, 282-301, and A.D. Olmsted, "Morally Controversial Leisure: The Social World of Gun Collectors," *Symbolic Interaction* Vol. 11 (1989), 277-287.

[7] Barney Glaser and Anselm Strauss, *The Discovery of Grounded Theory* (Chicago: Aldine, 1967).

asked respondents how they used guns, how they became interested in their gun sport or hobby, and with whom they associated. I took detailed notes during the interviews (as much verbatim as possible), then transcribed the interviews for analysis.

The Meanings Of Guns For Gun Enthusiasts
Shooting: Guns As Sports Equipment

Many gun owners may occasionally "plink" at tin cans. The shooters I interviewed were skilled marksmen who spent five to eight months or more per year competing in local, regional, and national matches. They identified themselves as athletes and viewed guns as sports equipment.

There are many different gun sports, each with its own type of target (e.g., clay pigeon, bull's eye, metallic silhouette), course rules (e.g., distances, speeds, number of chances or rounds), and gun requirements (e.g., barrel length, caliber, gauge). The shooters regarded the different types of guns (shotguns, rifles, pistols) as presenting different sports challenges. Shooters contrasted long and short-barreled guns. Some shooters preferred pistol shooting because the pistol's shorter barrel made attaining accuracy more difficult. A manager who served in the police reserve explained:

A pistol is more of a challenge than a rifle. A six-inch barrel compared to a 30 inch barrel. The longer the barrel, the more accuracy.

Other shooters preferred rifle shooting because they were drawn to the possibility of obtaining extreme precision, even at distances of 100 or more yards.[8] A physician said:

I shot some pistol competition, didn't like it. I changed to [benchrest] rifle. No other shooting allows that kind of accuracy.

A few shooting sports (or matches) require competitors to use standard guns (and ammunition), "out of the box," but most allow competitors to modify their guns and ammunition to improve speed, accuracy, or knock-down power. Most shooters did not shoot standard guns, then, but had their guns rebuilt, modified, or customized by master gunsmiths. Some did much of this work themselves. A pistol competitor described his gun this way:

[My gun was] special built for me by Bill Davis [gunsmith]. He converted it. Changed the barrel, put on different sights, had a cylinder stop put in it, ball and crane lock, made a one-inch Apex barrel to give it more twist, more spin, for greater accuracy.

Some rifle and pistol shooters also used custom ammunition. A pistol competitor explained how he experimented with various cases, powder charges, and bullets in order to improve the "group" — that is, reduce the distance between successive shots on the target:

Each gun has its own peculiarity and I worked out the load for that particular gun. We're talking about minute measurements in accuracy here. Say a gun shoots so that all its bullets will group within two inches on a target.

[8] See Richard Hummel "Anatomy of a Wargame: Target Shooting in Three Cultures, "*Journal of Sport Behavior*," Vol. 45 (1985), 229-244, for an excellent ethnography of high-powered rifle matches.

You can doctor the ammunition and maybe get an inch and three-quarters out of it — change the weight of the bullet, the powder charge, experiment with different cases.

The modifications shooters made to their guns and ammunition improved their performance, but they were improvements only in a highly specialized sense. Often, these "improvements" made a gun more delicate, more subject to stoppage or breakage, or heavier or bulkier than would be useful in the field or for self-defense. A trap shooter who made custom stocks explained how designing the gun to fit one sportsman often made the gun less useful to others:

People are built differently, need different forms, shapes of stocks. For example, I'm making a slender stock for a lady who has a small hand. I have a long neck, so I need higher comb on the stock. [If you bought a commercial gun without modification, you would get] the same stock, built to fit anybody, but no one in particular.

All sports involve sports equipment. Modifying and customizing this equipment to improve performance is an important part of competition.[9] The competitive shooters used guns as sports equipment, to test and develop their talent as athletes.

Hunting: Guns As Tools

Hunting is the gun sport with the largest following in the United States. But I found that many serious hunters do not regard themselves as "gun people." As one hunter put it, "I'm not a gun person, I'm a hunter." Hunters defined hunting as a means of putting meat on the table, a way of connecting with the natural environment, or a means to obtain trophies (notable body parts of the male of the species). They viewed hunting as part and parcel of rural culture. A hunter who grew up in the eastern part of North Carolina said:

Everybody in our part of the country hunts or fishes or both. It's heavily wooded, with lots of game. Guns are a part of the culture. It's a hand-me-down culture of outdoorsy interests.

Hunters believe they are among the few Americans who retain the skills that have historically enabled humans to survive in, and master, the "great outdoors."

The hunters used guns as tools, to bring down game and to protect themselves from danger in the out-of-doors. They appreciated guns that were well-crafted, but said that their main objective was to find a gun that was dependable and comfortable to use. They described their guns as "working guns." A farmer said:

I don't collect antiques or guns that won't fire. All of my guns are working guns. I still use the gun I bought when I was 16. I just put a new stock on it. The stock split.

Unattached to the guns themselves, most hunters used ordinary guns, purchased from local gun or sporting goods store. And, they usually used guns "as is" rather than

9 See Richard Mitchell, *Mountain Experience: The Psychology and Sociology of Adventure* (Chicago: University of Chicago Press, 1983).

52.

having them customized or modified. Indeed, one gunshop proprietor said that some hunters sold their guns back to him at the end of hunting season. He sometimes resold the same gun five or six times. Owners of stores that specialized in hunting guns added other merchandise to carry the business between hunting seasons:

> We had a small store. We just had hunting guns. But hunting guns are a seasonal business. We had to expand to get something to be able to carry the guns.

Most of the hunters did several types of hunting and therefore owned more than one type of gun. For example, a hunter might own two or three shotguns for wing (e.g., duck) hunting, and a couple of rifles for deer hunting. But the hunters felt guilty about owning "extra" guns they did not use. A writer said:

> I got rid of everything I wasn't using, didn't have time to keep clean.

A self-employed businessman rotated among his guns in an effort to use them all:

> I use one gun, take three or four deer with it, stick it back in the rack, try another.

In emphasizing that they were not gun people, the hunters explained that modern guns are only one means of hunting game. In North Carolina, hunting season for deer begins with bow hunting. Hunters may also use muzzleloaders and black powder (cap and ball) pistols to hunt deer before the modern firearm season begins. The hunters often cited their use of bow and arrow or muzzleloader to indicate that they were hunters, not "gun people." The proprietor of a small business said:

> Guns are a part of hunting, but I also hunt with bow and arrow and muzzle-loader, so you know I'm interested in the *hunting*.

When I asked a professor who hunted deer what he shot with, he corrected me by saying, "I hunt with a rifle, a bow, sometimes a shotgun." Hunters who took up bow and arrow or muzzleloader hunting often preferred these simpler technologies that brought them closer to the out-of-doors. A dentist who hunted duck and deer said:

> For me, hunting is not automatically associated with guns. I have been bow hunting for the last five years. I like the isolation.

The hunters were not the gun enthusiasts I expected them to be. They used guns often, but were not attached to their guns in the same way as were the competitive shooters or, as we shall see, the gun collectors. And because they were not interested in guns per se, they owned ordinary guns, not the more specialized or stylized sports equipment of the competitive shooter.

Collecting: Guns As Art, Artifacts, and Curios

The hunters and shooters used guns instrumentally, to support their activities as outdoorsmen and athletes. In contrast, the collectors said their guns were for "looking at," studying, and amassing as investments.

Some collectors were eclectic, collecting any guns they "liked." But most believed that "true" collectors have a theme or focus to their collection.[10] A media specialist

---

[10] See also Olmstead, Tonso.

who owned more than 200 guns said:

I tend to like antique military weapons, but I also have a general interest in a lot of guns. To a true collector, maybe I wouldn't be a collector because my collection is not specialized. I have some modern, some antique.

Most collectors collected a particular kind of gun, chosen for its beauty, historical significance, or design. They were not interested in "all the guns out there." Rather, they worked to fill gaps in their thematic collection and to upgrade quality or condition. A building contractor who collected antique Colts said:

I look for items I don't have, plus to upgrade the items I do have. The collection is never static.

Because of their thematic focus, collectors often owned many examples or variants of the "same" gun:

Years ago I collected Lugers. I had 120, 130 in all. They all look alike.

The collectors did not agree about which guns were most interesting or valuable. Some felt that times were "moving too fast;" hence, they "reached back to hold on to the past" and collected old guns that "had enough quality to last all this time." Often, they collected firearms that have come to symbolize particular historical events, eras, or persons — for example, the Colt single-action revolvers used during the settling of the West. A disabled farmer who rented tables at local gun shows said:

I collect Colt single action armys, made from the same mold from 1873 to 1980. The guns from the old cowboy pictures. Six-shooters.

Other collectors liked guns that incorporated particular design features (e.g., side-by-side shotguns; European "predecessors to cartridge arms"), or that they viewed as works of art (e.g., antique inlaid pistols). A physician who collected limited edition engraved commemorative guns said:

I think that my major interest in firearms is the technological and artistic. To me, it's just as much a work of art as a Picasso. An engraver is a highly touted artisan.

Similarly, a gunsmith who collected Parker Brothers shotguns from the 1880s proclaimed them the "epitome of gun craft in the U.S."

Regardless of the focus of their collection, the collectors collected not only the guns themselves, but also their stories. A pharmacist who had just bought his first antique gun, a ladies pistol, imagined a romantic history for his purchase:

I've traced it back to after the Civil War but before the turn of the century. I've convinced myself that it belonged to a river boat gambler who carried it up and down the Mississippi (laugh).

An electrical engineer described the research he had undertaken to learn the history of a Roth-Steyr semi-automatic pistol in his collection:

I'm researching a gun developed in Austria, a semi-automatic. It and two others ended up in Australia. Why Australia? I'm trying to research how it got there . . . I started writing letters around everywhere. Now I get letters.

The wife of one collector (who worked part-time as a gun broker) said she felt her husband collected guns "to have stories to tell." He smiled and added, "if you can sell the story, you can sell the gun."

Ironically, although many collectors owned particular guns because of their history of use, they rarely used the guns themselves. For example, the media specialist with the "eclectic" collection said:

Of the 200 or so guns I have, I shoot maybe 3 or 4. The rest are sitting in boxes, probably rusting (laugh).

Collectors of antique firearms worried that firing their guns would reduce their quality. Collectors of modern guns often did not even "open" their guns, but preserved them, closed and unloaded, in their original boxes. A physician who collected commemorative pistols said:

I never shoot them. The trade thing is "NIB" — new in the box. It loses its value if it's not in the original container and that container is not in original condition.

Instead, the collectors acted like curators, treating their guns as valuable museum pieces — artifacts, curios, or *objets d'art*. At gun shows, they often displayed their guns in locked glass cases, sometimes with papers of authenticity.

Unlike the hunters and shooters, the collectors did not care whether a gun was dependable or accurate as long as it was unusual, historically significant, artistic, or scarce. They saw themselves as historians and aesthetes who appreciated particular guns for their design and history, not for their use.

Rejected Meanings of Guns

The hunters, shooters, and collectors were highly committed avocationists. Most had been collecting, competing, or hunting for many years. All were "regulars" in their leisure social worlds; a few were "insiders" who professed their subculture's views via official and unofficial positions of leadership in local or national associations.[11] Yet the avocationists sometimes struggled with and against other meanings of guns. For example, most rejected that guns are "for men only," but admitted that they had always associated guns with manhood and male camaraderie. For example, a dentist who hunted said:

My wife and Nancy are the only women I've ever seen out there [hunting]. It is sort of a masculine phenomenon. When you're holding a firearm, for me it's an artistic feeling. But there's something about being a man holding a firearm, feeling it, that feels very right somehow.

In addition, while all of the respondents deemphasized the "weapon" aspects of guns, they said they would not hesitate to use a gun to defend themselves and their families. Several said that there had been times in their lives when simply having a gun available as a weapon had given them comfort.

Nevertheless, the gun enthusiasts believed that some uses and meanings of guns were superior to others.

[11] David R. Unruh, "Characteristics and Types of Participation in Social Worlds," *Symbolic Interaction*, Vol. 3 (1980), 115-129.

Talismans and Toys

The shooters, hunters, and collectors valued guns as leisure objects. But they also felt that guns were "serious business." Hence, they rejected two meanings of guns they attributed to more casual owners.

The respondents felt that many non-sportsmen buy guns "to feel protected." They described these people as viewing guns as "magic charms" or talismans that will "keep them safe" and "solve all their problems." They believed that people who treat guns as mystical objects may be more vulnerable with the guns than without them. A physician said:

I have a dealer's license and sell guns to friends who want them. I really chew them out when they buy them. I say, "Do you realize it's against the law to carry them concealed?" Number two, it's dangerous. At best, you could shoot yourself in the ass. At worst, if you pull the gun and don't use it, it can be used against you.

A pistol competitor who worked as a police officer put it this way: "owning a gun doesn't protect you any more than owning a violin makes you a musician."

The recreational gun owners felt that owning a gun was a "lot of responsibility," and that people should own guns only if they are willing to learn how to use them safely. They did not expect everyone who owned a gun to become a marksman, but they did feel that all gun owners should learn "proper respect for guns as tools," including "how to shoot, how to reload, and to check the gun." Several shooters felt that people should be tested on their safe handling of guns before being permitted to own them.

A second definition the gun enthusiasts rejected was that of guns as "macho toys." They felt that young men sometimes bought guns to feel powerful, displaying their guns as badges of their masculinity and toughness. The gun enthusiasts made fun of these gun owners, when they were not feeling personally endangered by them. A forester who hunted and also collected guns said:

They see an HK91 in a movie or on A-Team and want to have one. You'll see them at [gun] shows, very loud, wearing army coats, boots, a pistol on their hip into the gun show to show they have one, an authentic Rambo look-alike knife.

A competitive pistol shooter who was a police administrator contrasted his own attitude at the range with that of the "gun nut:"

I go out to the range and shoot. I go in a very disciplined manner, put my target up, blacken the sight, methodically go through a course of fire. Gun nuts may bring 5 or 6 guns — .44 Magnum, .357 Magnum, semi-automatic, some bring .22s, some bring .38s. They'll fire them fast, they'll fire them slow. They are fascinated with them more than really knowledgeable.

The respondents believed that the television and motion picture industries promote this view of guns as macho toys through such productions as "Rambo" and "Dirty Harry." They worked to dispel such imagery of guns and gun use in their own homes. A medical examiner who competed in pistol matches said:

I try not to look at firearms as a means of power. I have not introduced these ideas to my kids. TV does a good job of that. Firearms function as more a mental exercise. The gun enthusiasts used guns as leisure, but they did not trivialize guns by regarding them as toys with which to posture or play around. They believed that taking the mystery or mystique out of guns was essential to handling them properly. An actuary who collected antique Japanese pistols explained:

As soon as my boys had any understanding, I showed them where the guns were, how they worked. I tried to remove any mystery from the gun, keep it from being something to hide from Daddy.

Instruments of Violence

The gun enthusiasts disliked having others treat guns casually. But they were even more dismayed by what some perceived as a growing market for paramilitary products or assault weapons that some felt "don't have any place" in hunting, sport shooting, collecting, or even personal protection.

The gun enthusiasts felt that some people like guns for their "killing power." They referred to such people as "commandos," "paramilitary paranoids," or "survivalists." In distancing the recreational gun owner from these people, one shooter emphasized, "survivalists are not *hobbyists.*"

Several of the shooters and hunters did not go to local gun shows because they disliked seeing the display of paramilitary guns and paraphernalia. Others did not go because they disliked rubbing elbows with the "commando" element that also attended. The dentist who hunted said:

There are some people there [at the gun shows] that will scare the hell out of you. Wearing t-shirts that say, "Let's kill them all let God sort them out." I get very turned off by guns the whole purpose of which is to kill another human being.

And a gunsmith who competed nationally in trap and also hunted said:

I've never gone to gun shows. I never liked the paramilitary stuff. I never liked the military weapons, people-killing weapons. Never carry any here [in the shop], never work on them. Do work on some military pistols

Finally, the electrical engineer who collected Roth-Steyr pistols said that fellow-members of the National Automatic Pistol Club (N.A.P.C.) gave him a hard time because he also collected machine guns:

People in N.A.P.C. don't think too highly of people with machine guns. They think I'm a terrorist because I have machine guns. If I didn't have the Roth-Steyrs, they probably wouldn't accept me.

Members of all three groups of gun enthusiasts spoke out against the image of firearms as instruments of violence. But because the competitive shooters dealt with shooting most centrally, they had the most fully developed perspective on this issue.

The competitive shooters learned to be good shots, but they did not equate their marksmanship with training for combat or for killing. Rather, the competitive shooters felt they were *less* likely to perpetrate violence with their guns than others who had less shooting experience.

The competitive shooters believed that the "more proficient you get with firearms, the less likely you are to use them." A police administrator explained:

> If you are real proficient, you can wait longer, know that you have lethal force you can use, can strike where you want to.

One police officer felt that even the standard practical police match course that officers complete in is too stylized to prepare them to use a gun defensively. He took up combat shooting instead (in this sport, competitors move through an obstacle course of man-sized targets, some of which are "hostages" or "no shoots"). Yet he felt his combat raining prepared him to use restraint, not to use his gun as an assalt weapon:

> On the firing range you are constantly under stress. If you do well, it breeds confidence. If you have a confident bearing, you may not draw your weapon. With less confidence, you could use a weapon more quickly.

The shooters felt that competing taught them self-control, not violence. Thus, one shooter, a university student, compared shooting to meditation:

> I enjoy target shooting. It requires control, calmness, steadiness. It's like meditation in some respects. I don't see myself as a combatant.

Another shooter, a physician, felt the world would be a more peaceful place if more people stood at the firing line and fewer attended football games. The competitive shooters used guns a lot, but felt they taught them to become experts on gun safety and non-violence, not combatants.

DISCUSSION AND CONCLUSION

Mead taught us long ago that meanings are situational. Hence, we should not be surprised at the variety of meanings guns can have.[12] The hunters, shooters, and collectors enjoyed different gun activities, developed different leisure identities, and hence, defined guns in different ways. Shooters enjoy competing, see themselves as athletes, and outfit themselves with guns as sports equipment. Hunters enjoy surviving in and mastering the natural environment, take pride in being outdoorsmen, and value guns as dependable tools. Collectors like to study guns, view themselves as historians and aesthetes, and collect particular guns they value as art, artifacts, or curios.

Interestingly, the strongest attachment to guns occurred among gun collectors, the hobbyists who fired guns the least. The weakest attachment to firearms occurred among the hunters. It should not be surprising, then, that most hunters own ordinary guns; gun collectors' and target shooters' guns were extraordinary.

[12] George Herbert Mead, *Mind, Self, and Society,* Charles W. Morris, ed. (Chicago, University of Chicago Press, 1934).

The recreational gun owners recognized that guns have multiple uses and meanings that support different identities. Within their own social world, they worked to maintain a central, "good" meaning to guns, and to attenuate negative images and meanings. They expressed concern about people who are "fascinated" by guns, but who do not use them as sports equipment, tools, or curios. They rejected unserious uses and meanings of guns — as toys or talismans — and criticized those who value guns for their fire-power or as assault weapons. Serious gun hobbyists or sportsmen view gun ownership and use as activities imbued with morality.

Material objects have no inherent meaning. Rather, we give them meaning through our activities and associations.[13] This is as true for guns as for any other objects. The meaning of firearms varies even within a group as seemingly homogeneous as gun enthusiasts.

---

[13]Mead and Herbert Blumer, *Symbolic Interaction* (Englewood Cliffs, New Jersey: Prentice Hall, 1969).

Chapter 6

GUN OWNERSHIP AS SERIOUS LEISURE

by
A.D. Olmsted

Introduction

Social scientists, politicians, policemen, the mass media, gun owners and non-gun owners have been increasingly made aware of the social problem of firearm abuse in the United States. In all these groups, there is a material interest in maintaining a high profile, social problem approach to gun ownership.[1]

Firearms abuse, linked to firearms ownership, and hence to control of firearms ownership is a well documented political issue in the United States.[2] While Canada is not known for gun violence, gun ownership and control are considered social problems and become issues each time one of the vested interests examines them.[3]

Mass media news coverage, in addition to media use of gun abuse as entertainment, is typified by a cover story featuring pictures of guns.[4] Editorially, in Canada:

there is no room for handguns, rifles, or whatever kinds of firearms there are out there . . . the image of man the hunter . . . is threatening our planet . . . Gun collections should be displayed, not in homes, but behind locked glass doors in public museums as examples of artifacts no longer in use . . . sending a bullet into a target is an act of aggression and acquisition, similar in essence to other violent acts like rape, murder and the waging of war.[5]

This speaks directly to non-gun owners, and an adversary culture character-ized as

---

[1] R. Ogmundson, "Good News in Canadian Sociology" *The Canadian Journal of Sociology,* Vol. 7 (1982) 73-78.

[2] Robert J. Kukla, *Gun Control* (Harrisburg, Pennsylvania: Stackpole Books, 1973); and George D. Newton and Franklin Zimring, *Firearms and Violence in American Life: A Task Force Report to the National Commission on the Causes and Prevention of Violence* (Washington, D.C. : US Government Printing Office, 1969).

[3] Elisabeth Scarff and Ted Zaharchuk, *Evaluation of the Canadian Gun Control Legislation,* First Progress Report (Ottawa: Communication Division, Solicitor General Canada, 1981).

[4] See "Taking Aim at Handguns," *Life* (April, 1982), 30-36; "Machine Gun USA," (October, 1985), 46-51; and "The Other Arms Race," *Time* February, 1989), 19-25.

[5] Rosemary McCracken, "Guns Do Not Belong Here," *Calgary Herald* (January 20, 1986), A2.

upper-middle class, urban or urban oriented, college educated, internationalist, liberal or change oriented and unfamiliar with guns (especially handguns) and their wide range of legitimate, practical, recreational and symbolic uses.[6]

In their research roles, social scientists have performed credibly, disclaiming many stereotypes. Gun ownership is spuriously correlated with subcultures of violence.[7] Personality factors (fear, machismo, aggressiveness) are disproved by the finding that "there is no evidence that the *average* gun owner exhibits atypical personality characteristics."[8] Gun ownership is highest among white, middle to upper S.E.S. Protestants who safely and legitimately pursue personal hobbies or leisure activities such as hunting, sport shooting and gun collecting.[9]

This creates two difficulties. First, social scientists tend to be members of the adversary culture. Owning no guns, knowing no gun owners, "All good liberals favor stricter gun controls."[10] Not knowing the leisure worlds of gun owners, these social scientists will, in media or non-professional circles, continue to support the idea that there is no room for guns out there. Second, when a social scientist becomes convinced that neither the number of privately owned guns, nor gun control, are casually related to gun abuse he/she can make no easy policy recommendations.[11] Social science literature has not previously provided ethnographic research to allow the social scientist to subjectively understand why normal people are so passionately attached to guns as leisure accessories.[12] When social scientists speak publicly for gun

[6] William R. Tonso, "Media Culture and Guns," *The Quill* (March, 1983),18, and Edward F. Leddy, *Magnum Force Lobby: The National Rifle Association Fights Gun Control* (Lanham, Maryland: University Press of America, 1987),pp.29-50.

[7] Colin Lofton and Robert Hill, "Regional Subculture and Homicide: An Examination of the Gastil-Hackney Thesis," American Sociological Review, Vol. 39 (1974), 714-724; James E. O'Connor and Alan Lizotte, "The Southern Subculture of Violence Thesis and Patterns of Gun Ownership," *Social Problems,* Vol. 25 (1978), 420-429; Sheldon Hackney, "Southern Violence," in H.D. Graham and T.R. Gurr (eds.) *Violence in America* (New York: Frederick A. Praeger, 1969), pp. 505-527; and Raymond O. Gastil "Homicide and a Regional Culture of Violence," *American Sociological Review,* Vol. 36 (1971), 412-426.

[8] Edward Diener and Kenneth W. Kerber "Personality Characteristics of American Gun Owners," *The Journal of Social Psychology,* Vol. 107 (1979), 227-238.

[9] James D. Wright and Linda L. Marston, "The Ownership of the Means of Destruction: Weapons in the United States," *Social Problems,* Vol. 22 (1975), 93-107; Douglas R. Murray, "Handguns, Control, Laws and Firearms Violence," *Social Problems,* Vol. 22 (1975), 81-92; Diener and Kerber; O'Connor and Lizotte; and Alan Lizotte and David Bordua, "Firearms Ownership for Sport and Protection: Two Divergent Models," *American Sociological Review,* Vol. 46 (1980), 499-503.

[10] James D. Wright, "Second Thoughts About Gun Control," *The Public Interest,* Vol. 91 (1988), 23.

[11] Ibid., 23-39.

[12] James D. Wright, Peter H. Rossi, and Kathleen Daly, *Under the Gun: Weapons, Crime and Violence in America* (New York: Aldine, 1983).

controls the process has been referred to as sage-craft.[13] One author feels that the lack of studies is due to the fact that hunting is also "privately/personally abhorred, scorned and avoided by sociologists."[14] A perfect example of the social problem approach and personal opinions by social scientists occurs in a popular science magazine. In the article, this is the only reference to reasons for owning guns: "Most people who buy guns have no intention of becoming murderers — they buy guns to protect themselves and their families."[15]

I am a sociologist and a typical life long member of the leisure subculture of gun ownership.[16] In 1980 I began observing and interviewing while participating in the worlds of target shooting (standard pistol) and gun collecting. In this paper I will integrate a conceptual approach to serious leisure with evidence from observations and literature to show that gun owning leisure is comparable to other leisure activities, not deviant behavior.

Work, Casual Leisure and Gun Ownership

Although police, military and other occupational gun owners are excluded from this study, it may surprise many urbanites that guns are still civilian tools in the 20th century. Farmers and other rural residents are constantly plagued with small vermin — rodents and birds such as crows and magpies. Occasionally, larger problems arise; the bear, wolf, coyote or fox that develops a taste for farm raised meat. Badgers and skunks create their own problems — predation, many large holes and bad smells. Guns are efficient and often enjoyable ways for gun owners to solve these problems. Poison is too indiscriminate, and trapping or snaring is indiscriminate plus requiring skills which are often no longer available.

A US study reported that 44% of hunters in their sample hunted for meat.[17] In Canada, native people and northern residents are allowed special hunting rights in order to produce their own food. In economically depressed rural areas, hunting for meat is recognized as part of a pluralistic, labor intensive life style.[18]

Casual leisure in this study refers to gun ownership and use which involves low commitment, is a secondary activity, and/or has a low investment in skills, equipment and specialization. It is one end of a range of leisure activities, from casual to serious.[19] Often, where the sporting gun subculture is present, casual gun use is

[13] William R. Tonso, "Social Problems and Sagecraft: Gun Control as a Case in Point," in Don B. Kates (ed.) Firearms and Violence: Issues of Public Policy (Cambridge: Ballinger Publishing Company,1984),pp. 71-92.

[14] Richard Hummel, "Hunting and Fishing — But Not in Sociology," The Rural Sociologist, Vol. 3 (1981), 256.

[15] Nikki Meridith, "The Murder Epidemic," Science (December, 1984), 46.

[16] Lizotte and Bordua.

[17] Stephen R. Kellert, Hunting Survey (Washington, D.C.: U.S. Fish and Wildlife Survey, 1978).

[18] Wright, et.al, Under the Gun, 60.

[19] Robert A. Stebbins, "The Amateur: Two Sociological Definitions," Pacific Sociological Review, Vol. 20. (1977), 582-606.

similar to what is called "hitch-hiking" among car collectors: people going along with the group more interested in the opportunities for a social life than in the passion for the activity itself.[20]

Casual gun leisure involves plinking vermin, tin cans or variety targets instead of hunting or organized competitive target shooting. Buying a commemorative gun, keeping an inherited gun or buying an underpriced but attractive gun at a country or estate auction is casual gun collecting. It has been suggested that such casual gun ownership is extremely unnecessary. Hunting is an expensive and environmentally damaging way of providing food. However, gun ownership has social and symbolic meanings even at casual levels.

Fighting the "age-old range war" against gophers in Alberta keeps hunters sharp during the off season, is a great training and socializing ground for children, provides an enjoyable (casual) day of hunting, and controls gophers, our major field rodent.[21] This report called such varminting an annual tradition, and it is an ideal example of the work-casual leisure connection. Farmers fight this war as a secondary activity, using a .22 rifle carried in a vehicle or on a tractor.

Similarly, the casually collected gun may recall "important memories, relationships, and past experiences," often with a theme of recreation and kinship — grandad's gun or a boyhood rifle.[22] A firearms auctioneer claims his collection consists of one single shot Ace .22 rifle, similar to the gun with which he first learned to shoot and hunt.[23] A Canadian Pacific Railway member's issue commemorative may symbolize a career with the organization. Others may symbolize Centennials or just the mythical Winchester.

Wild game (country food) may be economically essential. It also has great symbolic and social value:

In a society where hunting is a central tradition, foods have a richness of meaning which stems from their procurement, distribution and preparation, as well as their eating...If hunting is more than the mere obtaining of food, then it follows that an evaluation of country produce does not thereby amount to an evaluation of the activity of hunting...There is no way one can evaluate a way of life, and there is no way to compensate for its loss.[24]

Group work such as barn raisings, quilting bees and group hunting have long combined survival, social interaction and symbolic meaning. Hunting tools —spears, bows and guns have become the javelins, bows and guns of Olympic events. Many people indulge in casual leisure, but in each field, a few will become serious leisure participants. While this term may appear paradoxical, casual and serious leisure

[20] D. Dannefer, "Neither Socialization nor Recruitment: The Avocational Careers of Old-Car Enthusiasts," Social Forces, Vol. 60, No. 2 (1981), 398.

[21] Bruce Masterman, "Age Old Range War Resumes," Calgary Herald (March 22, 1984), C4.

[22] Mihaly Csikszentmihalyi and Eugene Rochberg-Halton, "Object Lessons," Psychology Today, Vol. 15 (1981), 79-85.

[23] Bob Scammell, "Going...Going...Gun," Western Sportsman, Vol. 16 (1984), 68-72.

[24] Peter Usher, "Evaluating Country Food in the Northern Native Community, Arctic, Vol. 29 (1976), 105-120.

provides a compelling case that guns really do belong out there.[25]

Serious Leisure Gun Ownership

This section is a first step in examining gun owners as serious leisure hobbyists, using an analytic and sensitizing conceptual framework presented by Stebbins.[26]

Collectors

... develop a technical knowledge of the commercial, social and physical circumstances in which their fancied items are acquired. They also develop a sophisticated appreciation of those items, along with a broad understanding of their historical and contemporary production and use.[27]

One author has divided gun collectors into mechanics (technical knowledge), historians (social and historical circumstances), authors and romantics (historical and contemporary use) and artists (sophisticated appreciation).[28] Studies of gun collectors substantiate both the conceptual and insider view of gun collectors.[29] In addition, gun collectors are very similar to collectors of cars, stamps and beer cans and breweriana.[30]

Makers and tinkers are "such enthusiasts as inventors, furniture and toy makers, fly-tyers, automobile repairers, boat builders . . ."[31] If we compare handloading to flytying, and amateurs to professionals, the following distinguishing characteristics of gun makers and tinkers emerges. Doing these things for better and cheaper cartridges is a secondary activity for hunters, target shooters and collectors.[32] (Obsolete or black powder cartridges for collectors.) A handloader who is good enough to reload for others, but puts the money back into leisure gun owning activities is an amateur, and if he makes more than 51% of his income from handloading, he is a professional.[33]

Most gun owning, making and tinkering falls in the amateur category. Many of us handload, do routine maintenance or refurbish new additions to our collections. I own two percussion hunting rifles built from kits by a colleague. He also stocked two hunting rifles from 80% finished blanks. Payment goes to support hunting, target

[25] Robert A. Stebbins, "Serious Leisure: A Conceptual Statement," *Pacific Sociological Review,* Vol. 25 (1982), 272.

[26] Ibid.

[27] Ibid., 261.

[28] James E. Serven, "The Romance and Adventure of Gun Collecting," in James E. Serven (ed.) *The Collecting of Guns* (Harrisburg, Pennsylvania: Stackpole Books, 1964), 34.

[29] See Barbara Stenross in Chapter 5 of this volume and A.D. Olmsted, "Morally Controversial Leisure: The Social World of Gun Collectors," *Symbolic Interaction,* Vol. II (1988), 277-287.

[30] D. Dannefer; A.D. Olmsted, "Stamp Collectors and Stamp Collecting," paper presented at the Popular Culture Association National Meeting, New Orleans, 1987; and Michael P. Soroka, "In Heaven There's No Beer, That's Why We Collect It Here," paper presented at the Popular Culture Association National Meeting, New Orleans, 1987.

[31] Stebbins, "Serious Leisure," 261.

[32] Stenross; and Richard Hummel, "Anatomy of a War Game: Target Shooting in Three Cultures," *Journal of Sport Behavior,* Vol. 8 (1985), 131-143.

[33] Stebbins, "The Amateur," 601.

shooting and customizing his own guns.[34] While these and many other examples of amateur making and tinkering exist, I know of no individual whose ownership of guns is confined solely to this purpose. Further research may produce them. For the amateurs, making and tinkering definitely enhances their gun owning activities. Surveys have not reported making and tinkering as a motive for gun ownership, but they have not asked the question.

Activity participants (hunters) are people who:

steadfastly pursue a form of leisure for the development of skills and knowledge and for the personal enrichment it offers. Often the activity poses a challenge to be met, albeit a non-competitive one. When carried out continually and purposefully for these reasons, the following are among the things activity participants do: body building, backpacking,...bird watching,...hunting and fishing...[35]

Hunters as activity participants are discussed later. However, Stebbins choice of activities, and a purpose of this paper are well suited by a recent finding about hunters:

Our research has shown that hunters . . . do not differ from campers, hikers, anglers or any other group with common outdoor recreation interest . . . They are not bad mannered or bloodthirsty boors, as is so often depicted in the press or on television.[36]

In Canada, 71.5% of gun owners report hunting as the reason for owning guns. Similar results are reported from the US.[37] The strong presence of hunters in the conservation movement has been discussed by Reiger and Ward.[38]

Players (target shooters) of amateur sports and games represent serious leisure in that:

. . . Players are related to each other by a set of rules structuring their actions while they are engaged in the contest. [These activities] lack a professional counterpart . . . participation is continual and systematic. The aim is to acquire and maintain the knowledge and skills enabling the individual to experience uncommon rewards from the endeavour.[39]

Because of the extensiveness and diversity of target shooting, it is difficult to present a brief picture of its rules and structure. Trap and skeet shooting in the United States are discussed by Wellemeyer.[40] A recent summary of target shooting in Great

[34] Stenross.

[35] Stebbins, "Serious Leisure," 262.

[36] Daniel J. Decker and George F. Mattfield, "Beyond the Guns and the Game," The Conservationist (November/December, 1988), 3.

[37] Diener and Kerber.

[38] John F. Reiger American Sportsmen and the Origin of Conservation (New York: Winchester Press, 1975); and George B. Ward, "Guns and Game in the American West: The Role of the Sport Hunter in Conservation," in Ray B. Browne (ed.) Objects of Special Devotion: Fetishes and Fetishism in Popular Culture (Bowling Green, Ohio: Popular Press, 1981), pp. 151-167.

[39] Stebbins, "Serious Leisure."

[40] Marilyn Wellemeyer, "Bloodless Pigeon Shoot," Fortune (May, 1977), 100-136.

Britain is found in Baxter.[41] Current publications by the National Rifle Association, the International Shooters Union or the Canadian Federation of Shooting Sports will provide reliable information on most organized target matches.

These sources document the rules structuring target shooting. Its popularity is indicated by the continuous emergence of new types of competition, the Bianchi Cup for combat style handguns, The End of Trail for Western guns and the Coors Schuetzenfest for traditional single shot rifles. "Sporting clays" which duplicates hunting situations for shotguns has just reached Canada. The popularity of this event, plus traditional trap and skeet, is said to have "revolutionized" gun ownership in Great Britain.[42] Patterns of gun ownership among target shooters are discussed by Stenross.[43] (Although the Olympic rules separated them in 1984, men and women compete together in target shooting, where women are at no physiological disadvantage.)[44]

Qualities of Serious Leisure

Perserverance. Stebbins defines serious leisure perserverance as the ability to overcome difficulties such as weather, stage fright, embarrassment, fatigue and injury and other strains.[45] These unpleasantries discourage casual leisure participants.

Collectors are most likely to be embarrassed, often through misidentifying a gun. This can result in mislabelling a gun in your display. The 28th person to look corrects you, and you know the others are laughing. Comments like "Feeling generous today?" mean you have paid too much or sold for too little, often because of misidentification. Anxiety and a form of stage fright called choking up occur when making a bid at auction, or trying to set up a trade. In the latter case, few of us are familiar with haggling and swapping due to our fixed price economy. All serious collectors have misidentification stories, although many eventually say buying, selling and trading are an enjoyable part of collecting. Many deals may be ruined before this is achieved.

Hunters miss shots that they have made before and will make again. The reproachful look from your dog, who worked the bird perfectly, or your buddies, who drove the deer right past your stand, are embarrassing. Hunters catch a strange form of stage fright-anxiety called buck fever. Behaviour from visible shaking to ejecting cartridges without firing have been reported. The best duck blinds and deer stands seem to all be in the coldest spot on the coldest day. And the saying, "the fun is over when you squeeze the trigger" refers to the fatigue hunters feel when after hunting from sunup to near sundown they are faced with dressing out a big game animal and moving the carcass back to camp or the truck.

[41] Edward Baxter, "Invisible Sport," in Ken Warner (ed.) Gun Digest (Northfield, Illinois: DBI Books, 1984), pp. 217-225.

[42] Sidney DuBroff, "Revolution in Britain," in Ken Warner (ed.) Gun Digest (Northfield, Illinois: DBI Books, 1988), pp. 122-125.

[43] Stenross.

[44] Tim Pelton, "The Shootists," Science, Vol. 83 (May, 1983), 84-86; and Baxter.

[45] Stebbins, "Serious Leisure," 256.

Target shooters also miss shots. In the long range Bisley rifle matches (Baxter, 1984; Hummel, 1985) a miss was signalled from the butts by a red paddle known bitterly as "Maggie's drawers."[46] The only more embarrassing miss is to carefully squeeze off a shot, and see the marker come up on your neighbor's target. A form of nervousness known as "losing your concentration" can affect even the best target shooters.[47] The physical and mental effort required to fire your best shot 10 or more times a day is fatiguing. "The blokes who win all look like they had been dragged by the foot behind the machine of time . . ."[48]

Makers and tinkers like other craftspeople are embarrassed by the flaw in their product, which often cannot even be seen by others. The bad cut in wood or metal is a permanent reminder. Handloaders are publicly embarrassed by the "powderless load." This drives a bullet halfway down the barrel, or a charge of shot trickling out of the muzzle in front of competing target shooters, or fellow hunters. The concentration required to avoid such errors is physically and mentally fatiguing. Like a good auto mechanic, the inability to diagnose a problem is frustrating. First display or trial of a product is anxiety producing. What if it doesn't work, or people don't like it?

Careers "[Hobbyist] endeavors are enduring pursuits with their own histories of turning points, stages of achievement or involvement, and background contingencies." Many collectors interviewed for a recent study report boyhood fascination with a collectible firearm.[49] They were also members of the sporting subculture of gun owners, but this differentiated them, as the guns were not useful for hunting.[50] Gun collectors share this youthful fascination with car, stamp and beer can and breweriana collectors.[51]

Frequently, collecting careers are interrupted by family and vocational careers, and are resumed later, a pattern called "late blooming" by Dannefer.[52] Two main processes occur during collecting: organization and up-grading. The first is the creation of a collection e.g. all factory rifles in .250 Savage and .338 Winchester. Up-grading is replacing items with ones in better condition. One Colt collector said, "When I started, I hoped for one perfect specimen. Now I have nine." Collecting is interrupted by financial needs, divorces, transfers to other countries, but is usually

[46] Baxter; and Richard Hummel, "Anatomy of a War Game: Target Shooting in Three Cultures," *Journal of Sport Behavior,* Vol. 8 (1985), 131-143.

[47] Pelton, 84; and Baxter, 225.

[48] Baxter, 223.

[49] Olmsted, "Morally Controversial Leisure."

[50] Stenross.

[51] D. Dannefer, "Rationality and Passion in Private Experience: Modern Consciousness and the Social World of Old Car Collectors," *Social Problems,* Vol. 27 (1980), 392-412; Dannefer, "Neither Socialization nor Recruitment;" Olmsted, "Stamp Collectors and Stamp Collecting;" and Soroka.

[52] Dannefer, "Neither Socialization nor Recruitment," 398.

resumed when the crisis is solved. Most collections are dispersed by the death of their owner, but a visit to a good gun show will show you many proud and elderly gun collectors.

Hunters "Becoming a hunter in a hunting family is a process that begins at an early age. Older family members share stories . . . Family members share meals where game is the featured entree . . ."[53] This early interest is followed by an apprenticeship when children are too young to legally hunt and perhaps too unskilled. "The aspiring hunter seldom handles a firearm but typically has an active role as a game spotter or 'retriever.' The youngster also helps dress game, prepare meals and care for hunting equipment."[54] This practice (reported from New York state) is widespread in the hunting subculture. In Kansas

Year after year a young man must go on the hunt and be subjected to an initiation of sorts . . . Young hunters are often termed "bird dogs."[55]

In Saskatchewan, where I served my apprenticeship, we were told "you have to be a dog before you can be a man."

The active years of hunting are recounted verbally and in written form so often that "huntin' stories" have become a genre. It takes this form in the US:

1. The gun owner is a patriot
2. The gun owner is social
3. The gun owner appreciates nature
4. The gun owner is able to survive through his weapons
5. The gun owner respects tradition and the teaching of his elders.[56]

The first point is not universal — it is not present in the Canadian "huntin' story." Baloff recognizes this: "This is perhaps the weakest theme . . . [magazines] devote significant attention to international hunting . . . Canadians in particular. Indeed [they] take great pains to use the term 'North American.' "[57] Items two through four could summarize the research findings of Decker and Mattfield. Lack of time, loss of hunting companions and mobility interrupt and sometimes close a hunting career.[58] If a hunter is too old to take the field, he can close this career, and start new ones by telling his lifetime of stories to the children.

Target shooters With the increase in urbanization fewer target shooters are members of the rural-small town based sporting subculture of guns.[59] For those who are not, family membership in target clubs and family encouragement operate on the

[53] Decker and Mattfield, 6.

[54] Ibid.

[55] Kevin Jones, "Opening Day of Pheasant Hunting as Ritual in Kansas," paper presented at the Popular Culture Association National Meeting, St. Louis, 1989.

[56] Eugene G. Baloff, Chapter 12 of this volume.

[57] Ibid.

[58] Decker and Mattfield, 7.

[59] Alan J. Lizotte and David Bordua, "Firearms Ownership for Sport and Protection: Two Divergent Models," Vol. 46 (1980), 499-503.

same principle of socialization. Institutional exposure through groups such as Scouts, service clubs, Fish and Wildlife and gun safety courses may provide early exposure. Target shooters do excel at an early age and a relatively high number are women. George Genereux, Olympic Gold Medalist, trap shooting, 1952, won the Midwest International at age 13; Susan Nattrass, six times Ladies World Trap Champion, won her first World at 23, was fourth in the world at 19; Arnold Parks, rifle, won his first Canadian title at 18.[60] Mike Anti won a United States national rifle championship at age 15, and in 1983 it was estimated that four of the top ten shooters in the United States were female.[61] Linda Thom won Canada's first gold medal at the 1984 Olympics.

However, descriptions of the Queen's Plate winners (top rifle prize in the British Commonwealth) sum up the long careers of target shooters.

All the guys who win the Queen's have spent decades stockpiling the expertise and the luck it takes. They are hard, leathery old dudes who earned their victory . . . What a way to cap a life![62]

Baxter also comments "Mastery of the pistol comes from decades of hard work."[63] While all good things come to an end, target shooting careers may soon be extended by the introduction of Seniors' matches.

Makers and tinkers are currently an unknown career. There are hints that family and friends who are skilled at craftsmanship provide early interest and teaching. Skills and equipment grow over the years. What form of gun ownership focuses this interest on guns is unknown. As with many other hobby-crafts, work is seen as a definite interference. Makers and tinkers often see retirement as the time when they can achieve their highest goals. Further research is definitely needed here.

The next four qualities of serious leisure are discussed briefly, as *perserverance* and developing a *career* in serious leisure is the core of why some people "need guns out there."

Anti-gun attitudes simply provide additional "embarrassments" and gun controls become negative "background contingencies." This splits gun collectors from other collectors, hunting from other outdoor recreation, target shooting from other athletics and making and tinkering with guns from normal hobby crafts, creating small social worlds. Only within these worlds can leisure gun owners gain the knowledge to acquire durable benefits. Only in these worlds are the unique ethos and identification of gun owners recognized.

Effort ". . . Significant personal effort, based on special *knowledge, training* or *skill* and sometimes all three . . . differentiate amateurs and hobbyists from dabblers and the public."[64] The "gun literature" is full of advice, and tips and technical information

[60] Bob Ferguson, *Who's Who in Canadian Sport* (Prentice-Hall of Canada, Ltd., 1977).

[61] Pelton.

[62] Baxter, 223.

[63] Ibid., 225.

[64] Stebbins, "Serious Leisure," 256.

for collectors, hunters, target shooters and makers and tinkers. Good dealers, guides, coaches and master craftsmen can both socialize and help the individual to achieve his/her goals. Only personal effort and experience will provide the collector with the skills to research, identify, find and acquire not just the next item for the collection, but perhaps one previously not known. Successful hunting of game bears a strong resemblance to the steps taken by a collector. Only the individual target shooter can "psych himself up", maximize his strong points, minimize the weak ones and pace himself for the total match or event. The maker and tinker must learn how to deal with less than ideal tools and materials and to invent solutions to problems the literature or the master haven't mentioned. Most importantly, from a leisure viewpoint, all must learn to enjoy the experience, even when the immediate goal is not achieved. In the leisure world of sailboats the saying is "It's not getting there that's the point, it's being there."

Durable benefits ". . . are found by amateurs in their various pursuits: self actualization, self enrichment, recreation or renewal of self, feelings of accomplishment, enhancement of self-image, self expression, social interaction and belongingness, and lasting physical products of the activity."[65] Each of these benefits is worthy of a study in itself. The relevant social worlds provide interaction and belongingness for collectors, hunters, and target shooters.[66] No information is available on makers and tinkers, but observation has shown that they are valued members in each of the other worlds, plus their own. The more psychological rewards — self-actualization, self-enrichment, self-image, self-expression and feelings of accomplishment are partly covered below. The leisure or avocational nature of these activities create recreation and revival of self. It has been said for hunters: "When you are fed up with the troublesome present, take your gun, whistle for your dog, go out to the mountains."[67] Going to the gun room, the range or the shop equally apply. Durable benefits are obvious: the collection, the fine meal and the trophy head, the club colors and the match trophies and the fine guns, stocks or engraving created by the maker and tinker.

Unique Ethos ". . . Because of the previously mentioned qualities, amateurs, hobbyists . . . tend to develop subcultures composed of special beliefs, values, moral principles, norms and performance standards."[68] Sources already cited show that collectors are unique in their passionate attachment to individual objects and sets of

---

65 Ibid., 257.

66 Olmsted, "Morally Controversial Leisure;" Decker and Mattfield; Jones; and Baxter.

67 Jose Ortega Y. Gasset, *Meditations on Hunting* (New York: Charles Scribner's Sons, 1972), p. 128.

68 Stebbins, "Serious Leisure," 257.

objects. Through these objects they can know and demonstrate technological change, art, history and preserve a cultural heritage. Hunters are unique among current environmentalists in their belief that selective hunting, according to strict rules, is the best way to demonstrate human capabilities while positively knowing and experiencing their prey and the environment. Target shooters are unique in their belief that guns, rather than some other apparatus, are the best tool to demonstrate the athletic skills that humans can achieve through physical training, discipline and practice. Makers and tinkers believe guns are a good medium for demonstrating craft skills of wood and metal working, plus mechanical skills of diagnosis, repair and innovation.

Identification

Participants in serious leisure tend to identify strongly with their chosen pursuits. they are inclined to speak proudly, excitedly and frequently about them to other people, and to present themselves in terms of them when conversing with new aquaintances.[69]

Depending on his/her occupational, demographic and situational location, this is currently the most crucial test of the serious leisure gun ownership. Everywhere in the past, in small towns and rural areas today, we could proudly respond, "I am a gun collector. I collect...; I am a hunter. I hunt...; I am a target shooter. I shoot...; I am an engraver, wood worker, etc. I specialize in guns." This would/does gain some interest and respect in these areas. The only social danger was/is shared with other amateurs who "realize they are sometimes too enthusiastic about their avocations when discussing them with others."[70] As a sociologist in a large, urban university, identifying with guns is a daring and provocative response. I am much more likely to make it at a gun show, a gun auction or a target range. As in other forms of morally controversial leisure a gun owner must indeed be courageous to put forth this valued identity among urban, elite strangers, usually adversaries.[71] My hat is off to the enthusiasts who do testify, and the quality of the leisure experience that makes them do it.

Serious Leisure, Gun Ownership and the Domestic Arms Race

When this paper was first written, and then presented at the Popular Culture Association Meetings (Montreal, 1987) it contained a rather lengthy and laborious segment estimating the contribution of each of the serious leisure worlds to the rising number of guns in North America. Recent media controversies and splits among gun owners over Saturday Night Specials and semi automatic assault rifles have led me to drop this element. Although we Canadians can't carry either, I agree that it is difficult to distinguish Saturday Night Specials from trail guns.[72] I also agree with the editor who said (long before the controversy),

[69] Ibid.

[70] Stebbins, "The Amateur: Two Sociological Definitions."

[71] Olmsted, "Morally Controversial Leisure."

[72] Wright, 35-36.

Whatever you do, don't view this with alarm. [Assault rifle buyers] are the heirs of those fellows who soaked up about a million M1 carbines twenty years ago...those old carbines have not held up many liquor stores.[73] A recent "sensible guess" is that there are 150 million privately owned guns in the US.[74] Canada would probably add three to four million, of which just under one million are registered handguns. In both countries, the "fearful" growth rates, particularly in handguns, has been in the last twenty to thirty years. Comparing my 1961 Gun Digest to the 1989 edition produces some interesting non-controversial insights relevant to this discussion.[75] While the Gun Digest listings are criticized for being traditional "high end" guns, this guarantees that the guns listed are readily available in North America, and directed to a long term, stable market.

In 1961 the Gun Digest listed 21 handguns suitable for target shooting. These were all designed for standard bullseye shooting. In 1989, 47 target handguns were displayed, including 12 powerful single shot handguns designed for metallic silhouette shooting. These are also very popular with handgun varmint hunters. Many of the other guns are designed to be customized for various forms of practical pistol shooting matches. In 1961 only seven Colt or Colt style single action revolvers were shown. In 1989 there were 42 models of these guns listed. Target, single action, and single shot handguns are popular neither in crime fiction nor in crime fact. They are popular in hunting, target shooting and a combination of collecting and nostalgia.

In 1961, the Gun Digest listed three single action, percussion revolvers and seven single shot flintlock and percussion rifles. The 1989 listing is substantial: 21 single shot flintlock or percussion pistols and 26 percussion revolvers. There are 65 models of black powder rifles, either single or double barrelled, flintlock or percussion. There are ten black powder shotguns, again single or double barrelled, all percussion. All these guns are muzzle loaders. Seven Sharps type and one Remington rolling block black powder catridge rifles are also listed. 65 of the 132 muzzle loaders are available in semi-finished kit form.

Finally, in 1961, the Gun Digest listed 13 pellet and BB rifles and 15 handguns. In 1989 a bewildering array of 61 air powered handguns, 96 air powered rifles and two air powered shotguns are displayed. The word bewildering is used, because I could still recognize the Red Ryder Commemorative BB gun (much fancier than the one I inherited at age six), but the variety of power sources and projectiles is something else. Sufficient to say, these guns range from the inexpensive, stereotyped BB gun to refined, precise target guns and equally refined, but more powerful rifles (and a shotgun) suitable for hunting small game.

While it could be argued that even the airguns are simply an indicator of how gun crazy North Americans are, none of these firearms (or airguns) have a high crime

[73] Ken Warner (ed.) *Gun Digest* (Northfield, Illinois: DBI Books, 1984), p. 31.

[74] Wright, 29.

[75] John T. Amber (ed.) *Gun Digest* (Chicago: The Gun Digest Co., 1961); and Ken Warner (ed.) *Gun Digest* (Northfield, Illinois: DBI Books, 1989).

profile. If I had counted jogging shoes, skate board or tennis racquet sales, it would be an indicator of increased leisure activity. So it is with guns. Pellet guns for varmints and black powder guns for game are current specialized extensions of the hunter's skill. The use of handguns for both types of hunting is especially challenging.

... as the weapon became more and more effective, man imposed more and more limitations on himself as the animals' rival in order to leave it free to practice its wily defenses, in order to avoid making the prey and the hunter excessively unequal . . .[76]

Target shooting, and target shooters have incorporated the very precise air and black powder powered guns into their activities. In most cases, these are in addition to, rather than in place of, their main specialty. Collectors can now preserve their fine antiques, but still find out an Enfield musket, a Kentucky rifle or a Paterson Colt (replicas) can shoot as they did for the Union Army, Davy Crocket or the Texas Rangers. The increased specialization of hunting and target guns represents serious leisure. The number of black powder gun kits provide a feast for the maker and tinker. The estimated two million plus commemorative guns (half handguns and half rifles) provide instant collectibles for new or casual collectors. Air guns traditionally were used for new or casual shooters, and are still available to them.

These roughly documented increased in guns available also represent the one quality of leisure shared by casual (or secondary) and serious leisure practitioners. "A ninth benefit — self-gratification or pure fun . . . is the only one that is also characteristic of unserious leisure."[77] With the exception of the serious target airguns and firearms discussed above most of the guns listed here can provide either casual or serious gun owners with fun and self-gratification. Let us remember that even serious leisure provides fun. Given the number of new recreational guns it would not be surprising if they account for a far higher proportion of new gun purchases than the media have led the public to believe. Once again, the question is still to be asked.

Conclusion

This paper has advanced the discussion of gun ownership and analytic and sensitizing research concepts by giving examples of one to fit the other. In the advancement of research, it is a very short step. Nothing in the methodology prevents this material from accusations of advocacy research. Critics may simply search for examples of the obsessed collector, the rabid hunter, the macho target shooter and the fiendish maker tinker. Having shown that these types spend large portions of their lives perfecting their evil skills, the adversary might well conclude that the gun problem is even worse than they thought.

The big step is next. We must properly examine the conclusion-hypothesis suggested here. Are gun collectors simply collectors of guns, rather than cars or beer cans? Are hunters conservationists and environmentalists rather than killers? Are target shooters athletes rather than practice killers? Are makers and tinkers simply

[76] Ortega Y. Gasset, 53.

[77] Stebbins, 257.

craftsmen who work on guns? Including gun owners in studies of these categories is the necessary test. I believe social science will find it impossible to distinguish gun owners from practitioners of similar types of serious leisure, in their motivations, social interactions and gratifications. This belief, opinion or hypothesis can be tested by studying the behavior, not the guns.

Chapter 7

Gun Collecting in Western Canada:
The Influence of Popular Culture and History

by
A.D. Olmsted

Introduction

Comparing Western US and Canadian history and popular culture, an author asks How do you get from Tombstone to Moosejaw . . . from Fergusson's *The Conquest of Don Pedro* to Robert Stead's *Grain?* Probably you don't . . .[1]

Harrison sees the Hispanic world of Don Pedro as a world apart from both the Canadian and the American West. This difficulty can be overcome by considering the Canadian Metis as a culture within a culture in Western Canada.[2]

The second problem is that books such as *Grain* are not really Westerns. They are Northerns. "The Northern tends to be tight, gray, low-keyed, underplayed, avoiding melodrama where possible - sometimes it would seem, at all costs."[3] Not surprisingly, Canadians have turned, like many others, to Westerns as popular entertainment.[4] This opened the world of the popular culture Colt and Winchester to Canadian gun collectors.[5]

In Tombstone, Wyatt Earp is thought to have carried a single action Colt .45 revolver.[6] Near Moosejaw, Gabriel Dumont carried La Petit, his 1866 Winchester, during the Riel Rebellion. No mention is made of Dumont carrying a handgun. Even during a three month tour with the Buffalo Bill Cody Wild West Show, Dumont is

---

[1] Dick Harrison, "Crossing the Medicine Line: Problems in Comparing Canadian and American Western Fiction," in Lewis, Merril and Lee, L.L. (eds.) *The Westering Experience in American Literature* (Bellingham: Bureau of Faculty Research, Western Washington University, 1977), p. 48

[2] Joseph K. Howard, *Strange Empire* (Toronto: Swan Publishing Company, 1965).

[3] Leslie A. Fiedler, *The Return of the Vanishing American* (New York: Stein and Day, 1968), p. 17

[4] Wallace Stegner, *Wolf Willow* (New York: Ballantyne, 1973), pp. 49-56.

[5] William R. Tonso, "The Sixgun and the Popular Cultural West: Some Observations," paper presented at the Popular Culture National Meeting, St. Louis, 1989; and Richard Hummel, "The Rifle: Historical Facts vs. Popular-Culture Images," paper also presented at these 1989 meetings.

[6] Joseph G. Rosa and Robin May, *Gunsmoke* (London: The New English Library, 1977), p. 124.

pictured carrying only an 1866 Winchester.[7] Both men played a part in both the history and the myth of the Colt and the Winchester. Each is now represented by the commemorative guns discussed later in this paper. Collector's interest in these guns has created a symbolic network which easily encompasses the journey from Tombstone to Moosejaw, especially as the West has been defined in popular culture. This world, reflected in the collectible value of guns, is significantly at odds with history, particularly Western Canadian history.

Guns in Western History and Popular Culture

The "classical West" has been defined as a period from just before the Civil War to just before World War I.[8] For target shooting, the guns of this period are defined for the "End of Trail Shoot" as

... traditionally styled Old West single actions ... modern versions, copies and replicas of historic single action revolvers ....25 caliber or over. Rifles can be any tubular magazine lever action again .25 caliber or over ... Shotguns can be any double barrel 20 gauge or over.[9]

Exceptions are the Colt Lightning pump action rifle or the Winchester 1897 pump shotgun. This definition represents the Colt as sixgun for all seasons approach of popular culture.[10] It includes any lever action rifle, including Marlin, Winchester's closest competitor. Shotguns are recognized in their relationship to law enforcing and law breaking, which is consistent with their popular culture usage. Several historical realities, some in the US and Canada, some in Canada alone, are represented in the definition.

Although Colt single action revolvers (SARs) were popular in the US West, and considered an essential technology for the Great Plains there were many competing SARs.[11] In addition self cocking and double action revolvers made in England and the US were effective and functional six shooters throughout the classical western period. Guns by Dean, Adams and Webley fit this category and are mentioned because they were popular English sporting and military arms, familiar to many Canadians.[12]

Collectors of these British handguns comment that American popular culture often misleadingly supports the Colt myth.[13] Handguns always appeared in the

[7] George Woodcock, *Gabriel Dumont: The Metis Chief and His Last World* (Edmonton: Hurtig Publishers, 1974).

[8] Tonso.

[9] Mike Venturino, "High Noon Fever at the End of the Trail," in Phil Spangelberry (ed.) *The Complete Guide to Single Action Revolvers* (Los Angeles: Petersen, 1986).

[10] Tonso.

[11] Walter Prescott Webb, *The Great Plains* (New York: Grosset and Dunlap, 1973), pp. 167-178.

[12] Louis A. Garavaglia and Charles G. Worman *Firearms of the American West 1803-1965* (Albuquerque: University of New Mexico Press, 1984); and W.H.J. Chamberlain and A.W.F. Taylorson, *Adams Revolvers* (London: Barrie and Jenkins, 1976).

[13] Paul Trachtman, *The Gunfighters* (Chicago: Time-Life, 1974).

pictures, reports and popular fiction of the American West. Although handguns were frequently used in imperial exploring and military accounts, in pictures "swords, rifles and carbines are in considerable proliferation, but there are few revolvers."[14] In all the Sherlock Holmes stories, Dr. Watson's handgun was only referred to as his "old service revolver."[15] Frustrated Holmseans have been forced to deduce the various guns suggested in the Holmes stories.[16] Why, given that handgun production and use was high, is the handgun so invisible in British popular culture and history?

The simplest answer is that by the mid-19th century, the visible carrying of a handgun was not a positive badge of manhood or symbol of social status in Europe.[17] This attitude carried over from England and France to Canada. Illustrated popular histories, even of outlaws and lawmen in Western Canada seldom show handguns, and rifles and shotguns are infrequent.

Historically, in the Canadian West after 1874, carrying revolvers was banned by the Royal North West Mounted Police.[18] American ranch outfits were asked to check their handguns when in Canada on business.[19] The myth goes from Tombstone to Moosejaw, but real sixguns stop at the border.

By the time of settlement in Western Canada in the 1880's, the European hunting rifle had become, in reality and popular literature, the fine, handmade double rifle and single shot deer-stalking rifle. These were glamourous, expensive, and with the extinction of the buffalo, too much gun for Western game, although these guns were highly thought of in both the US and Canadian West.

The double rifle is the mythical gun of British popular culture and history. It, and its bolt action counterparts, were usually too expensive for settlers. Asked why he shot elephants with a .303 surplus Lee-Enfield, a Kenya farmer replied, "because it was the only rifle I had."[20] While a good gun making establishment had grown in Eastern Canada during the percussion era," Winchester, Marlin, Colt, Smith and Wesson and Remington moved in to supply the large quantities of arms required by the settlers of the land to the west of the Great Lakes."[21] In the American West, "after

[14] Garry James, "Six-Guns the Sun Never Set On," in Guns & Ammo 1984 Annual (Los Angeles: Petersen, 1984). p. 145.

[15] Ibid., 146.

[16] Garry James and Scott McMillan, "The Guns of Sherlock Holmes," in Guns & Ammo 1986 Annual (Los Angeles: Petersen, 1986).

[17] William R. Tonso, Gun and Society: The Social and Existential Roots of the American Attachment to Firearms (Washington, D.C.: University Press of America, 1982). p. 143.

[18] R.D. Symons, Where the Wagon Led (Toronto: Doubleday, 1973). p. 79.

[19] Ibid., 118.

[20] Finn Agaard, "Guns of the Kenya Settlers," in Guns & Ammo 1986 Annual (Los Angeles: Petersen, 1986), pp. 148-154.

[21] James S. Gooding, The Canadian Gunsmiths: 1608-1900 (West Hill, Ontario: Museum Restoration Service, 1962), p. 12.

the early seventies, the rifle, regardless of its make, was usually called a Winchester."[22]

By 1900, bolt action military rifles were well established in Europe and the West. Mauser, Lee Enfield and Springfield were issued in Mexico, Canada, and the US respectively. "Sporterized" Mausers were appearing in Canada by the turn of the century. Western men fought in wars with and against these rifles by the turn of the century. Like the double action Webley, the Short Magazine Lee Enfield Mark I No.s 1 through 5, was a British and Canadian standard issue from the 1890s to the end of World War II. Given the above mentioned popular culture reticence in Canada, the bolt action military rifle made no headway against the myth of the Winchester. It's presence in the Canadian West was enormous for hunting and target shooting. Only in the occasional popular culture Western do these rifles appear.

Double barrelled shotguns occupy a functionally strong but mythologically weak position in the American West. From the earliest explorers to the present, shotguns have served in defense, military and hunting roles.[23] In the 1830s "Josiah Gregg . . . noted that the frontier hunter sticks to his rifle, as nothing could induce him to carry what he calls the scatter gun."[24] By the classical western period "Scatter guns or shotguns were occasionally produced by the tenderfoots; but they, unless with sawed-off barrels, loaded with nails or buckshot, and in the hands of express messengers served for the westerner as objects of derision."[25] Hunting with shotguns does not figure in Western films.[26] With the possible exception of Greener, no named shotgun has emerged to equal Colt and Winchester. Frontier double barrelled shotguns tended to be English, and expensive in the US.[27] By the 1900s, cheap and efficient single shot and double barrelled shotguns were available, but anonymous in the Western myth.

Part of the rapid development of rim-fire cartridges, the .22 caliber was in use in Flobert target guns by 1845. In 1857, Smith and Wesson's First Model revolver introduced the .22 short to America. In 1877, Great Western Gun Works listed a .22 long, and in 1888 the .22 long rifle was being advertised by Marlin Ballard.[28] By 1890 every type of firearm was available in .22 rim-fire. Presumably its undramatic uses and users have made this incredible cartridge, and the guns chambered for it, a popular culture non-event.

Double action revolvers and semi-automatic pistols, with a few highly visible exceptions, have been excluded from the popular culture West, although just as in the

[22] Philip Ashton Rollins, *The Cowboy* (Albuquerque: University of New Mexico Press, 1979), p. 57.

[23] Garaglia and Worman, Chapters 2, 5, 15.

[24] Ibid., 69.

[25] Rollins, 57.

[26] Sarkis Atamian and Richard Hummel, "Portrayals of Sport Hunting in Popular Films," paper presented at the Popular Culture National Meeting, New Orleans, 1988.

[27] Garaglia and Worman.

[28] Frank C. Barnes, *Cartridges of the World* 3rd Ed. (Northfield, Illinois: Digest Books, 1972), pp. 271-272.

case of .22s and bolt action rifles, a convincing case can be made for their historical presence.[29] These handguns are the guns of urbanites, often concealed and seldom used. There is evidence that many of these guns were institutionally owned by banks, railways, etc. Others lived in drawers in bedrooms and businesses. In popular culture they are the gats, heaters and roscoes. When poor quality is imputed to them, they are Saturday Night or Suicide Specials.

To summarize, the six-gun mystique and the popular culture Western have substantially elevated the symbolic value of Colt single-action revolvers and Winchester lever action rifles over their many competitors and other types of firearms. Their visibility in the Western style has obscured similar types of guns in other cultures, such as the British Canadian tradition. Shotguns, double action and semi-automatic pistols have been symbolically downgraded, at the cost of historical accuracy. Guns for the popular .22 caliber have been ignored in popular culture. This is particularly evident in Western Canada, where the carrying of handguns has been systematically prevented and controlled since 1874 and the use of long guns has been as tools and leisure accessories.[30] After a brief discussion of gun collectors, collectible guns and methodology, we will examine the relationship between the popular symbolic value, the historical value, and the monetary value placed on collectible guns.

Gun Collectors and Collectible Guns

Gun collectors differ from other gun owners but are usually introduced to guns via the subculture of sporting gun use.[31] Except for this membership, gun collectors resemble other collectors such as car collectors and stamp collectors more than they resemble other gun owners.[32] It has been observed that gun collectors buy and sell more than other collectors.[33] Like car and stamp collectors, gun collectors are male, and begin at an early age. They have leisure careers as collectors.[34]

A noted gun collector and author reports the following subcategories among gun collectors:

THE MECHANIC - the problems of developing multiple fire and more efficient detonation have taxed the mechanical ingenuity of man for five hundred years.

[29] Tonso, "The Sixgun and The Popular Culture West."

[30] See Barbara Stenross in Chapter 5 of this volume.

[31] Ibid., and Alan J. Lizotte and David J. Bordua "Firearms Ownership for Sport and Protection. Two Divergent Models," American Sociological Review, Vol. 46 (1980), 499-503.

[32] A.D. Olmsted, "Morally Controversial Leisure: The Social World of Gun Collectors," Symbolic Interaction, Vol. II (1988), 277-287; Dale Dannefer, "Neither Socialization nor Recruitment: The Avocational Careers of Old-Car Enthusiasts," Social Forces, Vol. 60, No. 2 (1981), 395-412; and Olmsted, "Stamp Collectors and Stamp Collecting," paper presented at the Popular Culture National Meetings, Montreal, 1987.

[33] Robin Duthy, Alternative Investment (London: Michael Joseph, 1978), p. 162.

[34] See A.D. Olmsted in Chapter 6 of this volume.

Where could one find a more fascinating series of mechanical devices than the different mechanisms of firearms?

THE ARTIST - Look at the beautiful patterns worked with inlaid ivory in a Saxon dag. Examine the finely engraved designs . . . the intricately carved ebony stocks . . . the flowing lines - the perfect balance. Certainly this is the essence of art.

THE AUTHOR AND ROMANTICIST - what can have more romantic appeal than the vision of two stalwart gentlemen carrying their [dueling pistols] to the Field of Honor at dawn: there meticulously adhering to the Code Duello; to have their trial by combat to defend the honor of a lovely lady or cleanse a stain placed on their own honor?

THE HISTORIAN - The world's history has been molded by man's ability to develop weapons. The historical outline of man's past five hundred years lies clearly written in any comprehensive collection of guns. Since the invention of firearms, wars have been won or lost depending upon the ability to devise, manufacture and strategically use these weapons.[35]

These collector characteristics link with a set of collectible characteristics. The mechanic is interested in how a gun functions, how its mechanism evolved, and is this mechanism reliable. The Colt, and the Winchester have these characteristics. However, the development of the double action revolver (Webley) and the bolt action rifle (Lee Enfield or Mauser) have equally fascinating histories and mechanisms. Even within their categories, Winchester rifles are challenged by Marlin and Savage lever action rifles, while Smith and Wesson and Remington are arguably superior to Colt single action revolvers.

Both Colt and Winchester are famous for the refinement and beauty of their factory engraving, inlay, and stock wood.[36] Yet the artist may find this, and non-factory refinement, among the competitors. One prize winning display in Western Canada is of factory engraved Marlin rifles, and these are many delicately engraved, gold inlayed Webleys in beautifully crafted wooden cases.[37]

Good authors and historians must be able to research their collectibles. Colt and Winchester both have excellent record systems and have had many scholarly investigations which are available to their collectors. The researchability of a collectible is tautalogical. The more collecting, the more research. The more information available, the greater the collecting interest. Many collectors write up their specialties, thus becoming authors and historians. Again, the guns of the Western are firm competitors, but not uniquely attractive to collectors.

All categories of collectors are interested in the rarity of an object. However, rarity is a two-edged characteristic. The Golcher Kentucky rifles and the Hawken plains

35 James E. Serven, "The Romance and Adventure of Gun Collecting," in James E. Serven (ed.) The Collecting of Guns (Harrisburg, Pennsylvania: The Stackpole Company, 1964), p. 34.

36 R.L. Wilson, The Colt Heritage (New York: Simon and Schuster, 1978); and James E. Serven, "The Old Winchester," in John T. Amber (ed.) The Gun Digest 20th Ed. (Chicago: The Gun Digest Company, 1966).

37 William C. Dowell, The Webley Story (Leeds: The Skyras Press, 1962).

rifles have essentially all been collected or lost. Technical rarities, such as the Webley-Fosberry semi-automatic revolver were produced in such small quantities that they are virtually unavailable. At the other extreme, military rifles were made in vast quantities, and their value remains low, although research is creating more and more collectible categories. A similar phenomenon is occurring for shotguns, and even .22 caliber rifles. When duelling pistols and Paterson Colts are unavailable new collecting action emerges. As certain models, particularly of Colt and Winchester, become so rare, replicas, reissues and commemoratives are being produced.

Particularly for gun collectors, the recognition factor is important. All collectors are frequently perceived as odd and obsessive. Gun collectors face particularly harsh criticism.[38] Among other strategies, collectors of relatively obscure guns are advised to have a few guns people will recognize. Colts and Winchesters clearly shine here, due to their incredible exposure in the Western popular culture.

Guns which have recognizable marks need not be recognizable themselves. Adams revolvers and Lee Metford carbines clearly marked Royal North West Mounted Police are recognizable, and have a higher value to collectors and non-collectors. An Isaac Hollis and Sons percussion shotgun is recognized as old and somewhat refined. The same gun made for and marked by the Hudson's Bay Company has popular historical recognition. In the US a Texas Ranger Krag-Jorgenson carbine and a Wells Fargo shotgun would produce the same effect.

For the author, the historian and the public, from Natty Bumpo through Wyatt Earp and Gabriel Dumont to Dirty Harry and Rambo, recognition is largely a function of symbolic values created by popular culture. For popular culture guns, the trail from Tombstone to Moosejaw, with Colts and Winchesters, is the most clearly marked. It can also be traced through the economic values assigned by gun collectors.

Methods

Little is known of gun buying patterns, which are seldom publicly observed.[39] This is partly due to the fact that public gun auctions are rare in North America, although dealer-collector auctions are a significant part of most collectors' worlds.[40] Central to this paper are the gun auctions regularly held by the Haynes Auction Company, Red Deer, Alberta, Canada.[41] These began in 1966 and the last auction studied for this paper was number 62. Each gun sold at 12 auctions held in 1983-1984 was recorded by maker, model, type, caliber and price. Observation was unobtrusive as all data but the price was present in the auction catalogue, and most auction goers record prices on their catalogues. Data were subsequently computer coded, entered and analyzed.

---

[38] Olmsted, "Morally Controversial Leisure."

[39] James D. Wright, Peter H. Rossi, and Kathleen Daly, *Under the Gun: Weapons, Crime and Violence in America* (New York: Aldine Publishing Company, 1983), pp. 118-119.

[40] Norm Flayderman, *Flayderman's Guide to Antique American Firearms* (Northfield, Illinois, DBI Books, 1983), p. 20.

[41] Bob Scammell, "Going...Going...Gun," *Western Sportsman*, Vol. 16 (1984), 68-72.

All sale items are unreserved, that is they must be sold to the highest bidder at that particular auction.

In addition to being publicly observable, auctions are important in that they flourish in situations in which conventional ways of establishing price and ownership are inadequate either because costs cannot be established, the item is old or used, there is something special or unusual about the item . . . When this occurs, auctions are seen as socially acceptable — and hence legitimate — means for establishing the value and allocation of objects.[42]

Obviously, many of the auctioned guns were old, used, special and unusual. Gun collectors are finding it increasingly difficult to justify their activities.[43] Prices are difficult to establish in Western Canada as most dealers and price guides are from elsewhere (Eastern Canada and the US). Besides overcoming these difficulties, and most important for this study, the auction scene collectively and socially defined the economic value of the guns.

The author is a lifetime Western Canadian gun owner, student of Western history and gun collecting, a consumer of popular culture, and gun collector.[44] Participation in the gun owning subculture turned to participant observing and interviewing in 1980. Membership in collecting and target shooting clubs, subscriptions to local gun newspapers and magazines and attendance at gun shows have produced quantitative validation of the quantified data presented here.

TABLE I
Total Firearms Sold at Haynes Auction, 1983-84

Type of Firearm	N Firearm	% Firearm	% Dollars	Av Price
Rifles and Carbines	1,811	46.8	55.0	256
Handguns, all types	1,402	36.0	26.7	159
Shotguns, all types	611	16.0	16.0	218
Miscellaneous, all types	45	1.2	2.3	378
	3,869	100.0	100.0	216

42 Charles W. Smith, *Auctions: The Social Construction of Value* (New York: The Free Press, 1989), p. x.

43 Olmsted, "Morally Controversial Leisure."

44 A.D. Olmsted, "Mixed Bloods in Western Canada," in J.S. Frideres (ed.) *Native People in Western Canada: Contemporary Conflicts* (Scarborough: Prentice-Hall, Canada, 1983); and "Morally Controversial Leisure."

The Guns at Auction

Data presentation will use the following format (see Table I). The type of firearm, rifle, handgun, shotgun, is presented. The 1,811 rifles seems reasonable for the real West, at 46.8% of all firearms sold during the study. Rifles are relatively expensive, with the highest average price (excluding miscellaneous) $256 per unit. (All prices are in 1983-84 Canadian dollars.) 55% of the money spent at the auctions was spent on rifles, reflecting their importance. Although Mr. Haynes has said he has no objection to people recording actual dollar amounts, he does not announce them. For this reason, dollar amounts are not presented here.[45] It is not surprising that rifles are plentiful and expensive, as they are in demand by collectors, hunters and target shooters.

The presence of 1,402 handguns, 36% of the total firearms, average price $159, is surprising. The number and value is too low for the popular culture West and the number is too high for the Canadian West, with the strict control on handguns. Four reasons account for the large number of handguns. First, in the British, urban tradition, Canadians own handguns, they just don't display them, personally, or in historical or popular culture accounts. Second, handguns are very collectible. In addition to having all the collectible virtues of guns, they are the miniatures of the gun world. Third, collecting (and target shooting) are the only legitimate reasons for owning handguns in Canada.

Finally, with increasing controls and anti-gun sentiment in Canada, sales outlets for handguns are declining rapidly. These guns could, at one time, be purchased from mail order and other department stores, hardware stores and sporting goods stores. They are now available only through highly specialized gun stores. The auction setting provides an efficient, secure, anonymous and legitimate setting for buying and selling handguns in Western Canada.

The 611 shotguns in Table I rank lowest in number, and price. This conforms to the classical Western mystique, but violates both Western and British Canadian reality. Collectors and hunters both respond to this inconsistency. Speaking of pre-1900 "Damascus" barreled shotguns

. . . if a home was to have one firearm it would most likely have been a shotgun/fowling piece . . . these antique American shotguns have not been of high interest to the antique arms collector . . . exceptions are famous makers (Colt, Parker, Remington, Winchester . . . [shotguns] are akin to the suicide specials by being . . . unique in that they have almost no historical significance![46]

[45] Scammel, 69.

[46] Flayderman, 591.

TABLE II
Handguns Sold at Haynes Auction, 1983-84

Type of Handgun	N Handguns	% Handguns	% Dollars	Av Price
Single Shot Pistol	55	3.9	4.6	190
Semi-Automatic Pistol	391	17.8	25.3	144
Semi-Auto Military Pistol	139	9.9	17.9	266
Single Action Revolver	131	9.3	20.2	344
Single Action Revolver (mil)	13	0.9	2.7	469
Double Action Revolver	594	42.6	25.6	96
Double Action Revolver (mil)	79	5.6	3.3	94
	1,402	100.0	100.0	159

By 1882, Remington was advertising fluid steel shotgun barrels.[47] Unlike Damascus barrels most of these would safely shoot the new smokeless powders. Double barrelled shotguns, and their loads have changed little since then. If a hunter is happy shooting his father or grandfather's double, especially a fine one, then he is in no way handicapped in his sport. In keeping with the European-Canadian tradition and elite popular culture view of bird hunting shotguns are viewed more positively by the non-gun owners.[48] Fine shotguns are often kept as family heirlooms and status symbols. Less refined guns are often referred to as "homesteader commemoratives" by Bud Haynes.

The types of handguns in Table II are probably a reasonable representation of handgun distribution in Canada. Production of single action revolvers had nearly died by 1940. Military production has long been centered on double action revolvers and semi-automatic pistols. The recent revival of single action Colts, their replicas, and the Ruger single action is linked directly to the Western movie, and the TV Western.[49] Even with current production, Colt and other single action revolvers do not have high production numbers, with the exception of the modern Ruger Blackhawk.[50]

[47] Ibid., 165.

[48] Tonso, Gun and Society; and Hummel, "The Rifle."

[49] Phil Spangenberg (ed.), The Complete Guide to Single Action Revolvers (Los Angeles: Petersen, 1986), pp. 2-3.

[50] L.R. Wallack, "Thirty Million Handguns," in Ken Warner (ed.) The Gun Digest (Northfield, Illinois: DBI Books, 1985), p. 109.

TABLE III
Colt and Other Single Action Revolvers sold at Haynes Auction, 1983-84

	N Single action	% Dollars	% Dollars	Av Price
Colt	59	41	66	574
Colt Competitors	33	23	14.9	232
Colt Replicas	36	25	10.4	148
Ruger (Innovation, evocation of Colt)	16	11	8.7	278
	144	100	100.0	356

However, to reiterate a theme of this paper, "While blazing its way through thousands of movies and TV Westerns [the Colt single action army] has earned the distinction of being the world's most recognizable gun."[51] While Colt has also entered the commemorative market, there were not enough in the sample to warrant separate discussion. Percussion Colts had a similar low frequency. Even with this lack in the sample, the data are clear. Although few in number (131) single action revolvers were most valued by buyers (average price $344). (To be classified as military revolvers, issue marks had to be present.) These raised the average value to $469. Together, 146 single action revolvers made only 10.2% of the handguns sold, but 22.9% of the dollars spent on the handguns sold. Double action revolvers, 48.2% of the sample, made up only 28.9% of the dollars spent, with an average price of $95.

Turning to Table III, Colt, Colt replicas and Rugers make up 77% of the single action revolvers and 85% of the dollars spent on single action revolvers. Given a similar range of age and history, Colt competitors were valued at less than half than Colts ($574 vs $232). The competitors included 11 different makers, led by Smith and Wesson and Remington. Fourteen different makes of replicas were sold, none dominating the sample. The Colt is still king among Western Canadian gun buyers.

For later discussion it should be noted that Webley double action revolvers, civilian and military (N = 81, average price $76) fell a distant third behind Smith and Wesson (N = 73, average price $178), and Colt (N = 97) ($178). Among semi-automatic military pistols, Luger led in average price ($405) and was second in number (21) while Colt led in number (57) and was second in average price ($307).

In Table IV and Table V, the picture of the classic Western rifle (popular culture version) is clear. The 570 lever action rifles represent 31.5% of the rifles sold and 52% of the money spent on rifles. In Table V, real Winchester tubular magazine lever action rifles and carbines, commemorative versions and replicas of Winchesters represent 83.3% of the lever action rifles and carbines. Thirty-one of the Winchester

[51] Spangenberg, 3. This source is a compact discussion of Colt, the guns in Table III and the popular culture influence.

competitors are lever action Marlins (also accepted by the End of Trail Shoot). Their 6% of the lever action rifles brings the Western lever action to 89.3% of the lever action rifles in the sample.

Only the popular recognition and reputation of the lever action Winchester can account for its enormous presence in the sample. While many of these rifles were produced, the production numbers are matched by the predominantly bolt action military rifles which represent only 18.4% (N = 33) of the rifles sold and 6% of the money spent on rifles. The average military rifle price of $85 represents the result of large numbers produced and little collector interest.

While many hunters still speak favorably of the old "thirty-thirty," bolt action rifles are the most common hunting rifle today. Like the Marlin, Savage, Browning and other lever action competitors, bolt action rifles offer modern cartridges and easy mounting of telescopic sights. Only recent Winchester model 94s offer these features to hunters.

Built on the basic model 1894 frame, Winchester commemoratives offer instant stories to new collectors. Their names (only a few listed here) and their features reflect the popular culture West, more than its history. The Royal Canadian Mounted Police commemorative is the model 1894 with a full military stock, .30-30 caliber, imitating the 1876 carbines in .45-75 caliber actually issued to the R.C.M.P. The series named after Plains Indian tribes all have neat brass tacks in the stocks. The lore of guns says that such tacks indicate Indian ownership. Usually stamped designs imitate the original engraving.

The high average price of the eight replica Winchesters is due to four of them being models highly engraved by European craftsmen. The replicas and the commemoratives are both based on, and contribute to the myth of the Winchester. However, the bulk of the real Winchesters sold show that the plain model 1892 and 1894 saddle guns were highly valued. Although Henry's, 1866s and 1873s brought high prices, the bulk of the Winchesters were the plain, everyday working "saddle guns." Winchester competitors, mostly Savage and Marlin were few in number (73), low in average price ($222) and contributed only 6.7% of the lever action dollars.

TABLE IV
Rifles and Carbines sold at Haynes Auction, 1983-84

Type of Rifle	N Rifle	% Rifle	% Dollars	Av Price
Single Shot Sporting Rifles and Carbines	306	16.9	10	157
Lever Action Sporting Rifles and Carbines	570	31.5	52	423
Bolt Action Sporting Rifles and Carbines	379	20.9	23	273
Military Rifles and Carbines (all types)	333	18.4	6	85
Semi-Automatic Sporting Rifles and Carbines	154	8.5	5.9	177
Pump Action Rifles	65	3.6	2.3	170
Doulbe Barrelled Rifles	4	.2	.8	970
	1,811	100	100	256

TABLE V
Winchester and Other Lever Action Rifles sold at Haynes Auction, 1983-84

Type of Lever Action Rifles and Carbines	N Rifles & Carbines	% Rifles & Carbines	% of Dollars	Av Price
Winchester[1]	302	53.0	58.1	464
Winchester Commemoratives	165	28.9	30.2	441
Winchester Competitors	73	12.8	6.7	222
Winchester Replicas	8	1.4	2.1	631
Lever Action Innovations	22	3.9	2.9	311
	570	100.0	100.0	423

[1]Henry rifles, the forerunner of the Winchester, are included with Winchester.
N = 4 Average price $3,175.

TABLE VI
Shotguns Sold at Haynes Auction, 1983

Type of Shotgun	N Shotguns	% Shotguns	% Dollars	Av Price
Single shot Shotgun	141	23.1	8.9	85
Semi-auto Shotgun	80	13.1	16.6	276
Bolt action Shotgun	33	5.4	1.4	58
Pump action Shotgun	147	24.0	21.6	196
Double Barrel Shotgun	173	28.3	32.3	248
Over-under Shotgun	28	4.6	17.4	827
Lever-action Shotgun	9	1.5	1.8	259
	611	100.0	100.0	218

The double barrelled shotgun (Table VI) fulfills nearly all predictions as a Western gun, its value (average price $248), ranks third behind Colt ($574) and Winchester ($476). Historically, its popularity is reflected by the 173 doubles making 28.3% of total shotguns and 32.3% of the total amount spent on shotguns. The average price, however, is exceeded by the very rare lever action shotguns ($259), (a Winchester influence); the very refined and elegant over-under shotguns ($827) and the currently popular semi-automatic shotguns ($276). Double barrelled shotguns remain nameless, in the sense that the 173 doubles in this study represent 98 makers. There were no Greeners, the closest to a generic Western shotgun name.

Four other categories round off the discussion of data. Military rifles, although well represented (N = 333), are low in dollars spent on rifles (6%) and lowest in average price ($85). Semi-automatic military pistols fare better, due to the recognizability of the Colt 1911-11A and the Luger.

.22 caliber guns (not shown are well represented, totalling 630. (For overall summaries, .22s are included in the relevant categories.) .22 lever action rifles and carbines (N = 23) have an average price of $224. This is the highest average price for a .22 firearm. .22 single action revolvers (N = 25) have an average price of $185, just behind .22 semi-automatic pistols ($198). While nearly replicating the Western ranking, the average .22 price (N = 630) of $110 reflects the reality of .22 production and cost. Few collectors put a premium price on the myths of their own boyhoods. Similarly, while Canadians buy and sell the low visibility pocket double action revolvers and semi-automatic pistols, the prices paid reflect their lack of mystique. Finally, the few (N = 4) double rifles in the sample commanded the highest average price, $970. This is a tribute to their desirability, not their historical presence.

Conclusions

Opportunistic research cannot speak directly of cause and effect. However, this study suggests that popular culture and popular history provide a recognition factor which strongly affects the value placed on guns. This is most apparent among collectors. The mechanic, the artist, the author-romantic and the historian each have a particular view of a collectible rifle. Historians and authors should have different views from Tombstone and Moosejaw, when experiences differed in the Canadian and United State's Wests. Values do not reflect this interest.

The Colt single action revolvers are the most prepotent firearm in the popular culture West. They were a significant technological advance in the settling of the Great Plains in the US. They could and need not be carried by Western Canadian settlers. English handguns, the double action Adams and Webley, had an intricate and fascinating technological history, and were the official handguns of the British Empire. Unlike the Colt, these revolvers had no popular culture or historical presence anywhere, although they were available and present in the West and elsewhere. Both types of guns, and their competitors, were available in sufficiently elegant forms to attract the artists among gun collectors. Again, prices do not reflect their historical presence and characteristics.

The high value placed on Colt single action revolvers by Canadian gun buyers-collectors can reasonably be attributed to the sixgun mystique created by popular culture. For these guns, it is the romance of the mythical West which triggers the romantic aspect of gun collecting. For other collectible handguns, such as Lugers and Colt 1911-11A semi-automatics, a similar recognition attraction principle creates high competition and prices. All other handguns, although historically present in the US and Canada, and at the auctions studied, create relatively, and sometimes absolutely, low values. Elegant, innovative or historically relevant, these "other" handguns have only low or narrow interest for collectors.

When the Canadian West was settled, the Winchester lever action, tubular magazine rifle filled real needs. It was accompanied by competitors such as Marlin and Savage, which were often as elegant, and arguably superior in technology. For hunting, the rifle's major function in Canada, the Winchester lever action was rapidly superceded by other technologies, such as the bolt action.

The auction results show that in both number and price, the classic Winchester is the most popular and most valued rifle. Winchesters commemorating Western popular culture cannot be fired or separated from their boxes and wrappings without losing value but are a major component of the Winchesters sold at auction. Guns such as La Petit and R.C.M.P. Commemorative use the limited popular culture of Western Canada. Winchester is still winning at Western gun auctions.

The only gun whose historical reality overcomes its negative popular culture mystique is the double barrelled shotgun. This may only be true in Canada, where a British tradition favoring the double is present. Despite strong technological competition and poorly developed collecting fields, this gun is popular at the auctions. As collecting interest increases, Westerns become more "realistic" and Colts and Winchesters more rare double barrelled shotguns may rise in collector value.

The pocket handguns of urbanites, the issue handguns and rifles of all soldiers and the .22 caliber guns of collectors past and present have relatively little value to collectors. Initial low cost and lack of rarity no doubt influence their value. Yet it is tempting to speculate on popular culture events which could increase their recognition and reputation factors. The importance of the .22 in boyhood, the Mauser rifle in the Boer War or a Mexican revolution could increase their reputation. It is probably too late, but remember what Dirty Harry accomplished for his guns.

When this paper was first presented in 1986, it ended with a note on the present and future relationship between popular culture and guns. Current media guns, in news, editorials, books, TV and movies are dominated by the military assault rifles and combat 9mm semi-automatics. AK-47 has become a more common symbol than Winchester. No single pistol is dominating like Colt, although with its military adoption by the US, the 9mm combat Beretta may achieve this position.

As always, public opinion is based on a few horrendous abuses of guns. It ignores the fact that popular culture has produced a new generation of collectors, neither more nor less deviant than those who followed the myth of the Western guns. The mystique of guns has changed over the last century. Gun collectors have not. They will continue to be influenced by popular culture and popular history, just as the collectors in this study have been influenced.

Acknowledgement: I would like to thank my wife, Noreen and my son Tony for their many hours of data collection, typing and data coding. Without their help this paper would not have been possible.

Part II ITS ENEMIES
Chapter 8

ASPECTS OF THE PRIAPIC THEORY
OF GUN OWNERSHIP

by
Don B. Kates Jr. and **Nicole Varzos**

INTRODUCTION

The most extended exposition of what we shall call the priapic theory of gun ownership appears in a book by Detroit psychiatrist Emanuel Tanay:

Passivity and insecurity are perhaps the two major characterologic features leading to the need for a gun. Alcoholism, gun ownership and various forms of risk taking are behavioral expressions of reaction formation toward passivity ... Clinical evidence indicates that guns are acquired not only for aggressive but for libidinal purposes. On a narcissitic level, the acquisition of a gun often serves to enhance or repair a damaged self-image. The owner's overvaluation of his gun's worth is an indication of its libidinal value to him. Most of the dedicated gun owners handle the gun with obvious pleasure; they look after the gun, clean, polish, and pamper it. The narcissitic investment in the gun is apparent in a great many cases ... The equation of the gun with the penis is attested to in many expressions. In fact, "to shoot off your gun" is, in colloquial language, a synonym for ejaculation ... In dreams gun and penis frequently represent each other.[1]

Except for two passing comments this theory seems to have been ignored in scholarly and public policy literature.[2] It is not even mentioned in the National Institute of Justice's 1981 encyclopedic overview, *WEAPONS, CRIME AND VIOLENCE IN THE UNITED STATES: A LITERATURE ANALYSIS AND RESEARCH AGENDA.*[3]

The priapic theory has nevertheless been extensively championed in popular

ACKNOWLEDGEMENTS

The authors wish to thank the following for their assistance: Professors David Bordua (Sociology, U. of Illinois), F. Smith Fussner (History, Emeritus, Reed College) and Ted Robert Gurr (U. of Maryland, Political Science); Ms. E. Byrd and Ms. S. Byrd, Berkeley, Ca., Mr. C. Spector, San Raphael, California and Ms. P. Kates, San Francisco, Ca. Of course for errors either of fact or interpretation the authors are alone responsible.

[1] Emanuel Tanay, "Neurotic Attachment to Guns," in E. Tanay (ed.), *The Fifty Minute Hour.*

[2] Bruce Danto, *International Journal of Offender Therapy*, Vol. 5 (1979), 135-146; and Barry Bruce-Briggs, "The Great American Gun War," *The Public Interest* (Fall, 1976).

[3] Herein cited in its later commercially published form as James D. Wright, Peter H. Rossi, and Kathleen Daly, *Under the Gun: Weapons, Crime and Violence in America* (New York: Aldine Publishing Company, 1983).

literature.[4] Among its most prominent proponents are Mike Royko (urging that gun owners "Be honest about how the long barrel of your pistol reminds you of your . . . well, you know"), Harlan Ellison, ("Daddy's surrogate penis, the bureau-drawer Luger"), W.H. Auden, Arthur Schlessinger Jr. and Dr. Joyce Brothers.[5] Correlatively Diana Trilling, describing the Jean Harris murder trial, asserts: that for some women "the idea of masculinity and fierceness are not to be disentangled from one another"; and that, by acquiring a gun Harris "was supplied what she'd been deprived of by biology."[6]

The present paper attempts to comprehensively examine the evidence for and against the priapic theory.

CAVEATS RE GUNS AND POWER

Initially we must emphasize Tanay's differentiation of the gun as instrument or symbol of power in general from the gun as a specifically priapic instrument or symbol. It is only the latter which concerns us because non-sexual relationships between gun ownership and power have received extensive study. Though considerations of space preclude our summarizing this voluminous literature, indicative of the variety and complexity of the power relationships are such findings as: that handguns are used in c. 581,500 criminal attempts and (by law abiding citizens) in resisting c. 645,000 crimes annually, with each group enjoying a much higher success rate (c. 83%) than do either criminals or resisters when armed with lesser weapons; that gun owners are less fearful of crime than non-owners living in the same area; and that 81% of Good Samaritans who came to the aid of crime victims or arrested their attackers

"own guns and some carry them in their cars." Unlike those who shirk involvement, they "are familiar with violence, feel competent to handle it, and don't believe they will get hurt if they get involved."[7]

---

[4] See Carl Bakal, No Right to Bear Arms (New York: Paperback Library, 1966), p. 88; Robert E. Burns, "Sex Education Belongs in the Gun Store," U.S. Catholic Vol. 4 (1979), 2; Charles McCabe, "A Signal on Guns," San Francisco Chronicle (January 27, 1982), 53; and Thomas Brom, Review of B. Gelb, Varnished Brass: The Decade After Serpico, California Lawyer (May, 1984).

[5] See n. infra; Harlan Ellison, "Fear Not Your Enemies," Heavy Metal (March, 1981), 35; and W.H. Auden, Arthur Schlessinger Jr., and Joyce Brothers as quoted in Bruce-Briggs, 59, and McCabe.

[6] Quoted in Lance K. Stell, "Guns, Politics and Reason," Journal of American Culture, Vol. 9 (1986), 72.

[7] Gary Kleck, "Guns and Self-Defense: Crime Control through the Use of Force in the Private Sector," draft manuscript, School of Criminology, Florida State University; J. DeFronzo, "Fear of Crime and Handgun Ownership," Criminology, Vol. 17 (1979), 331-339; J.S. Williams and J.W. McGrath III, "Why People Own Guns," Journal of Communication, Vol. 26 (1976), 22-30; and Don B. Kates, Jr., "On Reducing Violence and Liberty," Civil Liberties Review, Vol. 5 (1976), 58.

Space considerations also preclude more than mentioning the sex role-linked (but non-priapic) possibility that male feelings about the traditional male responsibility to defend the family contribute to gun ownership in a violent society. One might speculate that insecurity about their ability to perform this protective role might even affect some men's sexual performance. But that only emphasizes the irrelevance to our concerns of such an issue since: a) such insecurity feelings would apparently characterize gun owners less than non-owners; and b) the issue does not relate to any priapic aspect of guns. After all, it could be speculated with equal plausibility that unemployment (i.e. insecurity in the traditional male role of breadwinner) might affect sexual performance.

SUPPORTING EVIDENCE FOR
THE PRIAPIC THEORY

1. Freudian Origins Transmogrified —

Tanay cites Freudian dream interpretation regarding the priapic theory.[8] But an actual reading of Freud suggests a very different hypothesis. To the very limited extent that he addressed anything pertinent to the matter, Freud's concern was not with "neurotic attachment to guns" (Tanay's subject) but with neurotic fear of them. See *interalia* Freud's assertion: "The representation of the penis as a weapon . . . is familiar to us from the anxiety dreams of abstinent women [patients] in particular."[9]

Thus Freud's interest lay in what guns signify not to their owners, but to those (presumably non-owners) who fear them. Moreover his concern was not about guns *as guns* but about a miscellany of *dream objects,* including guns, which he felt symbolized the penis in a variety of ways. As stated in his 10th Lecture:

the sacred number *three* is symbolic of the whole male genitalia . . . the penis is symbolized primarily by objects which resemble it in form, being long and upstanding, such as *sticks, umbrellas, poles, trees* and the like; also by objects which, like the thing symbolized, have the property of penetrating and consequently injuring, the body — that is to say pointed weapons of all sorts; *knives, daggers, lances, sabers;* firearms are similarly used, [and particularly those which resemble the penis] on account of their shape . . . The substitution of the male organ by objects from which water flows is again easily comprehensible: *taps, watering cans* or *springs;* and by other objects which are capable of elongation, such as *pulley lamps, pencils which slide in and out of a sheath* and so on. *Pencils, penholders, nail files, hammers* and other *implements* are undoubtedly male sexual symbols, based on an idea of the male organ which is easily perceived.[10]

In the next paragraph Freud adds snakes, reptiles, fish, hats and cloaks, hands, feet,

---

8 Tanay, n. 6.

9 Freud and Oppenheim (1958 ed.: 33) See also Freud (1952 ed.: 507): "In the anxiety dreams of young girls, pursuit by a man armed with a knife or rifle plays a great part."

10 Sigmund Freud (Great Books ed.), *The Major Works of Sigmund Freud* (Chicago: Encyclopedia Britannica, 1952), p. 507.

balloons, aeroplanes, and Zeppelins to the list of phallic dream symbols. To realize the priapic theory's full irrelevance to any Freudian concern would require summarizing Freud in much greater detail than our present space permits. Suffice it to say that his system links dream symbolism to myth, folklore, philology, religion, art and primal language. A central tenet is that in primal man sexual interest became attached to work. Work became acceptable by being the equivalent to, or substitute for, sexual acts. Sounds and words uttered during work initially had multiple meanings (connoting both work and sex), but eventually were fixed to work. As time went on, the pattern repeated itself *ad infinitum* and serves as a guide to the preservation in dreams of the earliest conditions. It is as a result of this preservation that dreams so often involve sexual symbolism and why weapons and tools in dreams always stand for what is male. This symbolic relation is the residue of the ancient verbal identity.[11]

In sum, even for those who might deem Freudian theory "evidence", it offers (at best) no support whatever for the priapic theory. Indeed, to the extent that Freudian theory is at all relevant, it might imply that it is Tanay's own "distaste for guns" and "reluctance to touch" them which is neurotic and/or immature.

2. Owners' Behavior/Attitudes Toward Guns

As quoted earlier, Tanay offers two other supports for the priapic theory: first, that gun collectors "overvalue" the gun, "hand[ling it] with obvious pleasure, [they] look after the gun, clean, polish and pamper it . . . speak of their love and respect for guns." At the risk of belaboring the obvious, comparable behavior is exhibited by stereo, car and computer enthusiasts, collectors of paper back novels, coins, comic books, match books, political campaign pins or posters, statuary, furniture, model railroads, cut glass, etc., etc. — regardless of whatever monetary value the objects of their enthusiasm may actually have. Indeed, such collectibles as cancelled stamps, ancient coins (not made of precious metals), empty match books, old campaign pins etc. have literally no intrinsic function or worth except for the sometimes enormous sums that collectors who "overvalue" them will pay to possess them. Thus this first item of supporting evidence says less about gun owners than about Tanay's own ability to evaluate the thought processes of those who value an object he admittedly detests.

3. Clinical Evidence —

Tanay's other support consists in a vague mention of "clinical evidence." If this refers to his own experience, or to private communications from others, it is strange that he does not so state in a footnote — as he does on other points. Yet his reference cannot be to published clinical research: writing in the same year Bruce-Briggs was unable to find any such work; this is confirmed by our own review of the entire corpus of psychiatric literature from 1930 to date.[12] Nor does any such discussion appear in the general social scientific literature on demographic and motivational factors in gun ownership.

[11] Freud, *The Major Works of Sigmund Freud; Sexuality and the Psychology of Love*, P. Rieff (ed.) (New York: Collier); and with D.E. Oppenheim, *Dreams in Folklore* (New York: International Universities Press, 1958).

[12] Bruce-Briggs, 59.

This inattention to the priapic theory is really quite striking given the substantiality of this literature and its inclusion of warm controversies over the incidence of gun ownership in general and correlations to such factors as race, religion, regional socialization, military service, sex and fear of crime.[13]

In light of scholarly inattention to the priapic theory there may be some value in examining empirical objections to it even though there seems to be no countervailing evidence to support it.

OBJECTIONS TO THE PRIAPIC THEORY
BASED ON GUN PREFERENCE

The priapic theory is rejected on empirical grounds by Danto, a psychiatrist, director of the Detroit Suicide Prevention Center and advisor to the Detroit Police Department.[14] He makes the point that if priapic motivation or symbolism were important elements in gun ownership, large caliber and/or long barrelled weapons should predominate. Yet his study of gun homicide, accident and suicide found long guns far less frequently involved than were handguns; moreover, in Detroit, handguns with small bores and short barrels predominated over larger ones.

1. **Weapons preferences among criminal populations —**

An immediate difficulty with Danto's argument arises out of the atypicality of his sample. It is fallacious to make inferences about the psyches of *normal gun owners* from the gun preferences of the perpetrators of accidents, murders and suicides unless it can be demonstrated that such perpetrators are not atypical of the general population or at least of gun owners within it. As to suicides this can be demonstrated, Danto himself having shown a close resemblance.[15] But murderers and fatal gun accident perpetrators present a very different case. While these groups closely resemble each other, it is in atypical ways that sharply differentiate both of them from the norm, i.e. their life histories of felony, mental disturbance, alcohol

---

[13] For the most recent contributions to this literature see William B. Bankston, Carol Y. Thompson, Q.A.L. Jenkins and Craig J. Forsyth, "Carrying Firearms: The Influence of Southern Culture and Fear of Crime," paper presented at the American Society of Criminology Annual Meeting, 1986; Robert L. Young, "Gender, Region of Socialization and Ownership of Protective Firearms," *Rural Sociology,* Vol. 51 (1986), 169-182, and "Perception of Crime, Racial Attitudes and Firearms Ownership," *Social Forces,* Vol. 64 (1985), 473-486; O.C. Ferrell and William M. Pride, "Overview: Handgun Ownership Study Provides Some Surprises," (unpaginated manuscript, Texas A&M University, 1986); Paula D. McClain, "Firearms Ownership, Gun Control Attitudes, and Neighborhood Environment," *Law & Policy Quarterly,* Vol. 5 (1983), 299-324; Alan J. Lizzote and David J. Bordua, "Firearms Ownership for Sport and Protection: Two Divergent Models," *American Sociological Review,* Vol. 46 (1980), 2229-2244; and Wright, et al.

[14] Danto, 137-138.

[15] Ibid., 137; and Danto and Joan M. Danto, "Jewish and Non-Jewish Suicide in Oakland County, Michigan," paper presented at the American Association of Suicidology Meeting, 1981.

and/or drug dependency, auto accidents and spontaneous or irrational violence.[16]

Yet even if Danto's argument cannot be sustained by the data he himself cites, it may nevertheless be borne out by patterns of gun ownership and characteristics of the guns favored by the general gun owning population:

2. Hunting Arms —

The largest bore rifles, designed for hunting elephant, rhinocerous, tiger, lion and cape buffalo, are the .458, .460, .470, .577 and .600 "big game rifles".[17] The priapic theory would predict a large American market for such guns since they could be used to take the larger North American game animals including moose and bear. But the market is, in fact, so small that only the 458 is even manufactured in this country; and only it and the .470 are available in import catalogs, the .470 at prices running from $8,300.00 to $10,500.00 per gun. To purchase a gun in any of the other calibers an American would have to specially order it from a custom gunsmith or from Europe. The largest, most powerful rifle likely to be found in an ordinary American hunter's armory would be a 30-06 and the lowly .30-30 deer gun would be far more likely yet; the considerably more powerful .338 or .375 (suitable for big bear) would be uncommon and any caliber larger than these would be extraordinary.[18]

---

[16] Philip J. Cook, "The Role of Firearms in Violent Crime: An Interpretative Review of the Literature," in M. Wolfgang and N. Weiner, *Criminal Violence* (Beverly Hills: Sage, 1982), pp. 269, 271-272; Danto, 136-138; Don B. Kates, Jr., "Points of Comparison Between Banning the Handgun and Prohibition of Liquor," in Kates (ed.) *Firearms and Violence: Issues of Public Policy* (Cambridge: Bollinger, 1984), p. 145; and Gary Kleck, "Firearms Accidents," draft manuscript, School of Criminology, Florida State University, 1986.

[17] The numerical designations by which differed gun calibers are described refer to portions of an inch (in this case thousanths, although some designations are in terms of hundrenths, e.g. .38 revolver or .30 caliber carbine). Thus the diameter of a .600 is 600 thousanths of an inch, of a .577 is 577 thousanths etc.

Bore diameter is not the only index of gun power. A major element in killing power is velocity which is based on the amount of the propellant charge with which the bullet is launched. Even among guns having about the same caliber the standard propellant charges vary widely thereby producing fundamental differences in killing power. Thus, although by far the most common American hunting guns are in calibers approximating .300, their capabilities differ drastically because of their propellant differences: the .30 caliber carbine, having a powder charge of only 14.5 grains, is considered unfit for anything bigger than jack rabbits or perhaps peccary; the 30-30 with its traditional 30 grain charge is acceptable for deer and boar; the 30-06 or .308 NATO with 50 and 48 grains respectively are used to take even the largest and strongest game animals found on the North American continent. (It should be noted that, although the 30-06 and .308 are perfectly satisfactory for deer, elk, caribou, mountain goat and most bear some experts consider them only marginally adequate for moose and polar and Kodiak bears.)

[18] Neither of the authors of this paper has ever hunted nor wished to do so. For our assertions about hunting and the arms and ammunition used therefor we are indebted to advice given us by Mr. R.L. Wilson, historical consultant to Colt Industries, and two social scientists of sport, Profs. Sarkis Atamian (U. of Alaska, Sociology Emeritus) and Richard Hummel (Eastern Illinois U., Sociology).

Even the smaller big game rifles like the .338 are quite expensive, with the larger and more esoteric, such as the .470, .577 and .600, being extremely so. But Danto's point cannot be gainsaid on the basis that these weapons are beyond the means of the American public regardless of their supposed priapic appeal. On the contrary, the prohibitive costliness of these guns derives largely from this very lack of a market for them. Their power requires that these rifles be made in massive double or single barrel configurations. The single barrel design particularly is far simpler and more easily produced than the complex semi-automatic, bolt or lever action weapons favored by American hunters. While the big game rifles are too massive to ever be downright "cheap", if the market predicted by the priapic theory existed, they could be mass produced at prices comparable to popular American hunting arms.

(In this connection, yet another characteristic of the hunting culture cuts very strongly against the priapic theory: among hunters the emphasis is on accuracy and coolness under stress, on using *the smallest, least powerful rifle capable of bringing down the hunted animal with a solid hit.* Even American hunters who could afford to specially order a .577 or .600 would not appear with it on a bear hunt because to do so would inspire derision, not respect.)

Shotgun bores are sized inversely with 8 and 10 gauges being the largest ever made, 12, 16, 20 and 28 gauges being progressively smaller and the .410 smallest of all. Since no cost differential is inherent in these sizes, the priapic theory would predict that the 8 and 10 gauges would prevail. In fact, however, the 8 is almost unheard of today and even the 10 is far less common than the lowly .410.

3. Functional Explanations for Weapons Preferences

The evidence so far reviewed suggests function rather than priapic considerations as the basis for the selection, and therefore ownership, of hunting arms at least. The predominance of functional considerations may be confirmed by any number of additional comparisons. Moving from bore size to barrel length, the priapic theory would predict preference for the longest possible. But for both shotguns and rifles variance in barrel length appears to be simply a matter of function: those oriented toward close quarters hunting in heavy brush where a long barrel would be unnecessary and cumbersome choose 16-20 inch barrel guns (as do those who keep a shotgun or rifle or personal defense); but those interested in target and trap shooting and/or taking game at long range choose guns with a barrel length of 26 to 30 or more inches.

It might be objected that our testing assumes a false dichotomy: perhaps priapic motivation is not *alternative* to function in determining the caliber, length etc. of the guns people select; perhaps priapic motivation is only an *additional* factor unconsciously affecting the selection process. From this premise it might be speculated that priapic motivation unconsciously influences owners toward shooting sports in which functional considerations dictate having longer or larger guns. Or they might be unconsciously biased toward the largest, longest guns that would be functional in the shooting sport they adopt.

While this objection is not without theoretical force, it does constitute a major alteration in the priapic theory as presented in popular literature. Specifically it demotes that theory from being **the** explanation for people owning guns to the status of a mere tendency. More important this demotion only alters the terms of the inquiry slightly without changing the outcome: Even when demoted to a mere tendency the priapic theory ill accords with the observed facts of gun owner preference. There is not just a lack of preference for shotguns, the largest and longest of guns, over all others; even considering shotguns, rifles and handguns (and the different sports in which they are used) as separate and incomparable to each other, there is just no evidence within any of these categories of the preference for long barrels or large calibers which would be predicted if priapic considerations were an important factor.[19] *A fortiori* differentials in popularity between various shooting sports do not suggest that any part is played by unconscious desire to use large, long guns.

What is true of sporting arms is equally so of defense weapons. While there are manifest disadvantages, it is not impossible to adapt rifles and shotguns to office or home defense. Indeed they predominated in those roles in the Depression era and before when crime was no less rampant but the average person, having much less disposable income, had to make do with one gun for both sport and defense. As the growth of per capita incomes increasingly permitted, long guns have been replaced by handguns for home and/or office defense.[20]

Though the proliferation of these small (often short barrelled and small bore [4]) weapons defies explanation under the priapic theory, it is readily explicable by their great functional advantages over shotguns or rifles: 1) for technical reasons handguns are both far less subject to accidental discharge and 2) far less deadly if discharged, while at the same time they are 3) much easier to lock or secrete away from children; also 4) handguns are much easier to bring into play in a close quarters defense situation, and 5) when discharged at a criminal much less likely to penetrate all the way through, menacing innocent bystanders beyond him, nor do they scatter shot promiscuously around the room, while 6) because of their short barrels they are far less subject than long guns to being wrested away by a criminal. To illustrate the functional advantage of a handgun in the defense role it is necessary only to envision a housewife trying to keep a burglar at bay with a rifle held precariously in one hand

---

[19] The size of both the total American gunstock and the numbers of shotguns, rifles and long guns within it can not be determined with any precision. But it is generally agreed that the proportions are about one third handguns, one third rifles and one third shotguns. See, e.g. Wright and Rossi, 1983: ch. 2.

Based on figures from the federal Bureau of Alcohol, Tobacco and Firearms for the years 1973 through 1981, domestic handgun production approximated 16.4 million of which 7.4 million (45%) were in handguns of .32 caliber or below.

[20] Don B. Kates, Jr., "Handgun Prohibition and the Original Meaning of the Second Amendment," *Michigan Law Review*, Vol. 82 (1983), 263-264; and Bruce-Briggs, 37, n.l.

while dialing the police with the other.[21]

This is not to deny that rifles and shotguns may offer compensating advantages for the defender or for society at large. Discounting NRA-cited incidents in which handguns routed burglars without killing them, a spokesman for the National Coalition to Ban Handguns argues that "A twelve gauge shotgun" would have had the advantage "of permanently ending the intruder's crime career."[22] This and other functional issues between particular kinds of firearm may be debated at length. For present purposes it suffices to point out that in such a debate priapic considerations appear to play no part, whether conscious or unconscious.

In sum, factors that are purely functional in nature fully explain American gun preferences while the priapic theory not only fails to do so but is directly inconsistent with the observed facts in various respects. The priapic theory thus seems both unnecessary and implausible.

OBJECTIONS TO THE PRIAPIC THEORY BASED ON THE DEMOGRAPHICS OF GUN OWNERSHIP

It is well established that gun ownership varies quite substantially within differing American demographic groups. This is illustrated by the latest national survey of handgun ownership which is particularly detailed in its attention to this issue, having been done by market research specialists who were also examining into the ownership of other consumer items such as bicycles, compac disc players and various types of cameras. The survey's overview offers the following pertinent findings:

... persons with some college were more apt to own a handgun (21.3%) than those who never completed high school (14.2%). Nineteen percent of those with a high school diploma owned at least one handgun ... people with lower incomes were less likely to own a handgun. Twelve percent of those earning less than $15,000, and 16.5% of those earning between $15,000 and $20,000 owned guns. The highest percentage of [hand]gun ownership (23.7%) occurred in the $20,000 to $30,000 bracket. The rate seemed to stabilize around 21% after $30,000 ... more whites owned a handgun (19%) than non-whites (13%) ... more of the handgun owners were married (20.8%). Only 14.4% of those who were not married reported [hand]gun ownership ... Age also seemed to be a factor in handgun ownership ... fourteen percent of those under 25 owned a handgun, while 19.6% of those between 25 and 34 and 21.9% of those between 35 and 49, owned handguns. Only 16.9% of those 50 and older were handgun owners.[23]

We have eliminated from this quotation speculations about the reasons for the

[21] Ibid., 261-264; and Massad Ayoob, *The Truth About Self Protection* (New York: Bantam, 1983), pp. 332-333, 341-342, 345-355.

[22] S. Fields, *St. Louis Law Journal,* Vol. 23, (1979), 41.

[23] Ferrell and Pride.

observed differences in rates of handgun ownership between different demographic groups. While plausible, these speculations are irrelevant to our concerns which may be expressed rhetorically: Does anything in the priapic theory predict "that married whites with higher income and more education [would be the] most likely to purchase a handgun"?[24] Is there any reason to think these demographic groups more subject to priapic compulsion or symbolism than the unmarried, the non-white, the less well educated and/or the less affluent?

OBJECTIONS TO THE PRIAPIC THEORY
BASED ON WOMEN'S GUN OWNERSHIP

The growing phenomenon of female gun ownership was Danto's second reason for rejecting the priapic theory. Although the majority of gun owners have always been men, the fact of female gun ownership is well established. The standard academic history of American gun ownership notes that the first sporting events in which women received equal billing with men in America were the 19th Century shooting contests sponsored by gun companies which featured Annie Oakley, Pinky Topperwine and their respective husbands.[25]

1. Lack of Female Interest in Shooting Sports —
Yet the contrast to the present situation dramatizes the lack of female interest in the shooting sports nearly a century after Annie Oakley. In shooting contests today women score separately as well as jointly. This is not at all comparable to tennis where the actual tournaments are often separate, reflecting real differences in inherent strength. In shooting physical strength is not a decisive issue; indeed it is a sport that can be practiced by the elderly and is often recommended to stroke and other disablement victims as a form of physical therapy that helps build hand-eye coordination without undue physical stress.

Thus in shooting matches men and women actually shoot together; it is only the scoring that is differentiated for the purpose of specially encouraging women competitors. If a woman comes in first overall in any match or in the entire shoot, she is the winner; but because the women are also scored separately she can still win the special women's prize by defeating all other women even if she doesn't come in ahead of all other (male) competitors.[26] The lack of female interest in shooting sports which

---

24 Ibid.

25 Lee Kennett and James LaVerne Anderson, *The Gun in America: The Origins of a National Dilemma* (Westport, Connecticut: Greenwood Press, 1975), p. 136.

26 We are informed by Massad Ayoob, a police firearms instructor and nationally recognized shooting champion, that a secondary reason (or at least excuse) for the differential scoring in most shooting matches is that the difference in upper body strength between men and women may give men some advantage in a championship-level contest. Lt. Ayoob himself feels that most women's smaller stature and lower center of gravity gives them a compensating speed advantage in combat shooting.

this scoring differential suggests is confirmed by a current study of active shooters in North Carolina. Although Southern women are far more likely to own and even carry guns than their Northern sisters out of upwards of 100 North Carolina shooters whom Stenross and Brooks have identified, only one or two were women.[27]

2. Protection versus Sport as Reasons for Ownership

But the relative lack of female interest in shooting sports does not necessarily suggest an absence of guns among women. When the editors of *GLAMOR* surveyed their readership in 1982 they were appalled to find that two-thirds of the respondents opposed banning handguns and 50% actually owned them. Though there are obvious problems with such a sample, other evidence corroborates a large and increasing incidence of female gun ownership. Based on their seminal study of gun ownership in Illinois, Lizotte and Bordua feel that one half of all those owners who keep guns for protection only are women. They suggest that many of these owners are young Black women living as heads of household in high crime areas. This is supported by a Detroit survey of Black and White households that found that while the likelihood of household gun ownership did not vary much along racial lines, white gun owners were generally male but Black gun ownership was divided about equally between the sexes.[28]

The gun ownership gap between Black and White women may be narrowing (or may be limited to Detroit). National survey data analyzed by Young indicate that protection gun ownership by White women increased c. 25% in the years 1980-82.[29]

3. Penis Envy and the Demographics of Female Gun Ownership —

Of course the mere fact that many women have guns does not necessarily refute the priapic theory as Danto himself recognizes; cf. Diana Trilling's explanation of female gun ownership as penis envy. Freud felt penis envy natural to every woman and (depending on whether or how she resolved it) key to her progression toward what he saw as her sole or primary social role. As summarized by Cameron and Rychlak, Freud saw the psychically healthy female as naturally progressing from castration acceptance [i.e. of her lack of a penis] to penis envy to cathect father's penis and thereby take on the feminine role as father's lover to desire for a father substitute's penis to desire for a [male] baby.[30]

For those who find this persuasive, comparative analysis of female gun ownership would seem to offer a fairly easy test of the priapic theory: if gun ownership is priapic in nature women who had not adequately resolved their penis envy would neurotically tend to desire guns but women who had resolved it would fulfill

[27] Young, "Gender, Region of Socialization and Ownership of Protective Firearms," Bankston et al.; and Barbara Stenross and Jeanne Brooks, "The Committed Avocationist: Making a Career in Target Shooting," draft manuscript, University of North Carolina, Department of Sociology, 1986.

[28] McClain.

[29] Young, "Gender, Region of Socialization and Ownership of Protective Firearms."

[30] N. Cameron and J. Rychlak, *Personality Development and Psychopathology: A Dynamic Approach* (Boston: Houghton, Mifflin, 1985), p. 72.

themselves by having babies instead. It may be unfortunate that the empirical evidence to resolve this point does not exist; no study seems to have compared gun ownership among women who have and have not borne children. Nor is such a study likley to be undertaken since Freud's theory of penis envy seems unpersuasive (to say the least) today. Danto dismisses the penis envy explanation for female gun ownership, citing the tendency of modern psychiatric thought to reject the concept of penis envy altogether. In that connection Eysenck and Wilson inquire

Why penis envy anyway? Could this be male conceit on the part of Freud? . . . How can we say that the appearance of phallic symbols indicates penis envy rather than penis interest. It may be that women want a penis in them, not on them. A feminist version of the Freudian [vision] with a concept of "cavity envy" could be employed. Why not penis anxiety (the fear of growing a dreadful protuberance in their crotch).[31]

Moreover, even if the penis envy concept be accepted, it would not validate the priapic theory for that theory is inconsistent with demographic patterns in ways that penis envy can not explain. Studies demonstrate disproportionately high gun ownership among Mid-western Black (Detroit and Illinois) and Southern White women. The authors explain the findings of these studies as follows: 1) Black women, being more likley than other women to live in high crime areas and/or to have been victims of violent crime, are also more likely to see a gun as necessary for defense; 2) Southern White women, being much more likely than other women to have been socialized to guns as they grew up, tend more to own guns in later life. This is true not only as to guns owned for sport but also for protection guns since if they fear crime they are more likely to feel comfortable having a gun.[32]

Because these explanations deal with the observed facts they are necessarily more plausible than the priapic theory. Nor is its only difficulty that these explanations render the priapic theory superfluous. More important yet is that the observed facts render its postulates improbable: we are unable to envision any contortion of the priapic theory that explains why Southern White and Mid-western Black women are so much more subject than other women to penis envy as to be 35-45% more likely to own a gun.

IMPLICATIONS FOR GUN CONTROL
(OR BAN) LAWS

As some gun control advocates have recognized, if accurate, the priapic theory would foreclose virtually all gun laws.[33] It is thus ironic that exponents of the priapic

---

[31] H. Eysenak and G. Wilson, *The Experimental Study of Freudian Theories* (London: Methuen & Company, 1973), p. 167.

[32] Lizotte and Bordua; McClain; Bankston et al.; and Young, "Gender, Region of Socialization and Ownership of Protective Firearms."

[33] *Science News of the Week,* Vol. 93 (June 29, 1968), 614.

theory are almost exclusively advocates of gun control or even banning and confiscating guns. Stell accuses such exponents of being so enthralled with that theory as a

disparaging explanation for [gun ownership that they] neglect to take seriously its implications. [For] their theory [would] predict widespread violent resistance bordering on social revolution were [a gun ban] to pass[:] . . . male gun owners would be as violently resistant to enforcement of such legislation as they would be to mandatory castration. The theory's phallus-envy corollary predicts that women gun owners would [also] cleave mightily to the[ir] cold steel [penis] substitutes.[34]

Resistance far less serious than this would doom a gun law; in fact, the effectiveness of any gun law would rest on voluntary compliance by the non-criminal gun owners at least. Various factors make gun laws, particularly bans, even more difficult to force upon a resistant sub-population than was Prohibition.[35] Gun control or even ban advocates rarely discuss the issue of enforcement; they believe that, though criminals would not obey, most gun owners would because they are good citizens.[36] But, obviously, gun owners would not obey either if they did subconsciously view gun laws as a form of castration.

It may reasonably be objected that in no event would a gun ban be complied with by those who believe, whether rightly or not, that they have both constitutional right and urgent need to have a handgun for family protection; and even that sport owners would defy a fan.[37] But the impossibility of effectuating gun prohibition and confiscation does not necessarily apply against control-type approaches (e.g. licensing to assure competence and exclude juveniles and irresponsibles) since those are consistent with the felt need to keep a gun for family defense. Historically gun owners have been open to control-type approaches and polls consistently show that, in principle, most of them still are.[38]

[34] Stell, 72-73.

[35] The problems are illustrated by a comparison between the problems of enforcing Prohibition and those likely to be encountered with overcoming resistance to a handgun ban: (a) the current civilian stock of 60-70 million handguns would continue indefinitely unlike alcohol, continued consumption of which required drinkers to take the risk of an infinite succession of black market purchases; (b) to supply a demand for additional handguns, up to 20 million of the size used to kill John Lennon could be smuggled in yearly (using the current estimated rate of marijuana smuggling as a guide), (c) the cost of purchasing might actually decrease as the black market made available pot metal copies of modern handgun designs which are easily producible in a machine shop or good home workshop. Kates, 1981: 155-160.

[36] Kates, "Points of Comparison Between Banning the Handgun and Prohibition of Liquor."

[37] David J. Bordua, "Adversary Polling and the Construction of Social Meaning," Law & Policy Quarterly, Vol. 5 (1983), 349-350; Mark H. Moore, "The Bird in Hand: A Feasible Strategy for Gun Control," Journal of Policy Analysis and Management, Vol. 2 (1983), 187; and Kates, "Points of Comparison Between Banning the Handgun and Prohibition of Liquor," 148.

[38] Kates, 209-210; and "The Battle Over Gun Control," The Public Interest, No. 84 (1986), 42-43.

THE PRIAPIC THEORY AS EPITHET

How then do the anti-control fanatics who run the gun lobby mobilize gun owners so that legislators' mail always runs strongly against controls — often by margins of 50-1 or more? The key to the gun lobby's success lies in culture or moral conflicts which are far more important in defeating control initiatives than ostensibly criminological issues.[39] The fundamental concern of a very vocal sub-set of gun control advocates is cultural or moral rather than criminological and pragmatic. As a result they invariably, if unintentionally, play into the gun lobby's hands by addressing even the most modest control initiatives in moral and/or cultural pejoratives. Discussions that should center on how totally reasonable and unobjectionable the initiative is, instead turn into savage debates over charges that gun owners are stupid, ignorant, demented and sexually deviant, that gun ownership is "simply beastly behavior" and guns themselves both mechanism and symbol of the savagery lurking in an American soul that is "hard, isolate, stoic and a killer."[40]

The inevitable effect of such pejoratives is to drive gun owners into circling their wagons under the aegis of the gun lobby.[41] The inevitable result of that — when nearly half of all households contain a gun (in nearly 25% it is a handgun) — is the defeat of gun control. Though gun control groups do not seem to understand how counter productive this epithetical approach is (largely because it expresses their moral and cultural perspectives and those of their strongest supporters), the gun lobby clearly does. Not only does it faithfully summarize each pejorative anti-gun article to inflame any gun owner who missed the original publication, the gun lobby even goes so far as to reprint the most pejorative cartoons.[42] In other words, *the gun lobby is actually paying Oliphant, Herblock etc. royalties for penning anti-gun*

[39] Moore; Stell; and Kates, "The Battle Over Gun Control."

[40] The "beastly behavior" quote is from SCIENCE NEWS, (1968), 614, the other is D.H. Lawrence's definition of "the essential American soul" as applied by Prof. Hofstadter in "America As A Gun Culture", *American Heritage* (Oct. 1970), 82. For similar philipics see, *inter alia*, Braucher, "Gun Lunatics Silence [the] Sounds of Civilization and "Handgun Nuts are Just That — Really Nuts", *Miami Herald*, (July 19, 1982 and Oct. 29, 1981); Grizzard, "Bulletbrains", *Atlantic Constitution*, (Jan. 19, 1981); O. Demaris, *America The Violent*, ch. 12, Ellison, 1981, Wills, "John Lennon's War", *Chicago Sun Times*, (12/12/80); "Handguns That Kill", *Washington Star*, (1/13/81); and "... Or Worldwide Gun Control", *Philadelphia Inquirer*, (5/17/81).

[41] A sociologist interviewing active target shooters found many unenthusiastic about people who have guns only for protection and uncomfortable with gun lobby fanatacism. Yet each interviewee was an NRA member, being convinced that they and their sport were beset by implacable enemies from which only vigorous, united political action could avail. Stenross and Brooks.

[42] See e.g. GUN WEEK, Oct. 5, 1979 "National Coalition to Ban Handguns Labels Gun Owners 'Dumb Bullies' " (Dec. 21, 1979); "Gun Publications 'Porno' According to Chicago Trib Writer," —summary of nationally syndicated column by Bob Greene (Feb. 1, 1980); "Roger Caras Labels Gun Owners 'Collection of Psychotics,' " (Feb. 20, 1981); "Handgun Lovers Belong on Shrink's Couch" — summary of nationally syndicated column by Mike Royko (Jan. 19, 1982); "Writer Calls Gun Owners 'Traitors', 'Anti-Citizens' " — summary of nationally syndicated column by Garry Wills.

cartoons. The money is well spent. The gun lobby will continue triumphant so long as it can continue to mobilize millions of gun owners to contribute money, write legislators and otherwise vote and act to defeat regulation to which gun owners themselves have no innate objection. And gun owners will continue to so act at the gun lobby's behest as long as it can convince them they are a hated minority beleaguered by ferocious enemies.

CONCLUSION

Perversely enough, the cause of gun control suffers from the penchant of some of its own supporters for framing debate in pejorative terms including (though by no means limited to) pseudo-psychoanalytic claims of priapism or "paranoia".[43] Above and beyond its socially deleterious effect, the priapic theory is not only unsupported by the available evidence but contradicted thereby: it perverts Freud's general theory of the significance of various objects in all dreams into a special theory about gun ownership; it is unnecessary because other theories more plausibly explain ownership of various kinds of guns and it is inconsistent with the observed patterns of American gun ownership.

---

[43] Over a ten year period a California homeowner will spend 20 times more than the cost of a gun to insure against natural disasters (fire, flood, earthquake, hurricane, etc.) which are less than one tenth as likely as a criminal attack on the household. Thus while buying a protection gun may be an error (taking into account risks like accident, suicide etc.) it is clearly not paranoid, i.e. irrational reaction to non-existent or exaggerated danger. As noted in the text studies find gun owners to be less frightened of crime than are non-owners living in the same neighborhoods.

Chapter 9

Culture Conflict and the Ideology of Pariah Groups: The *Weltanschauung* of Gun Owners, Southerners and Cockfighters

by
F. Frederick Hawley

"A single zealot may commence persecutor, and better men be his victim." — Thomas Jefferson

Since 1973, I have been studying groups and behaviors commonly viewed as marginal or deviant through the use of participant-observation and other field techniques. While working on my master's degree in anthropology at LSU I investigated folk healing among a stigmatized group of rural Spanish folk in the upper Lafourche region of South Louisiana. Upon completing the master's program and after finishing criminology course work at Florida State University, an opportunity to investigate cockfighting, an illegal activity in all but four states, presented itself at a particularly propitious moment. From that time, in 1978, to the present I have seen countless cockfights, met hundreds of chicken men and their families and have seen more dead chickens than Colonel Sanders. During my recent sabbatical semester, I traveled to Puerto Rico, California, and Ohio in order to see cockfights, interview sportsmen and animal rights advocates, and to conduct research. My own state of Louisiana, having among the most lenient laws in the country, has afforded me easy access to cockfighters and their arenas. That notwithstanding, most Americans would regard the cockfighter as an atavistic type, if not an overtly criminal or deviant personality.[1] The media's linkage of cockfighting with the current pit bull phobia has strengthened popular perceptions about cockfighters and cockfights.

My interest in this subject and its peculiarly Southern rural and Latin milieux has led to contacts in yet another potentially deviant group — "hard core" gun enthusiasts and survivalists. While survivalism seems to be no more concentrated in the South than in other regions (the Midwest and West seem to be the "cultural hearth" of this activity), surely gun ownership is at least a superficial cultural trait in the South as numerous studies seem to indicate. This observation in no way indicates support for the highly ethnocentric Southern Violence Construct of Hackney, Gastil

---

[1] F. Frederick Hawley, "Organized Cockfighting," unpublished doctoral dissertation, Florida State University, 1982.

Gastil and others.[2]

On the contrary, much of my own research energies since 1982 have been involved in dealing with the ideological and normative content of the gun control issue. Furthermore, I have focused on the lamentable and stigmatizing consequences of the spurious and specious linkage of Southerners, violence and weaponry.[3] Although this may seem like tilting at the very windmills of academe, I have found ample support for my thesis in the more judicious and statistically sophisticated work of Wright, Rossi, and Daly and many others.[4] Despite persuasive evidence to the contrary, in both the popular and academic milieux, the stigma of "Southernness" lingers on. Collective adaptation to Southern ethnic identity will be a third focus of this paper.

Moral Crusades and Pariah Groups

The primary process at work in the creation of all three "pariah groups" was and remains the symbolic or moral crusade as described by Gusfield.[5] Gusfield's formulation of the "symbolic crusade," originally used in reference to the temperance movement, has been applied to the efforts of other "moral entrepreneurs" and is applicable to a greater or lesser extent to all the pariah groups presently being described.[6]

As Gusfield states, "[i]ssues of moral reform are analyzed as one way through which a cultural group acts to preserve, defend or enhance the dominance and prestige of its own style of living within the total society."[7] In order that a desired change take place one or two types of reform must occur, assimilative or coercive. The assimilative element of reform is a more sympathetic approach in which the deviant is encouraged to get on the band wagon for his own good and be "lifted" to a higher level of propriety or consciousness. This very patronizing position affirms the perception of status of the reformer, thus allaying status anxiety.

The coercive element of reform on the other hand "emerges when the object of reform is seen as an intractable defender of another culture, someone who rejects the reformer's values and really doesn't want to change . . . the champion of reform . . . sees the object of reform as someone who rejects the social dominance of the

---

[2] S. Hackney, "Southern Violence," American Historical Review, Vol. 74 (1969), 906-925; and R.D. Gastil, "Homicide and a Regional Culture of Violence," American Sociological Review, Vol. 36 (1971), 412-426.

[3] F. Frederick Hawley, "Organized Cockfighting;" "The Black Legend in Southern Studies: Ideology and Academe," North American Culture, Vol. III (1987), 29-52; and "Cockfighting in the Pine Woods: Gameness in the New South," Sports Place, Vol. I (1987), 18-26.

[4] James D. Wright, Peter H. Rossi, and Kathleen Daly, Under the Gun: Weapons, Crime and Violence in America (New York: Aldine, 1983).

[5] J.R. Gusfield, Symbolic Crusades (Urbana: University of Illinois Press, 1963).

[6] Howard Becker, Outsiders (New York: Free Press, 1963).

[7] Gusfield, 3.

reformer and denies the legitimacy of his life style."[8] Accordingly, the problematic social aggregation is seen as the enemy and the reformer, using law and force, takes the offensive. In all of the present cases, it is clear that the groups in question are clearly viewed as threats to the world view of the reformer as "[e]ach is a repudiation of the power and prestige" of the reformers' cultures.[9]

While Gusfield and others sees coercive reform as symptomatic of the decline of the reforming group's power and prestige — a last grasp at retaining dominance —the present cases indicate a different dimension of coercive reform. *Coercive reform can be and is being used to bring regional and rural cultural variants into the "mainstream" of urban-cosmopolitan culture.* This tendency has been noted by Bruce-Briggs in his critique of the "great American gun war."[10] Clearly, in this battle over firearm ownership, Southern ethnic manifestations, and cockfighting the reformers and objects of reform are polarized, and there is "little middle ground." Since in all three cases, "the coercive reformer reacts to nonconformity with anger and indignation, . . . hostility, hatred, and anger toward the enemy were [are] the major feelings which nurture[d] the movement."[11] Thus the objects of reform in the three present cases are subject to denunciation, distortion of views and life styles, misleading and sensationalistic media myth making, and academic, intellectual and popular stigmatization.[12] At present, all are under attack by organized media, self-appointed "moral entrepreneurial groups," and, in some cases, well- and ill-intentioned politicians and political groups.

Since the purpose of this work is to study the reaction of groups targeted for reform, I will assume that there is consensus in academe that the three groups in question are, indeed, besieged (or view themselves as such) to one extent or another. Certainly, the ongoing stigmatization of white Southerners and their symbolic universe in academe and the media has been described in an earlier work.[13] Similar processes have been discussed by Wright, Rossi, and Daly in reference to the gun ownership issue.[14] Even if one doubts this author's thesis, i.e., that the "Southern Violence Construct" is based upon ideological and media engendered imagery and serves both academe and popular prejudices rather than having any immanent, objective, or "scientific" validity — one cannot cavalierly dismiss the explicit text of articles in a wide variety of popular journals.[15] Typical of the "Black Legend" genre is a polemic which asserts that there is "some underlying world view that imbues the

[8] Ibid., 7.

[9] Ibid., 8.

[10] Barry Bruce-Briggs, "The Great American Gun War," *The Public Interest,* Vol. 36 (1976), 37-62.

[11] Gusfield, 112.

[15] Hawley, "The Black Legend in Southern Studies."

[13] Ibid.

[14] Wright, Rossi, and Daly, 120.

[15] Hawley, "The Black Legend in Southern Studies."

Southern character with a deep strain of intolerance for many of the human freedoms that Northerners accept as self-evident."[16] While *Playboy* is not a source frequently cited in academic treatises (at least, in ones not focusing on pornography), its circulation of 3.5 million and potential readership of 10 million make it a most influential source of information for an affluent, if not overly intellectually-inclined, youthful audience. The quotation cited above in an article in defense of sodomy, is typical of the misuse of social science and popular stereotyping. It is followed by a statement that Southern men are "very much afraid that America is trying to remove their balls . . . that at heart, is what the Southern emphasis on states' rights has always been about."[17] From Jefferson, through Calhoun to modern conservatism, the conservative tradition in the South is fostered then by castration anxiety. This is a pseudo-Freudian popular hit below the belt: a twist to Hackney's hoary argument that Southerners, having had changes imposed from outside since the 1860s, are paranoid.

Gun owners and cockfighters have been subjected to similar sexually-based vilification. The very nature of the objects of their interest seems to invite uninformed and sophomoric analysis by opponents. Geertz and Hawley have noted that while there is a sexual subtext involved in cockfighting, the authors would reply that sometimes a "cockfight is just a cockfight" or a gaming opportunity, and not an implicit homoerotic struggle a la D.H. Lawrence.[18] That general point of view has not deterred individual animal rights advocates who see cockfighters (and hunters and gun owners) as "insecure about their masculinity," or as "barbaric sexual deviates."[19]

Similarly, the attraction of some men and women to firearms and gun-related activity has invited ideologically-based insubstantial and perhaps unverifiable innuendo. In fact, as Wright, Rossi and Daly have pointed out although "virtually nothing of empirical substance is known about this topic [personality characteristics of gun owners]" . . . [T]he themes of speculative literature are well known and, with few exceptions, condemnatory and derogatory."[20] Explicitly pointing to the theme of weapon as "phallic symbol" the authors discount the pseudo-Freudian thesis and citing other studies, see absolutely no evidence for the validity of that peculiar view of the gun owner. What is implicit in the use of such speculation and stereotyping is the underlying presence of the vocabulary and highly charged emotional atmosphere of the moral and symbolic crusade.

The Genesis of Pariah Groups

Pariah groups, in this formulation, are groups whose world-view, once respectable, even dominant, is now regarded as an affront to the sensibilities or status of politically

[16] W.J. Lowe, "The Civil War of Sex," *Playboy* (June, 1987), 44.

[17] Ibid.

[18] C. Geertz, "Deep Play: Notes on the Balinese Cockfight," *Daedalus*, Vol. 101 (1972), 1-27; and Hawley, "Organized Cockfighting."

[19] F. Frederick Hawley, interviews.

[20] Wright, Rossi, and Daly, 120.

influential and articulate pressure groups and minorities within a larger society. In a more formal definitional sense, its members are usually of a lower "caste" and are regarded as "outcasts" by the dominant society and its ideology. Their problematic world-view may be derogated as "archaic," "barbaric," "reactionary," or just out-of-step. That certain groups would choose to not jump on the bandwagon of the American nation-state mythos is seen as manifest evidence of an underlying pathology or perverse, deviant *weltanschauung.* Thus, groups whose value system has been superseded, if seen as viable threats to the mythos of newly (or potentially) dominant groups or elites, become targets for intervention and amelioration. Therefore, the unassuming Amish, monastic orders, and folk healers, as quietist and non-threatening antitheses to the status quo, are generally ignored, or viewed as quaint examples of healthy "pluralism and value relativism" in action. The more overt and public the practice and symbolism of the antithetical group remains or becomes, however, the greater the threat perceived by moral crusaders and policy makers. This precipitates higher levels of activity in the mobilization of media, the molding of public opinion and lobbying of politicians by local elites and moral entrepreneurial groups.

It often happens, as in the present cases, that far from being a "new" form or manifestation of problematic behavior or attitudes, the antithetical group represents an anachronistic and/or unsympathetic order, and thus is viewed as both a threat to the status quo, as well as a threat to the sacrosanct ideal of evolutionary meliorism, i.e., progress, that typifies the ideology of the chamber of commerce, politicians, and other dominant economic elites. Not only do these groups represent a perceived threat to a changing socio-economic (often local) elite world-view, said problematic groups embody ideologies whose overt expression is viewed as having a negative impact on the placement of a new factory, expanded manufacturing plant or think-tank.

As such threats to "New South" boosterism, gun enthusiasts, cockfighters, and manifestations of white Southern ethnicity and historical piety, are seen by many local elites as very real dangers to local and regional progress. The cockfighter and the Southern ethnic enthusiast, are especially damning in their ongoing conceptual critique of the established order. To their antagonists, their very lifestyle may represent the antithesis of reason, nationalism, and the American way of life.

Such a dichotomization of ideologies may produce a number of untoward consequences as noted by Miller.[21] *Polarization* and *distortion of the opposition* are among the most obvious consequences germane to the cases in question. As polarization takes place, "the more necessary it becomes to view the proponents of opposing positions as devils and scoundrels, and their positions as dangerous and immoral . . ."[22] Furthermore, the position of the problematic group becomes deliberately distorted in order to make it more "susceptible to refutation . . . [o]ppositional viewpoints are phrased to appear maximally illogical, irrational,

[21] Walter B. Miller, "Ideology and Criminal Justice Policy: Some Current Issues," in Jim Munro (ed.) *Classes, Conflict and Control* (Cincinnati: Anderson Publishing Company, 1973), p. 18.

[22] Ibid.

unsupportable, simplistic, internally contradictory, and, if possible, contemptible or ludicrous."[23] The Southerner or gun owner as immanently dangerous and violent — as an enemy deviant — is a theme covered at length elsewhere.[24] Certainly, both sides in the debate over gun control have made ample uses of distorting their opponent's agruments and world-views.[25]

Catastrophism, a scare tactic useful in opinion molding is also in evidence, i.e., "terrible catastrophes will certainly ensue unless their [partisan's] proposals are adopted."[26] For example, racial discord will ensue or be exacerbated unless symbols of white ethnicity are removed. Another germane example noted is the assertion that cockfighting is degrading to society at large and produces a desensitized, violence prone individual — a danger to society at large. Although the oft-made assertion that the cockfight brings in "undesirable" elements and criminals is nowhere supported by any objective observers or by my own evidence, it continues to be a constant critique leveled by animal rights' partisans.

Catastrophism has dominated the gun control debate to such an extent that its further discussion is unnecessary. Few partisans on either side of these issues are susceptible to reason, in any case.

Part of the failure of reason in policy formation involving the present cases stems from *reverse projection* and *ideologized selectivity.* In the former process, one's potential allies are perceived as enemies due to highly emotionally charged commitment characteristic of the partisan's own point of view. That is, unless you are with us *in all particulars,* you are against us. Moderates on issues or those with no opinions are seen as "dupes" or having insufficiently heightened consciousness. On the part of the true believer, ideologized selectivity posits a one-issue orientation in which no other policy positions or issues are of interest. Indeed, both reverse projection and ideologized selectivity give rise to a mind-set that is impervious to reasoned discourse and that is threatened by any new information, particularly from scholarly or objective sources, a phenomenon which Miller calls *informational constriction.* Since the basic answers "are already given, in their true and final form, by the ideology: it [new information] is dangerous because evidence provided by new research has the potential of calling into question ideologically established truths."[27] Miller is particularly relevant when he states that exercises such as the present one —the examination of criminal justice policy in the context of ideological and political considerations — are threatening to the partisan *"because the nature of the analysis implies that ideological truth is relative."[28]*

In the field investigation of antagonists of cockfighting, and white Southern ethnic manifestation, the lines were clearly drawn. The attitude of "don't bother me with

23 Ibid., 21.

24 Hawley, "The Black Legend in Southern Studies."

25 Bruce-Briggs.

26 Miller, 20.

27 Ibid., 21.

28 Ibid., 20, emphasis added.

facts" or questions of ethical or value relativism was clearly evident in partisans opposed to all the problematic behaviors which I studied. *The fact that I purported to be studying these issues from an objective or scholarly point of view made me suspect,* or worse, one with the enemy. *If a scholar, with presumably the "right," progressive set of attitudes, could take an "appreciational" stance toward the group or behavior in question he must be in sympathy or one with the antithetical group.*[29] *I encountered this attitude from media (I was seen as an apologist for cockfighting and violence), animal rights groups who viewed me with outright hostility, and from patronizing politicians who seemed astonished that a representative of academe would not manifest the elite consensus progressive point of view on any of these issues. The fact of academic investigation threw them into confusion, consternation, and, in some cases, anger. In fact, many of my colleagues were more than a little discomfited by the subject of my research and by my "appreciational" stance toward said subject matter. Some were patronizing; others were and remain openly antagonistic.*

Local elites and media (often controlled by cosmopolitan elites) set the agenda, if any, for change. Groups whose world view is seen as anachronistic or problematic are targeted by change imposed from without by media blitzes which "raise the consciousness" of the community to evils posed by said groups or behaviors. "Myths" are created to "justify (1) the proposed moral environment, (2) the distribution of authority, (3) the proposed disposition of the deviant, and the moral superiority of the nondeviant (crusader),"[30] Thus, moral crusaders pressure legislators and politicians into passing new laws, or interpreting existing laws in such a way as to effectively stigmatize, ostracize, and criminalize the behavior of the problematic group. More importantly, as a consequence of a moral crusade, the world view of the antithetical group undergoes a symbolic degradation and delegitimization.

Groups undergoing stigmatization may respond in a number of different ways. Individuals within these groups may respond by ending their involvement with the activity in question. This has frequently been the case in states where the legal status of penalties against cockfighting has been upgraded from misdemeanor to felony status. Some gun owners and enthusiasts will sell or turn in their weapons, if the law or the spirit of the times so dictate. White Southerners will cease public avowal of an anachronistically conservative ethos. Some will enroll in diction courses to lose their regional accents   perceived affronts to elite ears, and thus, impediments to advancement within the existing socio-economic order. Thus, many of the individuals within stigmatized categories may accept new definitions of the social situation and get on the bandwagon, while others simply try to avoid contact with stigma symbols, signs and overt manifestations "that would call attention to or reveal a person's debased or deviant condition."[31]

[29] David Matza, *Becoming Deviant* (Englewood Cliffs, New Jersey: Prentice-Hall, 1969), p. 25.

[30] Erdwin H. Pfuhl, *The Deviance Process* (Belmont, California: Wadsworth Publishing Company, 1986), p. 82.

[31] Ibid., 159.

However, others will continue to carry out deviant and proscribed activities and hold problematic beliefs in secrecy. Cockfighters, Sons and Daughters of the Confederacy and more extreme ethnic consciousness groups frequently resort to this expediency. Gun owners more often take the offense and hold gun shows, go hunting, compete in public tourneys — avoiding (in their own minds and press releases, at least) linkage with criminal and extremist elements.

All three groups contain elements within their membership that disavow deviance and seek to render normal and morally acceptable that which has heretofore been regarded as abnormal and immoral. Through collective voluntary organizations they engage in *instrumental* (moral entrepreneurial) and *expressive* (favoring the furtherance of the problematic behavior) fellowship and activity.[32] Another dimension of voluntary organizations concerns their value orientation. While some groups are *conformative* and are in accord with basic values, others are "hostile to the major legitimate values and institutions of society," and are thus termed *alienative*.[33]

Gun enthusiasts, cockfighters, and white Southern ethnic enthusiasts generally favor expressive organizations with alienative values. While almost all would deny an alienative dimension in favor of a more conformative orientation to modern society, the troublesome fact remains that their ethos is anachronistic and by definition, antithetical to the idea of progress and the American way of life as perceived by media, elites and the general public. Therefore, the general orientation of most voluntary associations of this type might appear to be expressive-alienative, like the Old Order Amish and Black Muslims.[34] However, since all three groups have more instrumentally-oriented components or subgroups, e.g., UGBA, DOC, and survivalist groups, it might be appropriate to create a revised typology of deviant organizations. Such a typology would allow for anachronistic attitudes toward social values and instrumental-expressive activity orientation: that is, cockfighters and Southern White ethnic identity groups promote fellowship, problematic behaviors *and* try to legitimize or defend their point of view in legislatures and to the general public.[35] These organizations do not exist primarily for recreation or reification, but also as a buttress against the rationalizing spirit of the age.

As such they have official and unofficial lobbyists and paid for (campaign contributions) and true believing legislators who welcome the sub rosa support of highly organized and generous "PACs" formed under various spurious and misleading rubrics.

In many states cockfighters have been able to keep the classification of their pastime as a misdemeanor, or in four states, entirely legal. In Louisiana, for instance, game fowl enthusiasts and sympathetic legislators have passed a bill in the 1987 session specifically exempting cockfighting from animal cruelty laws. Moreover, even if cockfighting is defined as a felony in a given jurisdiction, a sympathetic local district attorney or sheriff may elect to adopt a policy of salutary neglect in which

---

32 Ibid., 173.

33 Ibid.

34 Ibid., 175.

laws are simply not enforced. In such instances, when arrests are made, the charges are frequently "bargained down" to misdemeanors such as disturbing the peace or keeping a disorderly place.

Cockfighters are pitted against some very adverse circumstances on local, state, and national levels. As the UB grows yet more urban, rural folkways are viewed with less nostalgia and sympathy. On the contrary strong antagonism exists between rural and urban interests in many states. In such state legislatures the dichotomy in voting patterns on cockfighting issues almost always reflects differences between urban and rural constituencies. Increased urbanization, rationalization, and the imminent economic demise of the remaining small yeoman farmer and his ilk doom the cockfighting fraternity to inevitable criminalization by the mid 1990s. Although they have been fighting an effective rear guard action their activities ring a discordant note with the progressive tenor of the modern American way of life.

In the case of firearms enthusiasts, such instrumental-expressive conformative groups such as the much maligned "gun lobby," consisting of sportsmen's groups, the Second Amendment Foundation, and the media whipping boy, the NRA, form a reasonably effective political and ideological arm. This one-issue alliance has managed to stymie and in some cases turn back elite-generated gun control legislation for decades. What is not generally known is that very alienative anachronistic and reactionary components contribute substantially to the coffers of these legitimate and public PACs. Most funding for gun ownership lobbies on the state and national level is derived from small contributions from a broad base of individual guns owners, sportsmen, and small gun clubs, however.

White ethnic enthusiasts may be conformative or alienative in terms of their attitudes toward dominant society. Their revered ancestral symbols such as the Confederate battle flag, Dixie, and various monuments are under attack from politicians imbued with a relatively new and growing political imperative the urban block vote. Another underlying problem with which these stigmatized groups have to deal is pervasive popular and academic imagery involving the linkage of violence, Southern ethnicity and irrationality.[36] The unrepresentative Southerner whose idiosyncratic defense of his popularly disdained cultural symbols (and indeed, very heritage) brands him even in his own state legislatures as an "enemy deviant," an anachronism to be swept under the homogeneous rug of evolutionary meliorism. That articulate enemy deviants get little access to media, or decision-makers is axiomatic. The media continues to dwell on popular imagery of brick throwing, racist, gap-toothed bumpkins from the back woods and extremist elements in their coverage of this and most Southern issues. That scholars have allowed such labelling and stigmatization to continue without scrutiny or criticism suggests the presence of certain similar biases inherent to academe.[37]

[35] Hawley, "Organized Cockfighting."
[36] Hawley, "The Black Legend in Southern Studies."
[37] Ibid.

117.

Voluntary associations of Southern ethnic enthusiasts have had little impact on state legislatures and none on the national level in decades. The retention of public Southern ethnic heritage seems to be more a matter of inertia on the part of state legislatures and perhaps a reluctance to take the step "the Great Repudiation" would ultimately imply to the white electorate. That is, such a step, no matter how sensitive to minority sentiment and thus laudable the motives, would send a clear and unambiguous message that white Southern heritage is worthless, an embarrassment, a barbaric episode, or worse. That few legislators have been willing to go so far in the name of progress or racial harmony is understandable.

Characteristic of the Ideology of Pariah Groups

Stigmatized individuals and groups may enter into combination to form legitimate fronts, fraternal organizations, or political action committees to further both instrumental and expressive aspects of their antithetical behaviors. The behaviors in question have given rise to a wide variety of groups with different motives, rationales and focuses, e.g., white ethnic enthusiasts can affiliate with the Daughters of the Confederacy, the KKK, or certain independent religious congregations. The game fowl fancier can jon a local "sportsmen's" club or the United Gamefowl Breeders Association (UGBA), a very well-organized and generously funded international instrumentally-oriented fraternal organization and lobby. The firearms enthusiast has similar choices, a local "gun club" and/or the NRA. Additionally, both cockfighters and gun owners have a very instrumental and activist print component. In all cases, the antithetical but valued behavior is to be preserved and defended in the group setting as well as in print.

As one might expect, the general ideology of such groups is typified by chronologically distinct stages. Early in the stigmatization process, as the group's dominance is being challenged, one sees a strand of bemused contempt for the emerging elites, their ideology, and their specific prescriptions for ameliorating the situation. This detachment gives way to strident defensiveness and aggressive attempts at preserving the status quo as the new elites gain in power and are able to legislate against the behaviors in question. Finally, the problematic group's behavior, now truly antithetical, gives rise to occult practice of said pastime and secret avowal of ideology and the recognition of very well-defined ethnic boundary maintenance cues and devices.

Pariah groups develop certain commonly held boundary maintenance devices that are tantamount to being characteristics. They include such items as such as individualism, authoritarianism, vitalism, symbolism, rationalization and proselytism.[38]

The individualism of the pariah groups discussed herein is related to Miller's

[38] Hawley, "Organized Cockfighting," 80.

118.

lower-class focal concern, "autonomy," and stresses the responsibility of the individual for his actions, his freedom of choice and his "frequently expressed resentment of the idea of external controls, restrictions on behavior and unjust or coercive authority."[39] The overt and uncompromising rejection of all gun control proposals by organized and unaffiliated gun owners and groups is almost a cliche. This stance has led to a generalized conceptual critique of federal authority that is manifested in other spheres of life and political discourse. Frequently, gun enthusiasts, like cockfighters, express a verbalized and unapologetic resentment of external controls.[40] Deriding the generic "mess in Washington" (substitute Baton Rouge, Jackson, etc.) members of Southern ethnic pride groups are similar to their confreres in the cockfighting and gun owners ranks.

Authorities at all levels, because they do not "understand" the importance of the sport or activity, are seen as unjust, arbitrary and intrusive. This is less true of more conformative groups such as the NRA and the DOC. Cockfighters and KKKers, representing alienative strains within the spectra of their peculiar group's disvalued activity and identity, are much more anti-authority than gun owners, per se. Geertz, in study of Balinese cockfighters, notes an anti-authoritarian component among that stigmatized group. Indeed, the cockfight is seen as affirming the social and psychic order while expressing resistance and resentment toward the imposed social order of the Indonesian nation-state: a similar theme noted by this author with respect to North American cockfighters.

Although these groups value individualism, they also place importance on a type of authoritarianism. Although this is a seeming paradox they value a different orientation toward authority, especially when the authority to be submitted to lies outside the sphere of the deviant activity. That is, like the Balinese described earlier, they celebrate the law and order and mythos of the *ancien regime,* and question the validity of the new realities in local, state and national politics. The authoritarianism which typifies the speech of cockfighters, Southern ethnic enthusiasts and gun owners is largely for public consumption. While the cockfighter, for example, may want his son to obey the law in the abstract, he teaches him to rationalize and institutionalize its evasion on a daily basis through word and deed. But then, "He's a good boy. Never been in trouble; doesn't use drugs."[41] The problematic activity and observances are seen as character building in a chaotic and anarchic milieu.

The ideology of all three groups is characterized by an anti-rationalistic vitalism. In all groups studied much weight is put upon ancestral piety and the importance of the ongoing problematic activity as a link to the ancestors. Thus, Southern "shintoism" is closely allied to the cockfighter's overt evocation of tradition as a defense of his activity. The firearms enthusiast is also tied to a tradition of gun owning freeholding yeomanry in the folklore of that group.

Like Nietzsche, the ultimate anti-rationalist, these groups may feel to one degree or

[39] Walter B. Miller, "Lower Class Culture as a Generating Milieu of Gang Delinquency," *Journal of Social Issues,* Vol. 14 (1958), 143.

[40] Hawley, "Organized Cockfighting," 89.

[41] Hawley.

another that "men were [are] dominated by irrational forces over which they could exercise only a tenuous . . . control. These irrational forces were [are] essentially predatory and even bestial. Men could [can] never fully divorce themselves from their barbaric past . . . ."[42] Cockfighters openly celebrate this irrational ethic while Southern ethnic enthusiasts and organized gun owners are more covert in their view of irrationalism. The myths of the latter groups place much value on more circumspect and symbolic observance of this particular link with the ancestors. However, it should be noted that this vitalism is the driving rationale behind less alienative observances of Southern "shintoism," such as Memorial Day's festivities and genealogical research.

Certain highly charged symbols serve evocative purposes among pariah groups. The gamecock is a walking, crowing, totem of masculine bravery, "gameness," and sexual potency. As such a number of contexts exist where emblems of cocks adorn items of clothing, cars, trucks, purses, and constitute the principle part of the interior decor of many cocker's family rooms. In Latin American settings studied (and in some Anglo-Saxon homes) such iconography resembles the cult of the saints with the characteristic colorful decoration reminiscent of a religious shrine. A number of sexual *double-entendres* exist concerning the proper placement of the "cock" in the symbolic universe of the cockfighter. Jungians would find this a particularly interesting and fertile heuristic avenue.

Among white Southern ethnic enthusiasts a number of symbols and icons occupy positions of importance. The primary symbol among this group is the star-crossed Confederate battle flag. Its time-specific linkage with overtly racist groups, activities, and attitudes during the 1960s has rendered it *hors de combat* and its public disavowal by elites is imminent. Moderate and liberal Southern ethnic enthusiasts have switched or are switching to the "Stars and Bars" or first flag of the Confederacy. This allows them to maintain a linkage to the ancestral past while disavowing the contemporary stigma which inheres to the Battle Flag. That the Stars and Bars is only marginally more acceptable to "new elites" and New South "boosters" is immaterial. A good faith gesture had been made and further compromise is unlikely.

Other icons include representations of Generals Lee and "Stonewall" Jackson. Usually absent are portraits or statuary of President Davis or any of the civil officers of the Confederacy. Davis' unpopularity during life has followed him over the decades to haunt him in the grave, evidently. Other frequently noted icons include actual reliquary and relics such as swords, pistols, shreds of uniforms, lead munitions, and paintings and daguerreotypes of revered ancestors. Numerous books on "the War," and evidences relating to it, cover the walls as do maps and modern examples of "Confederate Realism," a highly detailed genre of battle scenes and heroic deeds and individuals of the bellum period. Of course, the omnipresent blue-haired aunt

[42] D.A. Zoll, *Twentieth Century Political Philosophy* (Englewood Clifts, New Jersey: Prentice-Hall, 1974), p. 18.

has collected a exhaustive family history which may be portrayed in graphic or tree form over the fire place, nestled perhaps, over an actual or reproduction of a bellum period cap and ball rifle.

The iconography of the gun enthusiast is much more varied. Guns themselves may be displayed or paintings of classic firearms may cover the walls. Gun enthusiasts frequently wear clothing denoting their loyalty to a favorite calibre, weapon, or manufacturer. Their cars and trucks may have bumper stickers which display a truculent view toward changing gun ownership laws, or less antagonistically, may simply have an NRA sticker. The gun owner can find a wide variety of iconographic material at gun shows which are held frequently nation-wide. The gun as icon is continually reinforced by popular reading matter, cinema and television. These media-engendered images are inescapable.

All of these stigmatized groups are concerned with rendering their activity respectable and perpetuating their activity and belief system. Therefore, they engage in rationalization and proselytism. Cockfighters have an elaborate catalog of rationalization which emphasizes the historical importance of the sport, its character-building attributes, the belief that fighting is the appropriate activity for the bird, and a condemnation of condemnors.[43] These rationalizations help them neutralize the stigma of their activity in a way recognizable to Sykes and Matza.[44] Running through the essence of these arguments is a defensive and combative posture. Recruitment is usually familial with young rural males from lower-middle-class backgrounds as the most dominant new force. It should be noted that well-heeled cockfighters frequently form international networks of reciprocity and obligation.

The international commerce in firearms, being regulated by international and national law, has not given rise to significant activity among firearms enthusiasts. However, trading and selling goes on in gun shows, newspapers, bars, and in the classified adds. New members join the ranks of firearms enthusiasts through many channels. Many enjoy shooting while in the military; others learn as children while hunting with their male relatives in rural settings. Some buy a handgun for protection and become caught up in an "escalation of deviance." That is, they are questioned and criticized for their gun ownership and in reaction, intensify their identification with the problematic behavior and their involvement in the activity.

Gun owners frequently rationalize their ownership of weaponry in the following ways; self-defense at home, hunting, collecting, target shooting and the constitutional question.[45] Dogmatic gun owners regard the Second Amendment as an open grant empowering individuals to own almost any form of firearm. NRA members and leadership oppose any qualification of that interpretation no matter how seemingly reasonable it may appear. In this matter, they resemble a typical moral entrepreneurial group, which of course, they are.

Regarding oneself as a member of the group "white Southerners" involves a wide

43 Hawley, "Organized Cockfighting," 113-114.

44 G.M. Sykes and D. Matza, "Techniques of Neutralization," *American Journal of Sociology*, Vol. 22 (1957), 664-670.

variety of processes. For example, even though almost all members of this category are Southern born and reared, not all so reared become ethnically conscious. Examples of hypoethnicity or indifference (even self-hate) to ethnic backgrounds appears especially evident among Southern academics and intellectuals many who have traveled the last mile "north toward home" to more hospitable intellectual climes in decades past. On the other hand, the ethnic enthusiast, usually older and of upper middle class upbringing, remains local in orientation. His power base, superseded by new elites and their ideology, has been substantially eroded. He deals with attacks on his activities and world view in the following manner: through intensified display of totems on relevant holidays, verbal and written statements of hyperpatriotic tenor, and through involvement in certain low-key or highly expressive reaffirmation activities, e.g., joining Civil War battle recreation groups or Sons and/or Daughters of the Confederacy. Some express concern about deracination by joining extremist groups and going semi-underground. Most remain in the mainstream and continue a frustrating battle against the ongoing revisionist rewriting, reworking and reinterpretation of Southern history.

Through the processes described earlier, the pariah groups herein described develop certain common rationalizations to help them deal with disvalued identity. Like Sykes and Matza's techniques of neutralization, these adaptations involve reaffirmation of group (higher) loyalty, condemnation of the condemnor, denial of injurious conduct, and denial of victim. The formation of the pariah group itself is a further method of neutralization. That is, a collectivity of deviants presents a conceptual validity to the legitimacy and non-deviance of a given behavior. Moreover, through organizing, paying dues, and acting in all respects as a "normal" group, voluntary associations of deviants participate and partake in conventional activities. Ironically, this only exacerbates feelings of alienation and indignation when the primary focus or *raison d'etre* of these voluntary associations is branded as deviant.

Observations and Conclusions

As social scientists we are expected to be objective in the conduct of research. The *de requeur* notion of *praxis,* a relic of the 1960s, goes a step further and asks "whose side are we on?" That social scientists have been sympathetic to select "sides," i.e., deviant groups, social worlds and lifestyles is axiomatic. However, it should be noted that this "appreciation" has not been typified by evenhandedness in dealing with groups which most social scientists find antithetical to their personal ideology.[46] While groups which symbolize liberal sensibilities and tolerance in action such as homosexuals, street corner habitues, drug users, pimps, and delinquent street gangs have been studied with great sensitivity and sympathy, groups such as cockfighters,

45 Wright, Rossi, and Daly.

46 J.Q. Wilson, *Thinking About Crime* (New York: Basic Books, 1985); and Hawley, "Cockfighting in the Pine Woods."

white Southern ethnic activists and, to a lesser extent, gun enthusiasts are generally ignored altogether. By not presenting these groups at all, the social scientist ignores the normative critique of certain cherished ideological assumptions that these groups present. Thus, groups not studied due to their anachronistic or unsympathetic nature have no objective existence, and therefore no antithetical point of view with which to deal.

Value relativism, a liberal ideal which is in fundamental opposition to conservative moral absolutism, is applicable in all situations or none.[47] We are appreciational to the situations and realities of all marginal groups or none. As social scientists we may not wish to study groups which challenge our ability to be objective, but we are called upon to do just that — if for no other reason, to prevent media and popular distortion of the motives and activities of such pariah groups as described in this paper. This does not necessitate agreement with the group's tenets or full participation in its symbolic universe. It does mean, however, that groups which most social scientists, intellectuals, and elites abhor be treated with evenhandedness.

Additionally, the focus and method of the ongoing present study, a microstudy of elite/pariah group dynamics have generally been neglected by social scientists. Such research is time-consuming and involves rubbing shoulders with evasive and often unavailable politicians and unsympathetic and inarticulate (and indeed, at times unsavory) individuals. It demands immersion in social worlds in which the academic researcher may be viewed as a threat, an amusement or object of anger. In the conduct of this research the academic is not in control of events as he is in the classroom or office; the irregular occurrence of events should control the researcher. That said researcher should be flexible is obvious, but such flexibility requires considerable investment of time, money, interest and effort — all to the end of a not necessarily publishable research product. Researchers who have studied such groups from an appreciational stance have had difficulty in surmounting the largely ideologically-based critiques of certain journal reviewers. It is only in the area of gun control and gun ownership that articles critical of elite and academic consensus have recently made an appearance. That few of these articles proceed from normative theses is significant.

It might be argued that articles on cockfighters and Southern ethnic pride groups have not been written due to lack of interest or perceived lack of publication opportunities. In both cases, it is demonstrable that social scientists are letting ideology interfere with the free flow of ideas. Self-censorship may be an operable difficulty in the present cases.

Equally germane to the problems of studying pariah groups is the issue of access to local elites and special interest groups. While deviant groups frequently open their doors to the researcher, moral entrepreneurial groups are more circumspect. One can speculate that the stigmatized group feels that it has little to lose from such an investigation and that any objective study would be sympathetic.

[47] Zoll, 97.

The antipathy of moral crusaders to the field researcher and academic review is based on the moral absolutism of the entrepreneurial policy position. That is, there can be no "objective" study of such an emotionally charged issue. There is no middle ground, no appreciation for other positions, and certainly no time to be given to those who maintain a value relativistic position. To acknowledge the validity of such a research strategy would be to undermine the symbolic universe of the reformer — and thus stands as an entirely antithetical notion.

That politicians wish to evade close scrutiny of the genesis of their positions is an understandable phenomenon. There may be large campaign contributions or highly activist interest groups' expectations at risk. In any event, to expect candor and disinterested commentary from politicians is naive. The politician has nothing to gain and much to lose from academic analysis of his position. The greater relative credibility of the academic puts anything said by the policy-maker at risk or potentially in the public domain. Having to dispense with customary platitudes and slogans and get down to specifics for public consumption is a most distasteful prospect. The student of pariah groups should not expect serious and valid information from politicians, policy-makers and local elites.

The study of local moral crusades and crusaders is made more difficult by parochial thinking from most participants. The researcher's own ideology and research preferences may interfere with the conduct of sound and fair inquiry. Politicians and moral crusaders may have hidden agendas and occult motivations. Local elites may speak to the public or the researcher through politicians, special interest lobbies, the media, or not at all. Certainly, deviant groups may be most uncooperative. However, as noted above, pariah groups generally believe that, since they are currently misunderstood and on the defensive, objective academic scrutiny might help them regain some of the moral and political high ground that they had heretofore occupied and lost to the forces of progress. Therefore, paradoxically, a more sympathetic view of the pariah group's interpretation of events may emerge because that is the only real point-of-view that the researcher is allowed to assess from his participant-observation perspective.

The tendency to take the side of the pariah group, though understandable under the circumstances, is to be avoided. More creative attempts, most albeit futile, to get the policy elite's perspective, must be made. If success is not forthcoming, the final research product may validate the fears of the moral entrepreneurial group. That is, it may appear as an academic apologia for the pariah group's activity and world view. The researcher might be justified in pointing out that a lack of cooperation from the moral entrepreneurial group was instrumental in the perceived lack of balance in the final content of the research product. As mentioned before, the moral crusader will not be convinced, and will hate you the more for "validating" the antithetical group's symbolic universe.

The study of anachronistic and endangered marginal groups and folk is an area of social science that criminologists have largely abandoned to the tender mercies of more apolitical anthropologists and folklorists. Characteristically, they have focused on issues outside of the socio-political context of deviance, preferring to study the problematic group per se, before it vanished into homogeneity.

Thus, the role of ideology, local politics, and the policy preferences of local and national elites have not been studied to the same degree as have the *weltanschauungen* of deviant groups.

Such matters should concern the social scientist who values a truly inter-disciplinary approach to the study of deviant groups.

Chapter 10

The New Class and the California Handgun Initiative: Elitist Developed Law as Gun Control

by
Brendan F.J. Furnish

Introduction: In May of 1982, a Constitutional Referendum entitled the "Handgun Initiative," sponsored by the Center for Law in the Public Interest, qualified for the November ballot in California. Its sponsors (naming themselves "Californians Against Street Crime and Concealable Weapons"), had gathered 575,000 signatures in 150 days (346,000 signatures were necessary to qualify). If this initiative were to have been approved by the California electorate it would have provided, among other things, the following restrictions on handgun sales and ownership within that state:

1) All handguns not registered with the Attorney General by November 2, 1983 would become contraband.
2) The supply of handguns would be limited to those in circulation as of April 30, 1983.
3) No person could register more than one handgun purchased between January 1, 1982 and April 30, 1983.
4) The number of handguns that a dealer would be allowed to sell between November 3, 1982 and April 30, 1983, would be limited by the state.
5) After April 30, 1983 only registered handguns could be sold and any sales must have been made either through a licensed dealer or a police department. Conviction for illegal sales or transfer of handguns would lead to a mandatory one year jail sentence.
6) Persons who moved into the state after November 2, 1983 would have to legally dispose of their handguns within 45 days.
7) The carrying of an unregistered handgun (loaded or unloaded) would be construed as a felony and would require, upon conviction, a mandatory six month jail sentence.[1]

The initiative was the 15th Referendum on the 1982 California ballot, hence it was widely referred to as Proposition 15. If it had been ratified, this Constitutional Amendment would have sharply altered California's gun laws, and it would have

[1] March Fong Eu, *California Ballot Pamphlet for General Election,* (Sacramento: State of California Secretary of State Office, November 2, 1982); and Michael V. Franchetti, *Analysis of Handgun Initiatives* (Sacramento: State of California, January 29, 1982).

created a new and large governmental bureaucracy.[2]

Although the language of the initiative raised a number of questions regarding both its logical internal consistency and the general workability of the proposal, it was nevertheless certified to be placed on the ballot by a much larger than required number of qualifying signatures, (which cost approximately $1.00 apiece; at that time a phenomenal expense). Thus, with considerable initial success, the campaign got off to a strong start. It should be noted that in addition to the handgun initiative, there was also a nuclear freeze initiative as well as highly publicized races for U.S. Senator and for Governor. As a consequence, this election was to have both lots of publicity and a heavy voter turnout.

The handgun initiative campaign received wide by-partisan backing. Although the Republican candidates for Governor and U.S.Senate (both of whom subsequently won the election) did not endorse it, many prominent Republicans did, providing strong support for the initiative.[3] The initiative was also endorsed by an impressive number of celebrities. The evident effect of all this favorable publicity; was demonstrated in a series of initial polls. The first Field Poll (Field is a California pollster), indicated nearly two-to-one support for the initiative.[4]

This outcome is not especially surprising since for a number of years, national polls have indicated that approximately two-thirds of those sampled have favored stricter control over handguns.[5] Up to election day, most California polls (with the exception of the *Los Angeles Times* poll) showed the initiative as winning. Indeed, it was thought to be more than wishful thinking when the *L.A. Daily Journal* (a newspaper oriented toward the legal profession) editorialized that "Gun-control supporters have shown increasing sophistication in translating that concern into effective political support for tougher handgun laws. The California vote gives them an opportunity for their biggest popular victory ever."[6] Obviously, a victory for the California initiative would be a vindication of national polls which seemingly favored handgun control and could be a harbinger of future handgun control efforts in other states.

Despite such optimistic support, the measure steadily declined in the polls until it

---

[2] The State Attorney General estimated that implementation of the initiative would require a central office staff of more than 800 employees. Additional field workers would also be required (cf., Franchetti, 6ff).

[3] E.g., David Murdock, a wealthy Republican fundraiser, and Elliot L.Richardson, former U.S. Attorney General.

[4] Fred Epstein, "California Sticks to its Guns: How the NRA Got Voters to Say No to Handgun Control." *Rolling-Stone* (February 17, 1983), 19; and Michele Willens, "Shooting the Works in the California Corral," *California Journal* (June, 1982), 95.

[5] *Gallup Poll: Public Opinion 1983* (Wilmington, Delaware: Scholarly Resources, Inc., 1984); and Tom W. Smith, "The 75% Solution: An Analysis of the Structure of Attitudes on Gun Control, 1959-1979," *The Journal of Criminal Law and Criminology*, Vol. 71 (1980), 3.

[6] *L.A. Daily Journal* (October 25, 1982), 2.

had only weak support on election day. The results of the election were somewhat of a surprise to most observers, since the initiative lost by the rather ignominious margin of 63% to 37%. Interestingly, although the predicted success of the initiative was widely covered in the national media, its subsequent failure was essentially ignored by out-of-state media outlets.[7] Regardless of media attention, Proposition 15 suffered the same fate as that of the 1976 Massachusetts Handgun Prohibition Referendum which was also overwhelmingly defeated by the electorate.

Much of the post-election analysis focused on the fact that the opposition, led by the National Rifle Association, managed to outspend the initiative supporters by a margin of 3 to 1. Although there is some merit to this argument, it does not take into consideration the significant amount of free publicity in favor of the initiative, provided by sympathetic media outlets. For instance, it was rather striking that the CBS show "60 Minutes" just happened to run a segment which was powerfully condemning of handgun ownership only nine days before the election. It was estimated that two thirds of the California electorate viewed this show and that it caused a 4% drop in the initiative's opposition.[8] Likewise, the *Los Angeles Times* (estimated readership of 3 million) ran eight separate editorials, each enthusiastically supporting the measure.[9] Other media outlets made similar contributions. Accordingly, when the value of such free advertising is factored in, the spending differential is sharply attenuated. Bordua gives a detailed cost analysis of the proposition 15 campaign. He claims that the "gun lobby" expenditure was actually 1.29 to 1.64 times that of proponents.[10] This is a differential which Bordua claims is, by itself, insufficient to explain the magnitude of the initiative's defeat.

If the spending differential was not as salient as some thought, then there must be other causal reasons for the failure of the initiative to be approved by the voters. Given the consistency of the national polls which seemingly favor such restrictions, the failure to pass this referendum appears to be something of a conundrum. One possible solution would be to question the accuracy and validity of polling in regards to the gun-control issue: some sociologists have indeed raised significant questions

[7] See Edward F. Leddy, *Magnum Force Lobby: The National Rifle Association Fights Gun Control* (Lanham, Maryland: University Press of America, 1987), p. 122.

[8] Epstein, 58.

[9] Ibid., 21.

[10] David J. Bordua, "Adversary Polling and the Construction of Social Meaning: Implications in Gun Control Elections in Massachusetts and California," *Law & Policy Quarterly,* Vol. 5 (July, 1983), 345-366; and James C. Dutra, "Anatomy of a Landslide: Enough People Cared," *Gun Owner* (May/June, 1983), 21-24.

about this issue.[11] Another possibility, which forms the thrust of this paper, is to consider voter perception of the class and elitist elements that might have been present in this proposed law. We surmise that during the rather intense campaign for various referenda and candidates, California voters identified an elitist dimension within the handgun initiative and voted according to their elitist/class interests and positions.

We further propose that the handgun initiative is part of a larger outlook which Bruce-Briggs has termed "interdictionism" — the reduction of the criminal use of firearms by restricting and controlling the access to all citizens of firearms.[12] This outlook is a fundamental orientation of certain strategic, ruling elites, particularly the elitist group now known as the "new class." It is also, as Bruce-Briggs observes, a reflection of a fundamental schism in American capitalist society — a schism between the relatively inarticulate working class and much of the contemporary American bourgeoisie. This latter group strongly believes that uncontrolled gun ownership — especially if it means proletarian ownership — is uncivilized.[13] Indeed, as Tonso points out, many of the educated detractors of firearms believe the private ownership of guns is at best, an anachronistic residual of the frontier era, and at worst, represents severe psychological maladjustment.[14]

Law as a Response to Elitist Interests. Recent concern with the societal aspects of law has brought about the development of the critical legal studies movement. One orientation of this approach comes out of the social theories of Marx and Weber. As Unger has observed, this is a mode of historical and social analysis that has combined functionalist methodology with radical aims. Its thesis is that law reflects the social divisions and hierarchies inherent in capitalism.[15] Thus, the law in U.S. society can be construed as a representation of the interests of strategist elitist groups.[16] This mode of analysis has spawned a variety of theoretical notions which help to explain how the mechanism of elitist control is made operational in modern capitalist society. For

11 James D. Wright, "Public Opinion & Gun Control: A Comparison of Results from Two Recent National Surveys," *The Annals of the American Academy of Political & Social Science* (May, 1981), 24-39; Bordua; William R. Tonso, "Social Science and Sagecraft in the Debate Over Gun Control," *Law & Policy Quarterly* (July, 1983), 325-344.

12 Barry Bruce-Briggs, "The Great American Gun War," *The Public Interest* (Fall, 1976), 38.

13 Ibid., 16.

14 William R. Tonso, *Gun and Society: The Social and Existential Roots of the American Attachment to Firearms* (Washington, D.C.: University Press of America, 1982), pp. 15ff.

15 Roberto M. Unger, "The Critical Legal Studies Movement," *Harvard Law Review* (January, 1983), 563.

16 We accept Keller's definition of strategic elites here: "strategic elites, in our view, comprise not only political, economic and military leaders, but also moral, cultural, and scientific ones. Whether or not an elite is counted as strategic does not depend on its specific activities but on the scope of its activities, that is, on how many members of society that it directly impinges upon and in what it respects." Susanne Keller, *Beyond the Ruling Class: Strategic Elite in Modern Society* (New York: Random House, 1968), p. 20.

purposes of this paper, we accept the premises of this variant of critical theory and propose to utilize it to provide focus for this assessment.

The controlling function of the law has been evolutionary in nature, keeping pace with other institutional structures found in capitalist societies. Thus, law once took the form described in "institutional" legal theory in which the state and the laws rather directly served the "power elite." In modern capitalist societies the connection between the elite and state is deliberately obscured, with the ruling class resorting to various forms of governmental subterfuge in order to prevent the dissident elements of the working class from correctly viewing the connections between law and the controlling elite. Therefore, according to Chambliss and Seidman, U.S. society has evolved from "instrumental" to "structural" to "dialectical" forms of law: such changes appear to increasingly separate the capitalist elite from direct participation in the formation of law and the running of government, while at the same time assuring that the legal structure will always operate in the long-term interests of the ruling elite.[17] We submit that interdictionist law serves the interests of the controlling elite in certain determinate ways. Further, firearms laws appear to have undergone evolutionary changes that are strikingly similar to changes in the larger body of the law.

Interdictionist Law in the U.S.: A Brief Overview. It is frequently assumed that gun laws are a relatively recent phenomena in the U.S., and have come about because of the rapid expansion of urban areas. Indeed, the lower crime rates of certain urban areas in the northeastern region, particularly in New England, vis-a-vis the more violent areas of the southern region are frequently attributed to the effectiveness of the northern region's strict gun laws. However, as Kates has pointed out, the south was an early leader in strict gun laws.[18]

A critical examination of gun control laws — especially those supporting interdictionist policy — in both Europe and America, is illustrative of elitist regulation. Prior to the post World War II era, such interdiction came about in a fairly instrumental manner and exemplified how the old power elite used regulatory law to suppress political dissent. Thus, we are not especially surprised to learn that in the antebellum south, Blacks were legally denied the right to bear arms.[19] The slavocracy of the day rightly feared slave revolts and thus passed increasingly restrictive laws preventing Blacks from having access to firearms.

[17] William Chambliss and Robert Seidman, *Law, Order & Power* (Menlo Park, California: Addison-Wesley Publishing Company, 1982); and Chambliss and Milton Mankoff, *Whose Law, What Order?* (New York: John Wiley & Sons, Inc., 1976).

[18] Don B. Kates, Jr. "Introduction," *Law & Policy Quarterly* (July, 1983), 261; and Douglas R. Murray, "Handguns, Gun Control Laws and Firearms Violence," *Social Problems* Vol. 23 (October, 1975).

[19] Stephen P. Halbrook, *That Every Man Be Armed: The Evolution of a Constitutional Right* (Albuquerque: University of New Mexico Press, 1984), pp. 96-106.

During the Reconstruction period, the Federal government made a serious attempt, focusing upon the ramifications of the newly passed 14th Amendment as a way of allowing Black citizens to arm. Indeed, as Hallbrook points out, one of the reasons for the *passage* of the 14th Amendment was to grant the Southern Black population the right to own firearms.[20] Simultaneously, the Federal Government attempted to disarm the various Southern militia which formed the core of the Ku Klux Klan.[21]

Unfortunately, such efforts of assuring Black civil-rights in general were short lived. As a result of a series of political compromises, the Blacks began to lose political power in 1870 and by the 1880's had been largely forced out of positions of power and into the economic and political serfdom which extended into the 1960's. Starting in the 1870's, a series of "Black Codes" were implemented which, among other things, virtually disarmed the Southern Black population. The mechanisms for this varied, ranging from banning of pistol sales to all except "special deputies"; by imposing a "transaction tax" which poor Blacks could not pay; or by requiring the purchase of only expensive weapons such as the Colt "Navy" model.[22] The upshot of this was that the Southern Black population of this country was effectively disarmed and suppressed until the 1960's. Interestingly, as Kates has observed, one seldom discussed reason for the success of the 1960's Civil Rights Movement was the fact that by this period in time, the Southern Blacks were well enough armed to effectively thwart many of the Klan terror attempts.[23]

After the turn of the century, gun laws moved into a more "subjective phase." The passage of gun restrictions against the foreign-born, especially those from Eastern and Southern Europe is illustrative of this. From the 1880's to the mid 1930's there was a wave of xenophobia which sometimes reached almost hysterical dimensions. The Italians, who were stereotypically thought by many to be lazy, violent and anarchist, were made special targets of ethnic hatred. This led to the "red scare" of that era and climaxed in the Sacco and Vanzetti affair and the infamous Palmer raids of 1919-1920.

As a partial consequence of these xenophobic outbursts, almost all the various states passed laws prohibiting ownership of firearms by aliens.[24] In 1911 New York City passed the Sullivan Law, the most restrictive law of its time. Not surprisingly, the

20 Ibid., 108ff.

21 Ibid., Ch. 7.

22 Don B. Kates, Jr., *Restricting Handguns: The Liberal-Skeptics Speak Out* (North River Press, Inc., 1979), pp. 12-15; and Halbrook, 113ff.

23 Kates, *Restricting Handguns*, 189-193. Interestingly, Robert Sherrill claims that partly in response to the black unrest of the 1960's, Congress passed the Gun Control Act of 1968. Robert Sherrill, *The Saturday Night Special* (Charterhouse Books, 1973), pp. 200ff.

24 Kates, *Restricting Handguns*, 15-22.

city's business interests fought hard for its passage, allegedly as a means of reducing the hold-up rate. The mistrust of foreigners is pronounced in the newspaper articles regarding the new law. For instance, one writer exalts the fact that this law has "a specially stringent clause [that] relates to aliens" and makes it a felony for them to possess a weapon.[25]

At first it was relatively easy for non-aliens to obtain a permit to own a firearm, and at one time as many as 35,000 permits were issued [now it is almost impossible for the ordinary resident of New York City to obtain such a permit].[26] Interestingly, the first person arrested and convicted under the Sullivan Law was an Italian immigrant. Indeed, a close perusal of New York Times articles concerning the Sullivan Law, for the period from 1911 to 1913, indicates that over 70% of those arrested for violations of this law had Italian surnames. Predictably, during this period of anti-Italian racism, it was almost impossible for people of Italian descent to obtain weapons permits in New York City.

From the outset, the Sullivan Law did not reduce homicide and other weapons crime; it did, however, give the police a sufficient pretext to arrest undesirable aliens — especially those "anarchists" or "radicals" who might be suspected of being involved in labor unrest.[27] The early operation of the Sullivan Law provides us with an example of one of the major political implications of interdictionism: such laws can be selectively enforced in order to carry out political or ideological goals. As Kessler has observed, "Gun control laws that are seemingly nondiscriminatory and apolitical can be selectively enforced against persons who constitute a threat to the government."[28] Eight states and a variety of other jurisdictions followed New York City's lead in adopting similar legislation, always at the urging of the conservative business community which claimed that such laws were needed to reduce the frequency of armed robbery.

All too frequently the laws were utilized in a selective manner as an excuse to arrest "foreign-born radicals" who were involved in labor organizing; one should bear in mind that this was a period characterized by significant labor strife. As Leddy has pointed out, during the early part of this century, there was much agitation from the nation's business interests to pass a national "Sullivan Law". The clear intent of such lobbying efforts was to intimidate groups involved in labor union organization. Such efforts failed, largely because of a populist reaction against the "plutocratics" of the day.[29]

25 New York Times (August 29, 1911), 5.

26 Lee Kennett and James LaVerne Anderson, *The Gun in America: The Origins of a National Dilemma* (Westport, Connecticut: Greenwood Press, 1975), pp. 173-186; and Kates, *Restricting Handguns*, 15-20.

27 Kennett and Anderson, 185; and Kates, *Restricting Handguns*, 19-20.

28 Raymond G. Kessler, "The Political Functions of Gun Control," in Don B. Kates, Jr. (ed.). *Firearms and Violence: Issues of Public Policy* (Cambridge: Ballinger Publishing Company, 1984), p. 467.

29 Kates, *Restricting Handguns*, 17-22; and Leddy, 81f.

All of this suggests an evolution of interdictionist policy going from a direct prohibition of firearms for blacks and ethnics to a selective enforcement of interdictionist law which was allegedly developed to "reduce crime" (a claim that has yet to be empirically demonstrated as valid), and yet had as its latent target very specific populations.[30] The straight forward influence of the power elite is obvious in this. In more recent times, particularly since World War II, the direct control of the old moneyed elite in such matters has become notably blurred. This has happened for a variety of reasons, one of which is the intensifying class dislike of the opulent rich who have become increasingly invisible and now accomplish control through various types of proxies.

More to the point for this analysis, has been the rapid expansion of a well-educated middle and upper-middle class which have significantly changed many of our basic social arrangements. This, coupled with the explosion of electronic technology especially in the areas of information management and the media, has apparently brought about a major alteration of the class structure. The emerging "New Class" (or what Lebedoff has termed "The New Elite"), holds forth the possibility of a more penetrating form of elitist social control, far greater than that of the old moneyed elite and their rather crude control mechanisms, ever conceived of accomplishing.[31]

The New Class and Interdictionist Policy. Central to the social and economic structure of advanced capitalist, industrial societies is an enormous knowledge industry. The New Class consists, for the most part, of college and professionally trained individuals who, in Berger's words, "derive their livelihood from the knowledge industry [:] . . . people whose social position rests on the manipulation of symbols rather than on the manipulation of things."[32] Although the New Class has

[30] Among those who take an interdictionist position, it is axiomatic to assume that guns cause crime. There is, however, little in the way of empirical research to support this assertion. For instance, studies of the southern region of the nation, the center of the so-called "subculture of violence" have shown this thesis to be largely specious (e.g., Howard Erlander, "The Empirical Status of the Subculture of Violence Thesis," *Social Problems,* Vol. 22 (December, 1974); Jo Dixon and Alan Lizotte, "Regional and Subculture of Violence Effects of Gun Ownership: The 'Southern Subculture of Violence' Thesis Revisited," paper presented at the American Sociological Association Annual Meeting, 1982; and James D. Wright, Peter H. Rossi, and Kathleen Daly, *Under the Gun: Weapons, Crime and Violence in America* (New York: Aldine Publishing Company, 1983), pp. 13f). As a result of their massive search of the literature, Wright, Rossi and Daly conclude that "there is little or no conclusive, or even suggestive, evidence to show that gun ownership among the population as a whole is, per se, an important cause of criminal violence." Additionally, there is accumulating a body of research that indicates not only is such a policy ineffective against the target population of criminals, but that where it is extant, it is simply not enforced by the criminal justice system (e.g., Steven Steitz, "Firearms, Homicides & Gun Control Effectiveness," *Law & Society Review* (May, 1972), 593-613; and Murray).

[31] David Lebedoff, *The New Elite: The Death of Democracy* (New York: Franklin Watts, 1981).

[32] Peter L. Berger, "Ethics and the Present Class Struggle," *World View* (April, 1978), 2. See also James D. Hunter, "The New Class and the Young Evangelicals," *Review of Religious Research,* Vol. 22 (December, 1980), 155ff.

relatively high levels of education and income, it can be recognized not so much by its socioeconomic characteristics (as the older moneyed elite was) but rather by its relation to the culture. The New Class are "symbol specialists" — they are the people who manipulate the symbolic meanings which constitute culture. In short, they are in a position to provide us with our ideas. Although Bell has complained that the New-Class idea is a "muddled concept," and Kristol has allegedly tried to "define it away" nevertheless, there exists a significant and growing literature which seems to assure its place in sociological analysis.[33]

Membership in the New Class is largely determined upon employment in particular occupations and, more importantly proper educational attainment.[34] Equal consideration can be given to the perception that they are, *sui generis,* measurably intelligent; brighter, in fact, than the bulk of the masses. Moreover, most members of this group are keenly aware of their intelligence vis-a-vis the masses.[35] The powers and privileges of this class lie in their individual control of special languages, cultures, techniques and skills.[36] Belonging to the New Class implies a sort of snobbish arrogance, an orientation that Lebedoff expresses rather well when he indicates that those who do not fit into the self-defined category of New Class are "left-behinds." This includes not only the bulk of both blue- and white-collar workers, but also members of the old power elite who do not fit into the criteria of the New Class.[37]

Recently, Singer has added some conceptual clarity to the new class concept. Singer developed the term "university-oriented Americans" or "UOAs" in an effort to reinterpret the somewhat fuzzy notion of the new class. He agrees with most other commentators on the new class that:

> The people who work in all the industries that are in the idea business or any communication business are UOAs. Educators, publicists, media people, governmental elites, politicians who are respected leaders, . . . and the great bulk of academic experts and the clergy are part of UOA. . . . Thus virtually all

---

[33] Daniel Bell, "The New Class: A Muddled Concept," in B. Bruce-Briggs (ed.) *The New Class?* (New Brunswick. Transaction Books, 1979); and David Bazlon, "How Now 'The New Class'?" *Dissent*, Vol. 26 (1979). 443-449

[34] Carl E. Ladd, "Pursuing the New Class," in B. Bruce-Briggs (ed.) The New Class? (New Brunswick Transaction Books, 1979), pp. 119ff.

[35] Lebedoff, 16ff.

[36] Alvin W. Gouldner, "The New Class Project, 1," *Theory and Society* Vol. 6 (1978), 168ff.

[37] Lebedoff, 19ff. Bazelon suggests the following Class map for the contemporary U.S. situation (Bazelon, 448; see also Bruce-Briggs, 16-17): a) *The Over-Class:* This is essentially C. Wright Mill's Power Elite — the super rich; corporation and government bosses and the institutional elites; university and foundation chiefs. b) *The New Class:* The under-the-top people who make organizations work. c) *The Rentiers:* The paper-holders, the residual rich whose wealth is managed — as is everything else — by the educated/organizational New Class. d) *The Proprietors:* Owners who control what they own and actively make their place in the world today. e) *The Unionized Worker.* f) *The Underclass.*

the people who most Americans look to for the articulation of ideas, for thinking about the world . . . are part of category UOA.[38]

However, Singer points out that UOAs are a special class, not because they have had university training and know they are bright, but rather because people who make up this category tend to have a "professional" outlook toward life. They tend to use academia as a reference point for truth and wisdom. UOAs do not trust their own judgement, but rather rely on the ideas of their university-oriented peers. Additionally, UOAs are bound to specific locations; "the Northeast, California, big cities, and university towns". Finally, Singer claims that UOAs make up about 10% of the American population.[39] For purposes of this paper, we accept these ideas of Singer's as a definitive enhancement of the new class concept (although for purposes of compatibility with most sociological literature we prefer to continue using the term "New Class").

At present, the New Class works in a more or less symbiotic relationship with the old business class; however, there are growing tensions in the relationship. The New Class is an ascending elite that will be increasingly involved in a struggle with the old class for power and privilege. For now, the lines between the two are "porous and shifting", since the New Class needs the infra-structure which the old class holds, but cannot maintain without New Class participation.[40] The relationship between new and old class can be seen in the developers and promoters of the California Handgun Initiative. The Appendix lists a sampling of individuals who developed, contributed, or significantly promoted this initiative. This listing rather clearly indicates the mixture of new and old class discussed herein. The author of the proposition, a public interest lawyer, appears to well fit the criteria of being a member of the New Class.[41]

Kirkpatrick has criticized the New Class, complaining that in their role as culture specialists, they have brought a shift in responsibility for the quality of social life away from the family, individual and private groups to the government. Two arguments have been given to justify this: first, widely acknowledged social ills are not being satisfactorily met; and second, such transfers are seen as ways of promoting social justice.[42] In this, the New Class rather decisively sets the agenda for the society. In setting the agenda it also maintains the power to obscure policy failures of previous New Class attempts at social engineering.[43]

---

[38] Max Singer, *Passage To a Human World: The Dynamics of Creating Global Wealth* (Indianapolis: The Hudson Institute, 1987), p. 230.

[39] Ibid., Ch. 14.

[40] Berger; Gouldner; and Bazelon.

[41] Nathan Glazer, "Lawyers and the New Class," in B. Bruce-Briggs (ed.) *The New Class?* (New Brunswick: Transaction Books, 1979), pp. 89-100.

[42] Jeane J. Kirkpatrick, "Politics and the New Class," in B. Bruce-Briggs (ed.), *The New Class?* (New Brunswick: Transaction Books, 1979), pp. 42-48.

[43] Kirkpatrick feels that the New Class has within it the seeds of totalitarianism. As surely as the monopoly of power and wealth is dangerous to the rest of us, a New Class monopoly on meaning and purpose is incompatible with democracy, (Kirkpatrick, p. 48).

It is noteworthy that the existence of the New Class is becoming increasingly visible to the total society. This is, in part, an evolution of industrial society; it is also a function of critical theory itself which, as Gouldner observes, tends to block the repression of the New Class role in social change and help this come into public visibility.[44]

While still somewhat obscure, the relationship between the New Class, social policy failure and interdictionist policy may be gradually becoming more transparent. This seems especially to be the case in terms of New Class policies toward the underclass. It is rather ironic that although the New Class has been often characterized as having a quasi-socialistic, progressive orientation,[45] New Class people can be surprisingly racist, in an incipient, "liberal" way. Blacks, for instance, have often been allegedly treated by New Class policies in a condescending, patriarchal manner.[46] Likewise, New Class efforts to "deinstitutionalize" the insane (supported for instance by California's New Class ex-governor "Jerry" Brown) have created a subculture of mentally incompetent vagrants who help swell the ranks of the homeless in this country and lead in some significant ways to an increase in fear among the average citizens. The massive failures of the social agenda for the underclass over the past several decades has now led to one of the compelling, underlying reasons for New Class concern over gun control.

One can argue that much of our welfare and educational policy toward the underclass was in large part a creation of New Class ideas and policies.[47] Rather than acknowledging that such ideas and policies have been at least partially causal in both the disintegration of the Black family and the alienation of much of the poor from the larger culture (and thereby bringing about an enormous increase in violent crime) the New Class, with a strong vested interest in the welfare and criminal justice system, simply refuses to acknowledge these policy failures. Rather than concerning themselves with the structural reasons for Black crime, they propose instead a "quick track" fix in the form of gun control.[48] Such proposals are advanced even though

---

[44] Gouldner. See also Habermas, "Critical Theory as an Ideology of the New Class," *Theory and Society*, Vol. 0 (1070).

[45] This is not especially surprising; one recent study noted the bureaucratic staffs of both the Democratic and Republican parties comprise some of the " most liberal elites and their progressive view stand out most prominently on 'new liberalism' issues dealing with public and private morality." Eric M. Uslaner and Ronald E. Weber, "Policy Congruence and American State Elites: Descriptive Representation vs. Elective Accountability," Vol. 45, *Journal of Politics* (Feb. 1983), 183-196. Berger; Kirkpatrick; and Hunter.

[46] See Lebedoff, 182ff.

[47] Berger, 10; Glazer, 91ff; and also Eva Etzioni-Halevy, *The Knowledge Elite and the Failure of Prophecy* (London: George Allen & Unwin, 1985), pp. 60f.

[48] It is noteworthy that firearms crime is one of the leading causes of death for black male Californians age 14-44: this against the fact that firearms-related incidents rank as the 8th cause of death in the total California population.

there is strong evidence to indicate that the alienated poor and minorities would be the people least constrained by interdictionist law.[49]

It is difficult to refrain from speculating about the racist overtones of many of the recent gun control schemes. For instance, as Bruce-Briggs pointed out in his discussion of the debate over the so-called "Saturday-Night Special," this weapon (which as of yet remains impossible to accurately define in a technical sense) has been emphasized because it is cheap and is allegedly sold to a particular class of people who employ such weapons in "street crimes." The name itself is significant since it presumably refers to "Niggertown Saturday Night," a stereotypical time of merriment and violence among Blacks.[50] Outlawing the sale of such weapons would supposedly prevent them from being used in crimes. A similar logic was present in California's Proposition 15. By limiting the supply of handguns to those in circulation as of April 30, 1983, the law would have caused such firearms to become an inelastic commodity and would most likely double or triple the original price. This would essentially become a significant sales tax on such firearms and would most likely prevent much of the real target population of this initiative (Blacks and Hispanics) from purchasing handguns.

Leaving aside the ethics of such subterfuge, this strategy would still most likely have failed for two reasons: first, there is a significant market in both stolen and contraband firearms, which present attempts at interdictionist law fail to stem.[51] Secondly, as alluded to before, studies of such laws indicate that they are simply not enforced.[52] DeZee claims that, "Police are reluctant to enforce gun control laws, prosecutors do not always press charges and judges are unlikely to fully sentence individuals guilty of such crimes. This means that any conclusions concerning the effectiveness of gun control laws are rendered invalid by the actions of the criminal justice officials."[53]

Given all of the above, one wonders that if the manifest consequences of such laws are so questionable, then what possible latent consequences are present? We submit there are several plausible ways, beyond the alleged pretexts, in which gun control laws benefit elitist interests: especially the interests of the New Class. In the interests

[49] Steitz, 608ff.

[50] Bruce-Briggs, 49-50.

[51] See Wright, Rossi, and Daly, Ch. 9 for a detailed discussion of this. Also see James D. Wright and Peter H. Rossi Armed and Considered Dangerous: A Survey of Felons and Their Firearms (New York: Aldine de Gruyter, 1986), pp. 193ff.

[52] Paul Bendis and Steven Balkin, "A Look at Gun Control Enforcement," Journal of Police Science & Administration, Vol. 7 (1979), 439-448; Matthew R. DeZee, "Gun Control Legislation," Law & Policy Quarterly, Vol. 5 (July, 1983), 367-379; Donald T. Lunde, Murder and Madness (San Francisco: San Francisco Book Co., Inc., 1976), pp. 30ff; Steitz; Wright, Rossi, and Daly, 298ff.

[53] DeZee, 365-366.

of brevity, let us consider two such elements. The first reason lies in the possibility that interdictionist law is a form of "symbolic law." Chambliss and Seidman propose that symbolic law is a technique for persuading both dissident factions of the ruling class and the masses not to threaten stability by political, economic or revolutionary action. Such laws apparently respond to a particular demand without controlling the problem they are intended to control. "Symbolic law concerns laws that the legislature enacts but the members of the state do not enforce."[54]

Therefore, it may well serve the interests of the elite to allow the continuance of a large underclass, especially if the real resolution of the problem of the poor required a significant redistribution of wealth and power. If this underclass is restless and violent, then the passage of interdictionist law can be a relatively inexpensive means of providing an illusory resolution to this problem.[55]

The second reason that the elite benefit from interdictionist law lies in the possibility that gun control forces an increase in citizen tolerance of police power and abuses, which in turn may lead to the development of large bureaucracies — one of the things at which Kirkpatrick claims the new class does well.[56] For example, we need only look at the number and type of new class experts that are now involved in the criminal justice system. Gun control law considerably expands the need for such experts by creating an entire new class of criminal (sometimes these are formerly legitimate gun owners). Such expanding bureaucratic structures broaden the new class power base by providing legitimacy for controlling experts.[57] Thus the New Class benefits from tangible elements, such as the creation of new employment opportunities, but also benefits in intangible ways by creating situations for an entire new corpus of theoretical ideas which spring from basic societal unrest.

In this chapter, we have briefly looked at a few of the influences of strategic historic and contemporary elite groups upon firearms legislation. This chapter has been offered as a tentative and highly speculative exploration of some of these issues. Obviously much more rigorous work remains to be done in this area.

---

[54] Chamblis and Seidman, 314-316. See also Joseph R. Gusfield, *Symbolic Crusade: Status Politics and the American Temperance Movement* (Urbana: University of Illinois Press, 1969), pp. 180ff.

[55] See Bruce-Briggs, 60-61 for a related situation.

[56] Kirkpatrick, 42.

[57] Raymond G. Kessler, "Gun Control and Political Power," *Law & Policy Quarterly*, Vol. 5 (July, 1983), 383-384.

APPENDIX

Partial Listing of Media-Mentioned Framers and Active Sponsors
of the 1982 California Ballot Proposition 15,
the Handgun Initiative

John Phillips; attorney; Executive director of the Center for Law in the Public Interest; author of the Handgun Initiative.

Victor Palmieri; attorney; real-estate developer; former chairman of the parent company that owned the Pen Central Railroad; Staff Director of the Kerner Commission on Civil Disorders; former U.S. Ambassador for Refugee Affairs; Trustee of the Center for Law in the Public Interest; co-sponsor, with John Phillips of the California Handgun Initiative, and Chairman of the Campaign Committee.

Max Palevsky; industrialist; prime supporter of the 1972 George McGovern presidential campaign; Trustee of the Center for Law in the Public Interest.

David Packard; Chairman of the Board, the Hewlett-Packard Corporation.

William Hewlett, Chairman of the Executive Committee, the Hewlett-Packard Corporation.

Armand Hammer; Chairman of the Board, Occidental Petroleum Corporation.

Walter Gerken; Chairman of the Board of Pacific Murual Life Insurance Company.

Pete McCloskey, U.S. Congressman for California (helped John Phillips write the Initiative).

Peter Pitchess; former Sheriff of Los Angeles County; member of the Initiative Campaign Steering Committee.

Warren Christopher; former Deputy Secretary of State; member of the Initiative Campaign Steering Committee.

Edmund G. Brown, Sr.; former Governor of California; member of the Initiative Campaign Steering Committee.

Shirley Hufstedler; former Secretary of Education; member of the Initiative Campaign Steering Committee.

Philip Hawley; Chairman of the Board, Carter Hawley Hale Stores, Inc.; member of the Initiative Campaign Steering Committee.

MacDonald Beckett; architect; Chairman of Welton Beckett and Associates (designers of Century City and the L.A. Music Center).

Justian Dart; Chairman of the Board, Dart Industries; financial supporter of Republican Party candidates.

Elliot Richardson; former U.S. Attorney General and former U.S. Secretary of Defense.

Clark Clifford; former U.S. Secretary of Defense. Initiative Campaign Steering Committee.

Milton Eisenhower; educator; brother of the late President.

Averell Harriman; former Board Chairman, Merchant Shipbuilding Corporation; former Governor of New York; former Ambassador to Russia (1943-46), to Great Britain (1946); former Secretary of Commerce.

Irving A. Zoff; entertainment agent (Manager of the Eagles, Chicago and Jimmy Buffett).

Otis Chandler; publisher of *The Los Angeles Times.*

Jerry Weintraub; entertainment promoter.

Mike Beard; Executive Director, National Coalition to Dan Handguns.

Nelson T. "Pete" Shields; Executive Director, Handgun Control.

Chapter 11

FIREARMS' STEREOTYPES IN AMERICAN T.V. AND FILMS: "TRUTH?" AND CONSEQUENCES

by
Richard Hummel

INTRODUCTION

The debate over private access to firearms is mainly about the risks to the public resulting from such access to firearms. Each side of this debate has charged the other with misrepresentations of the facts about the nature, uses, and misuses of firearms.

Just where do the "facts" about firearms come from? How do citizens learn what they know about firearms? The options are limited:

1. One can have direct experience with firearms and become familiar with their construction and uses.

2. One can indirectly absorb impressions of their nature from portrayals of their uses and effects in fictional entertainment.

3. One can develop one's perceptions of firearms from reports of their involvement in real-life events, both anecdotal and distilled into official statistics, which are passed on by the news media.

Is there any possibility that one can escape forming some structure of impressions about firearms given their ubiquitous existence in the public arena? The probability seems quite low!

This chapter contends that the images of firearms portrayed in the fictional entertainment media of television and films are distorted, biased, and exaggerated in numerous ways. These invalid images hurt as well as help both sides of the firearms ownership debate. We will examine the sources of these incorrect images as well as their likely effects on public perceptions of the role of firearms in our culture.

COMMON STEREOTYPES OF GUNS IN THE ENTERTAINMENT MEDIA

The stereotyped images of guns in the fictional entertainment media exaggerate and, thus, distort the nature of firearms and their uses in various ways. Consider the following examples:

1. GUNS OF ALL KINDS ARE EXTREMELY EASY TO BUY, LEGALLY AND ILLEGALLY.

This stereotype is essential to those who press for more stringent control laws. The other side retorts that over 20,000 gun laws already exist in various jurisdictions, and enforcement of existing laws rather than new laws should be the priority. Does any audience ever see portrayed in movies or on television the ACTUAL procedure for buying a gun in today's America: the Federal form with its questions, the identification procedures, the waiting periods in many jursidictions? It is especially ironic that California, where many episodes of the fictional media are produced, requires a 15-day waiting period for the purchase of a handgun. Are Hollywood producers merely ignorant of their state's purchase requirements or are they intentionally overlooking that fact when their story lines have handguns involved in California settings?

2. THE TYPICAL GUN BUYER IS A PERSON WHO IS OBVIOUSLY DISTURBED, FRIGHTENED, ANGRY OR CLEARLY UNBALANCED IN SOME WAY.

Thus revenge, tragedy, crime or some other misuse of the gun almost certainly follows if the acquisition process is portrayed. Also, typically the gun buyer is portrayed as a first-time buyer. In fact, most gun purchases are made by those already owning firearms. Additionally, suicides with firearms are typically committed with firearms not purchased recently.

3. CHILDREN ALWAYS MISUSE CARELESSLY STORED GUNS AND HAVE TRAGIC ACCIDENTS AS A RESULT.

This stereotype undoubtedly leads many new parents to abandon ownership of guns when their children are very young. Parents are seldom, if ever, portrayed showing their children the safe use of firearms. The impression conveyed is that possession of arms in the presence of children is an irresponsible thing to do. The related stereotype also is promoted that children are unable to separate in their minds the "pretend" violence in the visual media and real life violence. Hence, children will attempt to kill something in real life with a gun if given any chance.

4. PEOPLE SHOT WITH GUNS ALMOST ALWAYS DIE, ESPECIALLY IF THEY ARE VILLAINS.

This stereotype overlooks the fact that the most controversial type of gun, the handgun, is the least lethal. Of those shot with handguns, over 90% recover. The recovery rate for shotgun and rifle wounds is only around 20%.[1] Since handguns are most often portrayed in the visual media, their lethalness is distorted. The "substitutability" hypothesis postulates that the surest way to increase the lethalness of firearms' wounds is to reduce the incidence of handguns, thus increasing the use of rifles and shotguns in violent encounters.[2]

---

[1] Carol Ruth Silver and Don B. Kates, Jr., "Self-Defense, Handgun Ownership, and the Independence of Women in a Violent, Sexist Society," in Don B. Kates, Jr. (ed.) *Restricting Handguns: The Liberal Skeptics Speak Out* (North River Press, 1979), p. 166.

[2] Gary Kleck and David J. Bordua, "The Factual Foundations for Certain Key Assumptions of Gun Control," *Law & Policy Quarterly,* Vol. 5 (July, 1983), 273.

5. GUNS ARE UNERRINGLY ACCURATE IN STRIKING THEIR IN-TENDED TARGETS, ESPECIALLY IN THE HANDS OF THE "GOOD GUYS."

This stereotype suggests that the accurate use of guns is no problem. The reality is that marksmanship is a skill requiring substantial practice. Statistics from our 20th century wars suggest that perhaps millions of rounds of ammunition are expended to inflict one battlefield death. Handguns are especially difficult to shoot accurately and proficiency in their use is a hard-won skill. The one-handed, off-handed hit with the sixgun, from the back of a running or rearing horse, is pure fantasy, unless you happen to be Annie Oakley! Likewise with rifles from horses! The accuracy misconception is related to the fact that the recoil of real guns is not typically portrayed in the visual media. There is no Newton's Law on television and in movies. In fact, learning to counteract the effects of recoil is part of the training necessary to use guns.

Rifle shots at incredible distances with no telescopic sights are another dimension of this stereotype. Even with telescopic sights, rifles are difficult to use accurately if the telescope has not been carefully adjusted.

6. GUNS HAVE INEXHAUSTIBLE SUPPLIES OF AMMUNITION IN THEIR MAGAZINES.

This stereotype increases the sense of threat represented by firearms. They can just keep on shooting! In fact, reloading is a rather cumbersome process in most instances; ammunition is bulky as are extra magazines to hold the ammunition. The portrayal of automatic arms is especially guilty of this misrepresentation. The normal magazine of a submachinegun will be emptied in 2-3 seconds if the trigger is held back. The first shot may be an aimed and accurate one; the rest of the magazine will cut an arc above the target. In other words, the difficulty of controlling an automatic firearm when firing is almost totally ignored by the visual media.

7. THE PRESENCE OR POSSESSION OF A GUN TENDS TO STIMULATE ITS USE IN MOSTLY NEGATIVE WAYS.

This stereotype stems from the increasing appearance of automatic type weapons the "aggression-eliciting effects of the presence of weapons" on research subjects.[3] However, attempts to replicate this work have turned up opposite results: in the presence of weapons, provoked aggression often is associated with the studied, careful, intentional avoidance of the use of weapons.[4] Those who create the story-lines for the visual media almost never include gun uses which are pro-social, helping rather than hurting, defending rather than attacking, defusing rather than escalating a hostile encounter, reassuring rather than unbalancing its possesser.

[3] L. Berkowitz and L. LePage, "Weapons as Aggression-Eliciting Stimuli," *Journal of Personality and Social Psychology,* Vol. 7 (1967), 202-207.

[4] Desmond Ellis, Paul Weinir, and Louie Miller III, "Does the Trigger Pull the Finger? An Experimental Test of Weapons as Aggression-Eliciting Stimuli," *Sociometry,* Vol. 34 (1971), 453-465.

8. HANDGUNS ARE JUST AS POWERFUL AND DESTRUCTIVE AS LONGGUNS.

The existing recovery statistics reveal that 90% or more of all persons shot with handguns recover from their wounds while only 20-30% of those shot with longguns recover.[5] The above stereotype neglects to distinguish between types of firearms and levels of power possessed by those arms.

9. AUTOMATIC WEAPONS ARE INCREDIBLY DESTRUCTIVE AND INCREASINGLY USED IN CRIMES.

This stereotype stems from the increasing appearance of automatic type weapons in portrayals of armed violence in the fictional media. Their pyrotechnical effects are spectacular indeed. Automatic arms can be collected by private citizens who must comply with very stringent licensing procedures. Such possession has been legal for more than 50 years. Although automatic weapons seem to be used increasingly in the "drug wars", there is no evidence that licensed collectors are a source of such arms.

10. GUNS ARE SYMBOLS OF POWER, FORCE, IMPENDING VIOLENCE, DESTRUCTIVENESS.

This stereotype is more contextual than substantive. It concerns the style with which the guns are portrayed in the media. Consider how close-up shots of guns are used. They typically convey a sense of menace, impendinq violence — a revolver being loaded and its cylinder or loadinq gate being snapped shut, the magazine of a semi-automatic pistol being jammed "home", a long, sinister-looking cartridge sliding into the breech of a rifle, the startling "clack-clack" of a riot shotgun being pumped into a state of readiness. Do we ever see guns shown as art objects, mechanical marvels, or any other positive image? Seldom in my experience!

11. AMERICA IS MORE VIOLENT THAN EVER WITH AN INCREASING DEPENDENCE ON PRIVATE ARMAMENTS IN THE HANDS OF ITS CITIZENS.

This stereotype emerged with the elaborate post mortems conducted after the shocking, violent incidents punctuating the 1960's. Gerbner, et al find evidence that media fictional content contributes significantly to perceptions of the amount of violence in society:

... in prime-time television drama aired from 1969 through 1977, 64 percent of major characters and 30 percent of all characters (major and minor) were involved in violence as perpetrators, victims, or both. According to the 1970 census, there were only .32 violent crimes per 100 persons. In the world of television, therefore, one has between a 30 and 64 percent chance of being involved in violence, but in the real world only a one-third of one percent chance.[6]

5 Silver and Kates.

6 George Gebner, Larry Gross, Marilyn Jackson-Beeck, Suzanne Jeffries-Fox, and Nancy Signorielli, "Cultural Indicators: Violence Profile No. 9; Violence on the Screen," *Journal of Communication*, Vol. 28 (Summer, 1978), 194.

Sources of Fictional Media Stereotypes

What are the possible sources of these distorted images of firearms which appear in the fictional media? One study of the various actual uses made of firearms in recreation, hobbies and occupations suggests an answer:

> There is a disturbing schizophrenia . . ., a strange and irrational divergence between the media's almost universally anti-gun journalistic coverage and its wholehearted fictional commitment to the gun as THE power and glamour object, and the resultant middle-ground reality gap is communicated to media consumers. . . . (T)he shared pool of knowledge about gun lore, craft, technology, use and the places guns occupy in people's lives, originates in the realm of the fantastic as presented by Hollywood. With such origins, this knowledge may or may not reflect reality with any accuracy, but it is all that is available through the media, and in a lot of places it cannot be checked by observation. . . . (M)ost media professionals were born to the urban middle-class life and . . . their social milieu is not the America in which guns are familiar objects of daily life.[7]

Thus, the foregoing statement alleges that those responsible for producing the fictional media distort the nature of firearms out of ignorance or ideological myopia. Of course, the driving, guiding "engine" of the dramatic themes in fictional episodes may also overcome concerns for accuracy in representation of firearms. The entertainment media are in the business of attracting audiences for their sponsors. Audiences are attracted by the exciting, unusual, dramatic themes which are the stable fare of the entertainment media. Firearms are often the tools of good versus evil in these stories. Regardless of the source, these stereotyped images may be the only experience with firearms that a sizeable portion of the media audience ever receive.

Consequences of Firearms Stereotypes in the Fictional Visual Media

Direct evidence of the effects of these stereotypes on media audiences is not available. However, indirect evidence may be extracted from studies of effects of portrayed violence on the subsequent behaviors of audiences. A generation of empirical studies has attempted to illuminate the issue. Although the evidence is equivocal, the common wisdom accepts the anti-social behavioral effects of excessive

---

[7] Patrick Carr and George W. Gardner, *Gun People* (Garden City: Dolphin-Doubleday, 1985), pp. IX-X.

violence appearing in the entertainment media.[8] An obvious implication of this "wisdom" is that portrayals of violence with firearms may provoke some real instances of "copycat" firearms use.

Another provocative line of investigation has examined the effects of television viewing on the perceptions of the audience regarding the existence of various kinds of risks in the real world. This research has concluded that people who watch the most T.V. are more likely to perceive themselves as the eventual victims of violent or property crimes than are those who consume less T.V.[9] These results, however, have not been replicated by other researchers in cultures outside the U.S.[10] What I find illuminating about Gerbner's work is something he and his colleagues do not pursue in any detail. Their studies demonstrate that heavy viewers of television (more than 4 hours per day) are more likely to overestimate the dangers of various situations and the occurrence of various events than are light viewers (2 hours or less per day). However, they neglect to reflect on the fact that sizeable proportions (typically around 50%) of their light viewers also overestimate the risks discussed: percent of people involved in violence; how often police are required to use force; how often police shoot fleeing suspects.[11] In short, perceptions of social reality are distorted by light viewers as well as heavy viewers. Is that a result of television viewing? In a later report, Gerbner, et al, in fact, suggest that television is a cultural influence which no one escapes:

> Our approach reflects the hypothesis that the more time one spends "living" in the world of television, the more likely one is to report perceptions

[8] A. Bandura and R.H. Walters, *Social Learning and Personality Development* (New York: Holt, Rinehart and Winston, 1963); S. Feshbach and R.D. Singer, *Television and Aggression* (San Francisco: Jossey-Bass, 1971); R.D. Parke, L. Berkowitz, J.P. Leyens, S. West, and R.J. Sebastian, "The Effects of Repeated Exposure to Movie Violence on Aggressive Behavior in Juvenile Delinquent Boys: Field Experimental Studies," in L. Berkowitz (ed.) *Advances in Experimental Social Psychology*, Vol. 8 (New York: Academic Press, 1957); P.H. Tannenbaum and D. Zillman, "Emotional Arousal in the Facilitation of Aggression Through Communication," also in Berkowitz; M. Carruthers and P. Taggart, "Vagotonicity of Violence: Biochemical and Cardiac Responses to Violent Films and Television Programs," *British Medical Journal*, Vol. 2 (1973), 384-389; and William J. McGuire, "The Myth of Massive Media Impact: Savagings and Salvagings," in George Comstock (ed.) *Public Communication and Behavior*, Vol. 1 (Academic Press, Harcourt Brace Jovanovich, 1986), pp. 175-257.

[9] George Gerbner and Larry Gross, "Living with Television: The Violence Profile," *Journal of Communication*, Vol. 26 (Spring, 1976), 173-199; and Gerbner, Cross, Michael F. Eleey, Marilyn Jackson-Beeck, Suzanne Jeffries-Fox, and Nancy Signorielli, "T.V. Violence Profile No. 8: The Highlights; Sex, Violence and the Rules of the Game," *Journal of Communication*, Vol. 27 (Spring, 1977), 171-180.

[10] J.M. Wober, "Televised Violence and Paranoid Perception: The View From Britain," *Public Opinion Quarterly*, Vol. 42 (1978), 315-321; and Anthony N. Doob and Glenn E. MacDonald, "Television Viewing and Fear of Victimization: Is the Relationship Causal?" *Journal of Personality and Social Psychology*, Vol. 37 (1979), 170-179.

[11] Gerbner, Gross, Signorielli, Jackson-Beeck, and Michael Morgan, "The Demonstration of Power: Violence Profile No. 10; Growing Up with Television," *Journal of Communication*, Vol. 29 (Summer, 1979), 191 and 194.

148.

of social reality which can be traced to (or are congruent with) television's representation of life and society. . . .

At the same time, we must acknowledge that even those whom we designate as "light" viewers may be watching up to 14 hours of television each week! Further, few people — even the "absolute" non-viewers — may be able to avoid or escape the consequences of living in a television saturated society. . . .[12]

Consequently, it seems reasonable to postulate that distorted perceptions of social reality are also likely to result from witnessing stereotypical portrayals of firearms as cultural artifacts by the visual media.

I contend that the stereotypes of firearms identified above are likely to lead viewers with no direct experience of firearms to view them as overly dangerous, too easy to use, too easy to acquire, exerting anti-social effects on their possessors, etc. These distorted impressions do not necessarily line up support for one side or the other of the gun-control debate. The heightened sense of risk associated with firearms in these stereotypes buttresses the arguments of the anti-gun forces. On the other hand, the distortions regarding the ease with which firearms can be used may encourage naive citizens to acquire arms for self-protection, thus reinforcing the pro-gun position.

Effects of Experience with Firearms: An Hypothesis

What effects on perceptions of firearms result from audience members having had some experience with firearms? Audience members who have had direct contact with firearms are able and likely to discount the distortions contained in the media images. Those with no direct contact have no reality checks to insulate them from gradually absorbing the images available in the visual media.

As a partial test of this hypothesis consider some data from a study which examined problems with traditional means of public opinion polling.[13] The subjects of this study (N=467) were nonprobability samples of students in three different institutions in Illinois. I have no reason to assume the samples from the different institutions differ significantly from the parent student populations; however, some unrecognized systematic distortion may exist. Included in that study was a rough measure of familiarity with firearms: "When growing up, did your family own firearms?" If media effects and other sources of information regarding firearms aside from direct experience are distorting the "facts" about firearms in only random ways, then responses to the following assertions about the role of firearms in American culture should exhibit only random differences or no differences at all when we compare responses of those with some firearms experience with responses of those with none. In other words, distorted images can convey two false impressions: firearms are more dangerous than the facts support; firearms are less dangerous than

[12] Gerbner, Gross, Morgan, and Signorielli, *Violence Profile No. 11: Trends in Network Television Drama and Viewer Conceptions of Social Reality 1967-1979* (Philadelphia: The Annenberg School of Communications, University of Pennsylvania, 1980), p. 31.

[13] Richard L. Hummel, "Bullets, Blades and Black Belts: The Sociology of Self-Defense," paper presented at the Popular Culture Association National Meeting, Montreal, 1987.

the facts show. If experience with firearms reduces the likelihood of distorted perceptions which exaggerate rather than underestimate the dangers, then the differences in the following data should tend to fall in one direction only.

Table 1 contains "agree" responses to a number of firearms' issues elicited from subjects with and without family experience with firearms.

TABLE 1: FAMILY EXPERIENCE WITH FIREARMS AND OTHER ATTITUDES

OPINION ITEM	NO EXPERIENCE WITH FIREARMS	EXPERIENCE WITH FIREARMS
	% Agreeing	% Agreeing
1. Firearms should be much more difficult to buy in our society.	84.8	71.0
2. Firearms are misused way too much in our current culture.	90.6	79.8
4. The misuse of firearms is primarily due to the influence they have on people who possess them.	78.0	65.1
5. I would prefer to live in a society where fewer people own firearms.	78.5	57.0
6. Knowledge that my neighbors own firearms makes me very nervous and worried about the safety of my family and the whole neighborhood.	38.0	12.2
27. Handguns make me nervous when I see them in person.	62.5	40.5
28. I intend to teach my children the safe use of firearms.	41.4	72.4
29. I was carefully taught how to use firearms safely.	25.7	64.1
30. I plan to teach my children to avoid ownership of firearms because of dangers of accidents.	51.6	25.1
31. I am afraid to have even unloaded guns around the house.	46.9	14.8
32. I am afraid to keep a loaded gun around the house.	74.5	55.5

33. I would be uneasy visiting a friend if I knew s/he had a loaded firearm in the house.	33.5	21.4
35. Keeping a firearm in my home reassures me and keeps me calm.	21.4	40.3
37. Firearms owned by citizens cause more crimes than they prevent through thefts of those arms, improper use by citizens, etc.	59.4	41.2
38. The protections, real or imagined, that firearms provide their owners are worth the costs resulting from their misuse, theft, etc.	17.3	27.2
45. If I had a daughter who worked in a dangerous area or during dangerous hours, I would urge her to take lessons in the use of a handgun to defend herself.	32.1	42.9
46. Women would be most likely to cause harm to themselves and others if they acquire handguns for self-defense.	28.4	21.9
50. The only purpose of a handgun is to kill things.	30.2	24.0
54. People who try to use handguns for self-defense are more likely to have them taken away and used against them.	49.2	41.1

There is no random pattern among these data. With every answer subjects with no direct experience with firearms manifest more fear regarding the presence, uses, and misuses of firearms than do subjects with direct experience. The probability of these consistent differences occurring by chance in this sample, when only random differences exist in the population, is less than 1 in a 100. (P .01).[14] Thus, these data support a linkage between experience with firearms and perceptions of firearms. (Recall, however, that these data are from nonrandom samples.) If you have had some direct experience with firearms, you are less likely to fear them. But why is lack of experience consistently associated with greater fears? My earlier argument contends that distorted usages in the fictional media seem a likely cause.

Summary and Conclusions

To review my argument: The fictional media content affects conceptions of reality among the audience regarding the risks and dangers in real life. Firearms are represented in the fictional media with various distorted stereotypes which especially affect perceptions of firearms held by media audiences who have little or no direct experience with firearms. These audiences are also the voters who are asked to judge measures calling for more stringent controls on access to firearms. If their conceptions of firearms contain exaggerated images of the dangers surrounding firearms use, as voters they are more likely to support additional control measures. Therefore, these distorted images of firearms represent more than just the exercise of poetic license in the pursuit of entertainment; but, in fact, weigh in on the side of the forces advocating increased controls over private ownership of firearms.

What is to be gained by more accurate portrayals of firearms and their uses: A reduced sense of the alleged threats they represent by their continued presence in our cultural inventory; a reduced level of violent themes in our media fare; a more neutral environment in which the debate over private ownership of arms can be carried on.

Chapter 12

Popular and Media Images of Firearms in American Culture

by
Eugene H. Balof

A Regional-Cultural Dichotomy: The McClure-Volkmer Act

Throughout 1985 and into 1986, the nations' attention was focused on the most significant piece of gun control legislation since the sweeping Gun Control Act of 1968. The new bill, officially termed the Firearm Owners Protection Act, and more popularly known as the McClure-Volkmer Act, represented what some saw as a counterrevolution in the gradual shift to greater federal regulation of firearms. The bill, which carried the endorsement of the National Rifle Association but less than total support of NRA membership, modified in a number of significant respects the 1968 Act. Among the changes wrought by the new law were greater freedom for interstate transfer of firearms and legalization of mail order of ammunition following verification of the purchaser's age and legal ability to purchase ammunition and components. A further, although less publicized aspect, was a ban on the private acquisition of new automatic weapons (machine guns). This provision was added to the legislation in the House of Representatives and accepted by the Senate, where the NRA did not actively oppose it. Other gun owner groups opposed the bill on this basis less from a fondness for increased fire power than from fear that the bill's restrictions might weaken the strict defense of Second Amendment freedoms to keep and bear arms. Opposition was thus motivated more by ideology than by any real fear of loss of personal liberty.

Among opponents of firearms ownership, the McClure-Volkmer Act was seen as a significant defeat. Various unsuccessful attempts were made to amend or gut the bill's more objectionable features. Despite opposition, the proposal finally cleared the U. S. House of Representatives by a 292-130 vote on April 10, 1986, was approved by the Senate in a voice vote, and was signed by President Reagan on May 1986.

As the most significant piece of federal firearms legislation of the decade, McClure-Volkmer attracted much interest and lobbying efforts from all sides, and individual votes on the measure were significant in many 1986 House election campaigns. It could well have been termed a bipartisan vote, for not only were the sponsors from different parties but voting cut across party lines. Republicans largely supported the bill while Democratic voting patterns were far less uniform. One aspect of voting in the House that went relatively unnoticed was the distribution of support. Pro gun support was heavily rooted in the nation's west, south, and rural areas. States of the Old Confederacy were particularly solid, with representatives from that region voting "aye" or announced as favorable by an astonishing margin of 101-13. Of the "nays", more than half came from the increasingly cosmopolitan and urbanized state of Florida. If Kentucky and West Virginia are added to the tally, the South Congressional delegations voted an even more impressive 112-13. (See Appendix).

Further evidence of voting support comes from analysis of two sharply divided states, Illinois and New York. Each contains a major urban center at one end of the state with rural hinterlands across much of the rest. Downstate Illinois, just as Upstate New York, is rural Republican, with only Democratic enclaves in St. Clair county and Buffalo to disturb the clarity of each state's political map. Illinois Republicans, largely from the state's corn and hogs belt, voted 5-2 for McClure-Volkmer, while New York's suburban and upstate Republicans were an even more solid 13-1. Illinois Democratts on the other hand, voted "no" by a 13-1 count. The New Yorkers were again more unified, the Democrats castinq 17 "no" votes against a single "aye".

While party affiliation is suggestive of voting patterns, geography is more useful. In seventeen states, all Democratic party congressmen broke ranks to vote "yes". Each of the seventeen unanimous states was southern or western.

Although both regions of the nation can no longer be seen as purely rural in population, with the growth of sprawling boom towns in Denver, Phoenix, Atlanta, and Miami, the South and West remain rural in character. The cowboy image is deeply rooted in the nation's folklore, and the urban cowboy may serve as a vicarious masquerade for the harried commuter in Dallas or Houston. More subtle but deeper may be the South's attachment to what historian Clement Eaton has called the "Country Gentleman ideal", a preference for rural living, even at the price of reduced economic means, that rendered the South of the last century a land of farms and small towns rather than one of cities.[1] Firearms ownership remains an essential element of both the myth and actual history of rural America, from tales of the mountaineers who mowed down the King's regulars at New Orleans in 1815 to Wyatt Earp facing down evildoers at the OK Corral. Under these conditions, the attachment of rural Americans, and those whose frame of reference remains rural, to guns makes gun control an altogether unappealing social option. Bob Dix, cartoonist for the *Manchester* (New Hampshire) *Union-Leader* posed this attitude in a splendid if unsubtle cartoon depicting a menacing figure labeled "Anti-Gun Crowd" pointing to a hunter, shouting "We've got to get guns out of the hands of these nuts." Particularly arresting is that the hunter, leaning against a tree in the forest, possesses a straight-jawed, manly profile, his rifle to one side and his loyal dog at the other.[2] To Dix, and

[1] Clement Eaton, "The Country Gentleman Ideal," in Monroe L. Billington (ed.) *The South: A Central Theme?* (New York: Holt, Rinehart and Winston, 1969), p. 48.

[2] Chip Elliot, "The Case Against Gun Control," in David L. Bender and Bruno Leone (eds.) *Crime and Criminals* (St. Paul: Greenhaven, 1984), p. 157.

millions of other Americans, the gun is a source of virtue, be it sport, recreation, personal protection, or simply pride of ownership. Research by Barbara Stenross has shown that while reasons for ownership vary rather widely, in fact, to the extent that owners may have little in common, a common assumption remains that it is fully proper and fitting to own as many guns as one wishes so long as use remains within legal limits.[3] Other researchers have noted the association, particularly in the South, of guns with purposes of sport, outdoor recreation, and protection.[4]

Examiners of the cultural implications and associations of guns have tended to focus on the gun owners themselves rather than on the media influence and choices of the owners. Although general interest media, particularly at the national level, tend to ignore non-criminal uses of firearms, an impressively long list of national and regional magazines serves the interests of the gun owner and outdoor enthusiast. These can be divided into three rather discrete groups. Best known are general outdoor magazines, including *Outdoor Life, Field and Stream,* and *Sports Afield.* These publications focus on hunting and fishing activities, and to a lesser extent the boating, camping and backpacking activities that support hunting and fishing. A tacit assumption of these journals is that guns play an essential role in the natural world, and by their age (some of these magazines have been publishing continuously for over a hundred years), circulation and presence on virtually every newsstand in America play an essential role in the culture of the gun owner as naturalist. Indeed, the most prestigious job in firearms journalism may be the position of shooting editor of *Outdoor Life,* a post held for decades by the late Jack O'Conner and presently by Jim Carmichel.

A second category is the more specialized field of hunting magazines. Some of the more prominent examples include *American Hunter* (published by the National Rifle Association), *Petersen's Hunting,* and *North American Hunter.* As may be expected, the amount of space devoted in these magazines to guns and gun issues is significantly greater than in the general outdoor press. This is not to suggest that guns are a dominant topic, in fact their role is more one of a tool than the central purpose of the sport. This editorial choice is consistent with Stenross' findings about the hunters.

The third area of the shooting press is those publications specifically concerned with the guns themselves. These are technical, specialized treatments of tools. The purpose of the firearm may vary, be it hunting, target competition, protection, or military. Publications of this category include NRA's flagship *American Rifleman, Guns and Ammo, Shooting Times, Rifle, Handloader,* and a host of sporadically published magazines, annuals and guides.

[3] Barbara Stenross in Chapter 5 of this volume.

[4] Jo Dixon and Alan J. Lizotte, "Gun Ownership and the 'Southern Subculture of Violence,' " *American Journal of Sociology,* No. 2 (1987), 383-405; Lizote and David Bordua, "Firearms Ownership for Sport and Protection: Two Divergent models," *American Sociological Review,* Vol. 45 (1980), 229-244; and James D. Wright, Peter H. Rossi, and Kathleen Daly, *Under the Gun: Weapons, Crime and Violence in America* (New York: Aldine, 1983).

From these publications comes the gun owners view of him- or herself, although admittedly in an idealized sense. (The addition of the *her* to the previous sentence is inserted not merely to avoid the fatal sin of sexism. An increasing number of articles in these publications are written by or for women, particularly in the specialized hunting magazines.) This world view is frequently subtle and secondary to the purpose of the information presented, but at times the message is central, reaching its highest expression in a modernized version of what formerly was called the "huntin' story".

THE HUNTIN' STORY AS A GENRE

The huntin' story does not have to be about hunting, although most are in some sense. The huntin' story may be about a particularly useful piece of equipment, a famous firearms shooter or designer, or a piece of what might be termed peripheral equipment. Many huntin' stories are about wildlife. Three examples from three different publications illustrate some of the dimensions of this genre.

Gregory Miller, in *North American Whitetail,* a magazine whose masthead proclaims "The Magazine Devoted to the Serious Trophy Deer Hunter", described techniques of using evidence from trees and saplings to locate deer. Although nominally technical and instructive, Miller clearly telegraphs his views of hunting, guns, and the outdoor world in his opening paragraphs:

I had been in my tree stand only thirty minutes when I first heard the buck coming. He was making no apparent attempt to be quiet, but he was also in no big hurry. In fact, I could hear the deer breaking branches and busting brush for at least 25 minutes before I got my first look at him.

As he stepped clear of the thick tamarack on the edge of the swamp, only 30 yards separated us. At that . . . The time was 5:25 p.m. on October 25, 1986. The place was Douglas County in the northwest part of my home state of Wisconsin.[5]

Although Hemingway's reputation as the premier writer of huntin' stories seems unlikely to be challenged, Miller's narrative, really unnecessary to an instructive article, places the reader in the frame of reference appropriate to the gunner's cultural world. As he takes the reader from the sighting of the buck to the weighing of the trophy, Miller establishes that we are in a world beyond the mere technical.

Later in his story, Miller, after describing some of the more useful and arcane elements of practical and theoretical woodcraft, describes another specific hunt, with all details of color, wind and sounds recalled, as well as the particular cartridge and bullet used (.270 Winchester, 130-grain bullet). Finally, he assures us that "Believe me, it's no real chore to learn how to 'read' and decipher buck rubs. And it's a weapon I think every serious buck hunter should have in his or her arsenal."[6]

Another technical article, this time about squirrel hunting, was written by Terry Madewell for *Alabama Game & Fish.* This publication and its fellows represent

[5] Gregory Miller, "How to 'Tree' a Trophy Whitetail," *North American Whitetail,* Vol. 5 (1987), 44.
[6] Ibid., 83.

something of a triumph of modern outdoor journalism marketing. Published by Game & Fish Publications of Marietta, Georgia, *Alabama Game & Fish* is a modular journal. Using a core of general articles, the central publisher fleshes out a state magazine with articles specific to the state or region. The result may be Alabama, Tennessee, Illinois, or Arkansas *Game & Fish,* but the general appearance, as well as many of the advertisements, remain the same. Game & Fish articles closely follow the huntin' story model.

Madewell begins:

I slipped into the woods as lightly as possible, trying my best not to alert any squirrels already up and moving about. I was a few minutes later getting into the woods than originally intended, and I felt certain some of the early risers had left the nest in search of something to eat.

I took about 30 small steps into the hardwood stand, then stopped to look and listen. The rain from the previous day had soaked the leaves and the damp leaf litter made my entry fairly quiet.[7]

Over a third of total column space in Madewell's article is occupied by the events of that autumn morning, the sights, sounds and smells which anyone who has experienced the woods and hunting can appreciate. Superficially, the introductory remarks would seem unnecessary to the article but they remain an essential part of the rhetorical form of the huntin' story.

A more traditional and unabashed huntin' story by James E. Churchill appeared in *Petersen's Hunting* and recounted the hunt for the largest bear ever taken by a hunter in the state of Michigan. In this form of story the narrative component, the telling of what the hunter/shooter did, can occupy the entire piece and in this case it does. But Churchill's opening paragraphs are scarcely different from the others:

It was nearly dusk in Michigan's Porcupine Mountains, and the lone hiker was awed by the brilliant sunset reflected in the clear, cold water of Lake Superior.

He dropped his backpack and walked a few steps to a better vantage point. Distracted by the incredible beauty of the panorama, he didn't hear the soft footfall behind him until the gigantic bear was only 10 feet away.[8]

Lest the reader develop premature sympathy for the bear, it should be noted that Churchill goes on to describe the bear killing the hiker, a constant reminder that while the natural world is beautiful and healthy, it can also be a very dangerous place. This is another essential facet of the huntin' story. The shooter does not bring death to the world, animals seldom die of natural causes, and the gun is just as much a part of the natural world as the tooth or the claw.

---

[7] Terry Madewell, "Tactics for Nut-Cuttin' Squirrels," *Alabama Game & Fish,* Vol. 9 (1987), 27.

[8] James E. Churchill, "Michigan's Biggest Bear," *Petersen's Hunting,* Vol. 2 (1987), 72.

To complete the narrative, after the killing of the hiker, the bear continued to wander until it encountered Ray Bray, an experienced hunter who through woodcraft, skill and marksmanship ultimately brought home a 506 pound black bear, the largest ever encountered in his home state.

The gun article in any of the three elements of the outdoor press may take many forms, depending in large part on the topic. After examination of over a thousand individual articles in national and regional magazines from 1982 to 1987, five distinct themes become clear. The majority of articles do not contain all of them, but elements are present in virtually all articles in the outdoor press. Taken collectively they form the assumptions and cultural heart of firearms ownership in America.

1. **The gun owner is a patriot.** This is perhaps the weakest theme, and appears most strongly in the gun-specific press. This can be easily explained by the fact that the categories of general outdoor and hunting-specific magazines are international. They devote significant attention to international hunting and activities by foreigners, Canadians in particular. Indeed, hunting magazines take great pains to use the term *North* American in general writing and in titles such as *North American Whitetail* or *North American Hunter*.

In the gun press, however, the patriotism theme is strong. Historical articles describe successful American use of arms in battle, an ongoing element of firearms mythology. Other articles note restrictions on gun ownership in other countries. Even the hunting press is not immune to this appeal. *North American Hunter* is currently running a series titled "How Good We've Got It" which contrasts the freedoms to own guns and to hunt that are enjoyed by Americans and Canadians compared to conditions in other democratic Western nations.[9] Another series, in *Rifle* magazine profiles "Famous Riflemen", frequently military or quasi-military figures such as Theodore Roosevelt, Sgt. Alvin C. York, and "Buffalo" Bill Cody.

Bearing arms is thus seen as not only a defense of the nation, but more importantly, the possession, use, and interest in arms is seen as a uniquely American (or perhaps North American) trait. The gun owner is an American just as the American is a gun owner.

2. **The gun owner is social.** This theme is an incongruent one, since few activities are more solitary than shooting, whatever the purpose or target, and the specific activity of hunting would seem to offer one of the few opportunities to escape crowds. Despite this, the community, family, and social relevance of hunting is a strong theme. "Deer camp" stories of past hunts are a staple item but are giving way to more family-oriented stories as the entry of more women into hunting and shooting displaces the male-bonding aspects of outdoor sports. This theme appears even in highly technical articles. In an article on the 7x57 Mauser cartridge, a topic sufficiently arcane to all but the most dediated shooters, Finn Aagaard, one of the most prolific writers for NRA publications, noted the preferences of his wife and son

---

9 Tim Eisele, "How Good We've Got It," *North American Hunter* (November/December, 1987), 32-35.

regarding the cartridge for hunting use.[10] Another common theme is the author's reference to a favorite gun or cartridge having been a gift of a father or relative, or may express the hope that a new purchase will serve one's son as well.

The emphasis on social aspects may be more than myth, at least where hunters are concerned. A study of Wisconsin deer hunters indicated that enthusiasts rated "companionship with friends" as the sixth most important of twenty hunting satisfactions, while "companionship with family" ranked eighth.[11]

3. **The gun owner appreciates nature.** This is a far more common theme in general outdoor and hunting-specific publications than in the gun-specific press. This too is supported by actual attitudes. The Wisconsin study already mentioned showed "nature appreciation" to rank third among hunter satisfactions. Among waterfowl hunters exclusively, nature ranked first, ahead of other satisfactions such as hunting success.[12]

The nature appreciation aspects of gun use show most clearly in the formula huntin' story which by custom begins with a first person account of the author's personal experiences. The narrative component of the story is essential, for it serves to establish the author's membership in the society of those who understand the natural world. The gun is part of that world. Writer Gary Frederick describes a conversation between a father and son. When Tommy asks his father if he killed a deer, the father replies, "No, son, I harvested him, much like a farmer harvests his crop. This deer is part of God's crop that we are allowed to harvest so a healthy new crop can grow."[13] Other articles relate the efforts of current and past shooters to protect endangered species and expand wildlife knowledge.[14]

4. **The gun owner is able to survive through his weapons.** To some extent this represents technology triumphant, as modern weaponry enables the citizen to overcome the dangers inherent in nature. From this idea it is only a brief leap of logic to the firearm-as-protection theme which is found in the exclusively gun press, although the writing tends to emphasize the urban wilderness rather than the woods, and handguns rather than shotguns or rifles.

Consistent with this theme is a common formula article appearing throughout the shooting press, the question of what gun-cartridge combination is adequate in power for a specified application. These debates, which never seem to be resolved to anyone's satisfaction, underscore the almost universal theme of the gun owner's ability to control and protect himself in his environment.[15]

10 Finn Aagaard, "The 7x57mm Mauser," *American Rifleman* Vol. 11 (1986), 71.

11 Bob Jackson and Bob Norton, "Hunting as a Social Experience," *Deer & Deer Hunting*, Vol. 2 (1987), 40.

12 Ibid.

13 Gary Frederick, "The Greatest Gift," *Deer & Deer Hunting*, Vol. 1 (1984), 79.

14 Mary Nelson and Michael Vadine, "Who is Stealing Our Wildlife?" *American Hunter*, Vol. 5 (1985), 14-15; and Lonnie Williamson, "Is Acid Rain Killing Our Waterfowl?" *American Hunter*, Vol. 6 (1987), 24-25.

15 Richard P. Smith, "The 30-30," *Deer & Deer Hunting*, Vol. 2 (1986), 48-53.

5. **The gun owner respects tradition and the teachings of his elders.** Almost without exception, the entire outdoor press publishes numerous articles on the field's heroes of antiquity and more recent past. These may be hunters, shooters, designers, or a combination of all. Each is described in terms of a teacher or father figure, and those whose careers were less than successful are generally considered as being ahead of the times. The careers of Hiram Berdan, John Moses Browning, Theodore Roosevelt, Bill Ruger, Roy Weatherby, et al., are examined as role models of skill and dedication. The similarity to Horatio Alger stories is most striking, for the great majority of firearms designers in the United States of yesterday and today were self-made entrepreneurs. Being even today a specialized craft industry in which an individual can excel, the firearms industry offers products frequently designed and marketed by a single individual. In fact, in the past half century the principle battle rifles of the United States Army have been designed by two individuals, John Garand and Eugene Stoner.

Given this factual backdrop, the outdoor-shooting press strongly emphasizes the history of past practitioners as models. Little wonder that the shooter feels kinship with past hunters and shooters and sales of books by long-since deceased or retired persons remain strong in the shooting media.[16]

To summarize, the outdoor press offers a cultural outlook that emphasizes the congruity of the gun both with nature and with virtue. Firearms are not simply a nasty solution to a nasty problem, but are in and of themselves a positive good.

NATIONAL MEDIA CULTURAL ASSUMPTIONS

Views of guns and gun owners as presented in the national media are far less clear. Criticism of the national media has been an ongoing concern since Vice President Agnew's charges of nearly a generation ago, but in recent years the critics seem to have been gaining. The National Opinion Research Center reported in 1983 that only 13.7% of the general public expressed "great confidence" in the press, while television rated but 12.7% confidence.[17] Particularly critical cases have been made against network television news reporting of defense and economic issues.[18]

It is far more difficult to identify media views of firearms questions. Critics have noted a strong identification of newspaper editorial policies, particularly those of major urban dailies, with anti-gun groups.[19] To a great extent, however, media coverage reflects sins of omission rather than commission. Peaceful firearms uses receive scant coverage. Although target shooting and other competitive shooting

---

[16] Elliot, 157.

[17] William A. Henry III, "Journalism Under Fire," *Time*, No. 25 (1983), 79.

[18] Joshua Muravchick and John E. Haynes, "CBS vs. Defense," *Commentary*, No. 3 (1981), 44-55; and Paul H. Weaver, "The Networks vs. Recovery," *Commentary*, No. 1 (1984), 35-40.

[19] William R. Tonso, "Guns and the Media," *American Rifleman*, No. 4 (1986), 42-43, 78-79, and Paul Blackman, "Mugged by the Media," *American Rifleman*, No. 6 (1987), 34-36, 80-81.

sports attract large numbers of devotees, the results of such events are rarely reported. There is some justification in the journalistic sense for this preference. Few sporting events are poorer suited to the spectator or more esoteric to the casual observer. Similarly, the non-lethal use of firearms for personal defense is a less newsworthy story than a mass murder for the simple reason that no one is hurt. Standard practice dictates that blood equals ink, and a deterred crime is not a particularly newsworthy event. Nonetheless, the relative absence of hunting-related articles in the general media seems unusual.

In his exhaustive study of the coverage of the Tet offensive in Vietnam in 1968, Peter Braestrup, found that errors and omissions were produced less by conscious bias than by the cultural view and work habits of journalists.[20] A similar case may be coverage of firearms issues. To a great extent, media leaders share a background quite unlike that of the general public and particularly unlike the world described in the outdoor press. In 1981 Lichter and Rothman published a study of the characteristics of the media elite, "journalists and broadcasters at the most influential media outlets, including the *New York Times,* the *Washington Post,* the *Wall Street Journal, Time* magazine, *Newsweek, U.S. News and World Report,* and the news departments at CBS, NBC, ABC, and PBS, along with major public broadcasting stations." Persons responsible for news content were sampled.

Backgrounds of media elite were most atypical of the nation as a whole. "Geographically, they are drawn primarily from the northern industrial states, especially from the northeast corridor. Two-fifths come from three states; New York, New Jersey, and Pennsylvania. Another 10 percent hail from New England, and almost one in five was raised in the big industrial states just to the west-Illinois, Indiana, Michigan, and Ohio. Thus over two-thirds of the media elite come from these three clusters of states."[21]

This provides some quantification of Theodore White once called the "Perfumed Stockade", a "twenty block by four block area in which all the communications in America are gathered into the single most complicated switchboard of words, phrases, an ideas in the world."[22] The concept of urban, northeastern America, New York in particular, wielding sinister and disproportionate power is hardly a new one, but not utterly without some basis. Lichter and Rothman summarized the personal backgrounds of the media elite: "(S)ubstantial number of the media elite grew up at some distance from the social and cultural traditions of small town 'middle America'. Instead, they were drawn from big cities in the northeast and north central states."[23]

[20] Peter Braestrup, *Big Story* (Garden City, New Jersey: Anchor, 1978)

[21] Robert S. Lichter and Stanley Rothman, "Media and Business Elites," *Public Opinion,* No. 5 (1981), 43.

[22] Theodore H. White, *The Making of the President 1964* (New York: Signet, 1965), p. 86.

[23] Lichter and Rothman, 43.

In consequence it is hardly surprising to discover that differences exist between media and the public, especially gun-owning public, on firearms issues. A 1985 study found 78% of print journalists at the 621 most read newspapers favored stricter handgun controls.[24] Despite some problems with public opinion polling on gun control issues, this was clearly a much higher level of support for legislation than with the general public.

It seems extremely unlikely that any methodology will be discovered to reliably measure media treatment of firearms ownership for the simple reason that so little ever gets printed. But this is not necessarily a case of bias. It may instead reflect editorial choices of what is newsworthy or interesting. Nonetheless, the gap between the outdoor media and general national media seems an impossible one.

IMPLICATIONS

Perhaps the most disappointing aspect of the national debate on firearms ownership is that there is no national debate on firearms ownership. Developing consensus on guns as well as on other controversial social issues may seem impossible. But the cultural milieu of the guns as revealed in contrasting media treatments suggests that even reasonable dialogue may be quite difficult. General semanticists have long argued that debates without common ground on the meaning of essential terms are seldom fruitful.[25] Such seems to be the case with guns and might well be extended by implication to include all hunting activities as well. In the outdoor/gun media, firearms are an essential and virtuous part of the natural world, reinforcing the simple pleasures of nation, family and friends. "Gun control" means restriction of those liberties and denial of those virtues. Analysis of media coverage of firearms activities gives little encouragement to any notion of reasoned debate and/or understanding of such votes as McClure-Volkmer by the national media. Future researchers might well examine the growing influence of cable television and expanding national coverage by local television to determine if the urban-Northeastern orientation of national media will remain. New technologies and deregulation may well create a new media less concentrated and more compatible with the attitudes of gun owners and outdoor enthusiasts in general.

[24] William Schneider and I.A. Lewis, "Views on the News," *Public Opinion*, No. 4 (1985), 7.

[25] William G. Hardy, *Language, Thought, and Experience* (Baltimore: University Park Press, 1978); and J. Dan Rothwell, *Telling It Like It Isn't,* (Englewood Cliffs: Prentice-Hall, 1982).

Appendix

Votes and Declared Preference on H.R. 49,
Firearm Owners Protection Act
U.S. House of Representatives

	Yes	No		Yes	No
Alabama	6	0	Montana	2	0
Alaska	1	0	Nebraska	3	0
Arizona	4	0	Nevada	2	0
Arkansas	4	0	New Hampshire	2	0
California	23	22	New Jersey	6	8
Colorado	5	1	New Mexico	2	0
Connecticut	2	4	New York	14	19
Delaware	0	1	North Carolina	11	0
Florida	11	7	North Dakota	1	0
Georgia	10	0	Ohio	12	9
Hawaii	0	2	Oklahoma	6	0
Idaho	2	0	Oregon	5	0
Illinois	8	12	Pennsylvania	16	7
Indiana	8	2	Rhode Island	0	2
Iowa	5	1	South Carolina	6	0
Kansas	5	0	South Dakota	1	0
Kentucky	7	0	Tennessee	8	1
Louisiana	8	0	Texas	23	4
Maine	2	0	Utah	3	0
Maryland	4	4	Vermont	1	0
Massachusetts	1	9	Virginia	9	1
Michigan	8	9	Washington	6	2
Minnesota	6	2	West Virginia	4	0
Mississippi	5	0	Wisconsin	8	1
Missouri	6	3	Wyoming	1	0

Chapter 13

MEDIA BIAS IN COVERAGE OF GUN CONTROL: THE PRESS EVALUATES THE POPULAR CULTURE

by
David B. Kopel

INTRODUCTION*

Gun owners frequently assert that the press in the United States in biased in favor of gun control. While it is easy for critics of the media to point out inaccuracies in individual stories, proving more systematic bias is difficult.

Even proof that the media is unfair to one side of an issue does not necessarily prove imbalanced reporting. Perhaps an anti-hunting program such as CBS's "The Guns of Autumn" was slanted. But CBS's coverage of animal rights activists might be as distorted as its coverage of hunters. If the media portrays hunting as sick and animal rights as silly, hunters cannot claim an unfair media tilt against them.

Sometimes both sides of the gun debate find the same flaws in press coverage, such as insufficient coverage of the self-defense issue. Gun advocates contend that the press does not mention the high frequency with which guns are used in self-defense. Gun control advocates complain that the press does not adequately inform the public how dangerous self-defense gun ownership is. The press, in its own defense, might point out that self-defense is often inaccessible as a news story. The police beat — filled with reports of gun crime — is the first assignment for many reporters. On the other hand, if a citizen brandishes a handgun and frightens away a criminal on a deserted sidewalk, the police (and hence the reporter) may never hear of the incident.

In a psychological study of classroom teachers, the teachers were given student papers to grade. Students with popular names such as "Sarah" received relatively higher grades. The exact same papers received lower grades (from other teachers) when the purported student's name was an unpopular one, such as "Herbert."

A similar study in newsrooms would give reporters two press releases with similar facts; one press release would emphasize the pro-gun side, the other press release would emphasize the anti-gun side of the same facts.

In 1978, liberal pollster Patrick Caddell released a poll regarding public attitudes about gun control. In the late 1970's, conservative pollster Richard Wirthlin released two polls about gun control. Although Caddell and Wirthlin came from different

* Thanks to Professor Guido H. Stempel III, of the E. W. Scripps School of Journalism, Ohio University, for his thoughtful criticism of an earlier draft of this article.

political backgrounds, both pollsters found nearly identical results. Thus, in some important ways, the Caddell and Wirthlin polls were similar story events. Yet these events received very different treatment.

THE SURVEYS COMPARED
Similar Pollsters with Similar Methods

In many respects, the pro-control and anti-control surveys were mirror images. The Caddell study was conducted by Cambridge Survey Reports, Inc., a liberal polling institution headed by Pat Caddell. The survey was sponsored by the Center for the Study and Prevention of Handgun Violence (hereinafter "the Center" or "CSPHV") a relative of America's leading anti-gun lobby, Handgun Control Inc.[1] The Caddell Survey was used by its anti-gun sponsors to support their arguments in favor of gun control. The Center released its results on the 10th anniversary of Robert Kennedy's assassination — one day before a House of Representatives vote on national gun registration.[2] Other parts of the study (not released to the public) involved marketing research for anti-gun media campaigns, such as testing which spokesperson for gun control would be most effective.[3]

Similarly, the pro-gun polls were conducted by Decision-Making Information (hereafter DMI), a conservative polling group headed by Richard Wirthlin. The surveys were sponsored by the National Rifle Association and the Second Amendment Foundation, the nation's leading pro-gun organizations. The first poll was released in 1975, partly to counter pressure for gun controls following the assassination attempts against President Ford. The most thorough DMI survey was released in March 1979. Whenever DMI data was released, leading pro-gun Senators and Representatives announced the results.

Methodology was similar too. The Caddell Survey sampled 1500 adults between April 20 and May 15, 1978. Only four days after the Caddell survey was completed, the second DMI survey began, and ran until June 9, 1978. DMI conducted further polling in December 1978.

The only notable methodological difference was that Cambridge surveyed all

---

[1] The Center was founded by Milton Eisenhower in 1968. As the Chairman of The National Commission on the Causes and Prevention of Violence in the 1960's, Eisenhower had produced a report urging substantial tightening of gun controls.

[2] The proposed Bureau of Alcohol, Tobacco and Firearms regulations would have: 1. Required manufacturers to use a unique serial number on every firearm; 2. Required manufacturers and dealers to promptly report thefts to the B.A.T.F.; and 3. Required quarterly reports to the B.A.T.F. of all sales by gun manufacturers, importers, and dealers.

[3] Cambridge Reports, Inc., *An Analysis of Public Attitudes Toward Handgun Control*, A10, A12 (June 1978).

adults, while DMI surveyed only registered voters.[4] Accordingly, DMI's sample was slightly older, whiter, and more middle class. Since attitudes about gun control do not correlate strongly with socioeconomic status, the somewhat different composition of the samples was probably insignificant.[5]

In the late 1970's, Patrick Caddell was the leading liberal pollster. He had advised the McGovern campaign in 1972, the Carter campaign in 1976, and became an important White House advisor. Richard Wirthlin, while not as famous as Caddell, was the New Right's top pollster; he would play important roles in the New Right's successful election campaigns of 1978 and 1980.

Both Caddell's and Wirthlin's companies were highly regarded. Still, both could be suspected of ideological taint.

Similar Results

When the two expert pollsters surveyed public attitudes about guns and gun control, they found consistent results. In *Under the Gun: Weapons, Crime and Violence in America*, sociologists James D. Wright, Peter Rossi, and Kathleen Daly analyzed extant research about gun control under a grant from the National Institute of Justice. Wright, Rossi, and Daly studied the Caddell and the 1979 Wirthlin polls, and found them reliable, despite the potential for ideological bias.

Almost always, the Caddell and Wirthlin surveys reached consistent results. Both surveys reported that about 40-50% of U.S. households owned some kind of gun, and about half of those households owned a handgun. The two surveys agreed that about 7% of adults carry a gun on their person, and that 40% of handgun owners bought their weapons mainly for self-protection. About 15% of all registered voters or their families had used a gun in self-defense, including brandishing. Caddell reported that 2% of all adults had personally fired a handgun in self-defense; Wirthlin found that 6% of all registered voters or their families had fired a gun in self-defense.[6]

The two surveys also produced mostly similar results about gun control. Regarding mandatory prison sentences for criminals who use a gun, Caddell found 83% support, and Wirthlin found 93% support. Caddell found 62% of the population against a ban on handgun ownership, while Wirthlin found 83% opposed. 78% of Caddell's sample thought that gun control laws only affect law-abiding citizens; 85-91% of Wirthlin's sample thought registration would not prevent criminals from acquiring handguns.[7]

---

[4] James Wright, Peter Rossi, and Kathleen Daly, *Under the Gun: Weapons, Crime, and Violence in America* (New York: Aldine, 1983), p. 217.

[5] Ibid., 220.

[6] Ibid., 145.

[7] Ibid., 235-236. Wirthlin's sample group was consistently more anti-control than Caddell's, although usually by small margins. The difference might be attributable to different phrasing of the questions by the pollsters. Alternatively, the public might have been somewhat more in favor of gun control when Caddell was polling than when Wirthlin was polling.

Gun registration was a leading gun control proposal of the late 1970's. About half the Wirthlin and Caddell samples agreed that national gun registration might eventually lead to total firearms confiscation.[8] Requiring detailed record-keeping by gun dealers (an element of registration) was favored by 54% of the Wirthlin's respondents, and 49% of Caddell's.[9]

To the extent the surveys seemed to differ, it was usually because the pollsters had asked different questions. For example, 87% of Wirthlin's respondents thought that the Constitution guaranteed an individual right to own a gun, and 53% of Caddell's thought handgun licensing was Constitutional. The results were not necessarily inconsistent, in that the majority may have felt that the Constitution guarantees a right to own a gun, but that handgun licensing does not violate that right.[10]

Similarly, Caddell found 84% in favor of gun registration. Wirthlin asked if people would support registration if it would cost 4 billion dollars, and 61% said no. The majority then, favored gun registration, but not at a high cost.

The Wright, Rossi, and Daly study concludes:

Despite the occasionally sharp differences in emphasis and interpretation . . . the actual empirical findings from the two surveys are remarkably similar. Results from comparable (even roughly comparable) items rarely differ between the two surveys by more than 10 percentage points, well within the "allowable" limits given the initial differences in sampling frame and the usual margin of survey error . . . [O]n virtually all points where a direct comparison is possible, the evidence from each survey says essentially the same thing.[11]

There were, of course, important differences between the surveys. Caddell's was released at a time when gun control was already in the news, thanks to the Carter gun registration proposal. Several politicians appeared at the press release of the 1979 Wirthlin poll. Politicians did not figure as prominently in the release of the 1978 Caddell poll.

Simply because the polls were released on different days, the other world and national news competing for attention with the poll was different.

Still, the polls had a great deal in common. Analysis of the press treatment of the Caddell/Wirthlin polls, therefore, may roughly approximate a "Sarah/Herbert" experiment, testing press attitudes about gun control.

I contacted the firms which conducted the surveys, and organizations which sponsored them, to request newspaper clip files about the surveys. The items discussed below are all of those that were received. The discussion deals with wire service stories, staff-written stories, editorials, and letters to the editor from a large variety of written media, in order to assess the overall dissemination and reporting of the polls.

8 Ibid., 239.

9 Ibid., 237.

10 Ibid., 239.

HOW THE PRESS TREATED THE WIRTHLIN PRO-GUN SURVEYS

The notion that the American press is monolithically liberal, or monolithically anti-gun, is wrong. Every four years, a solid majority of American newspapers endorse the Republican presidential candidate — even if the candidate is headed for a landslide defeat like Goldwater, or is bitterly hostile to the press, like Nixon. Most of the newspapers that make up the conservative majority of the press are small town papers, and these papers often treated the pro-gun surveys very well. Several papers, including the *Salt Lake Sunset News*, the *Provo Herald, The American Fork Citizen, The North Las Vegas Valley Times-News*, the *Fallon Eagle Standard*, the *Newport Plain Talk*, and the *Murray Ledger & Times* ran a Second Amendment Foundation press release as a news article.[12] The press release quoted many anti-control statistics, omitted all the pro-control statistics, and led with quotes from the Second Amendment Foundation. The press release identified the author of the polls not as "Richard Wirthlin, the new Right's leading pollster," but merely "Decision Making Information, a California based polling firm."

It might be argued that the mere printing of these gun lobby press releases does not prove that the small newspapers were necessarily pro-gun. Because small papers have tiny staffs, they must rely on news items fed by public relations officers. Nevertheless, it should be noted that all of the headlines for the small town stories treated the news respectfully; the headlines were "Americans Oppose Gun Control," or even "Gun Control: Not Effective," rather than "Conservative Pollster Claims Americans Oppose Gun Control."

Some small papers used the DMI news as a springboard for their own pro-gun stories. The *Ardmoriete*, of Ardmore, Oklahoma editorialized against gun control, drawing extensively on DMI. The editorial did disclose that the poll had been commissioned by the NRA.[13]

In Sophia, West Virginia, *The Gulf Times* reported a new poll released by the NRA "that appears to conflict with previous polling on the subject." DMI was identified as "a polling company in Santa Ana, Calif." The article did a man-in-the-

---

11 Ibid., 240.

12 "Americans Oppose Gun Control Laws," *N. Las Vegas Valley Times-News,* (June 29, 1977); "Americans Oppose Gun Control," *Newport (Tenn.) Plain Talk,* (May 16, 1977), circ. 7,581; "Americans Oppose Gun Laws," *American Fork (Utah) Citizen,* (June 9, 1977), circ. 1,800; "Oppose Gun Laws," *Provo (Utah) Herald,* (June 14, 1977), circ. 23,212; "Gun Controls: Not Effective," *Salt Lake City Sunset News,* (June 7, 1977), circ. 6,118 — the Sunset News is not one of Salt Lake's two major dailies; "Americans Oppose Gun Laws," *Fallon (Nevada) Eagle Standard,* (June 29, 1977), circ. 2,906; "Nationwide Survey on Gun Control Released," *Murray (Ky.) Ledger & Times,* (Apr. 6, 1978), circ. 7,397.

13 "Poll Shows Opposition to More Gun Controls," *Ardmore, Okla. Ardmoriete,* (Mar. 23, 1979), circ. 12,935.

street survey of local residents, and found most of them opposed to gun controls.[14]

Not all small-town papers were uncritical towards DMI. Several small northeastern papers ran an editorial which took issue with parts of the poll. An editorial reprinted in several small papers noted that only 13% of respondents stated there are too many gun laws. Further, the results contrasted with Harris and Gallup polls, as well as a poll taken by "the liberal Cambridge Reports Inc." Nevertheless, the article quoted Sen. Steve Symms about the "ballot box . . . the jury box . . . [and] the cartridge box," and concluded that no further gun controls were necessary.[15]

Outdoors columnists solidly backed the DMI polls. In Elizabethtown, Pennsylvania's *The Chronicle,* the outdoors column touted the anti-control findings in detail. In the first paragraph, the NRA was identified as the sponsor, and "Dr. Richard Wirthlin" as the pollster. Wirthlin was not further identified as the leading New Right pollster.[16] Publications like *Tennessee Out-of-Doors* ran lengthy enthusiastic stories about the survey. "Dr. Richard Wirthlin" was quoted, but the NRA was omitted.[17] The South Dakota Department of Game, Fish, and Parks wrote a similarly zealous essay. Gallup and Harris were specifically criticized, and the NRA never mentioned.[18] Other outdoors columnists took a similar tack.[19] Some columnists, such as the *Houston Post's,* did advert to the NRA's role, while reporting the results with pleasure.[20]

[14] "More Gun Regulations Opposed," *The Gulf Times,* (Mar. 21, 1979). The article seemed to hypothesize that public opinion had changed since the Gallup and Harris polls were taken, for "88 percent now believe they have a right to own weapons." Further, "88 percent of the 1,500 registered voters surveyed said they had used a gun to protect themselves or their property." This sentence incorrectly implied that the gun owners had actually fired in self-defense, rather than merely keeping the weapon for self-defense purposes. Further, since far less than 88% of American families own guns, it would be impossible for such a high percentage to even possess for self-defense.

[15] *Corry Journal,* reprinted in "As Others See It: Anti-gun Control?," *Salamanca (N.Y.) Republican-Press,* (Mar. 28, 1979); "Gun Control Issue," *Ridgway (Pa.) Record,* (Mar. 10, 1979), circ. 3,753; "Gun Control Issue," *The (Scranton, Pa.) Evening Times,* (Mar. 13, 1979), 3.

[16] Brandt, "Another Public Poll on Crime and Gun Control," *The Chronicle,* (Apr. 26, 1979).

[17] "Do Americans Really Want Gun Control?," *Tennessee Out-of-Doors,* (Jan. 1977).

[18] "Survey Shows 76 Per Cent Against Handgun Ban," *Jim Peterson's Outdoor News,* (Feb. 20, 1976), 3.

[19] Kruse, "Right of Gun Ownership Backed in Poll," *Everett (Wash.) Herald,* (Apr. 27, 1979), 53,000 circ.; Seattle metro area, "Outdoor Recreation Writer".

[20] Bob Brister, "NRA gets bigger, tougher on gun laws," *Houston, Texas Chronicle,* (May 22, 1979), circ. 322,762; Putnam, "Outdoors in Hanford County," *Bel Air (Md.) Aegis,* (Mar. 22, 1979), 4, Baltimore metro area.

Editorial pages of larger metropolitan dailies are usually considered hotbeds of anti-gun extremism. Yet even here, one could find some favorable mention of the DMI polls — albeit not by staff writers. Letters to the editor about gun control often discussed DMI, and so did guest columnists.[21]

John Lofton, a conservative syndicated columnist, authored an editorial contending that handgun ownership for self-protection is especially important for the poor and for minorities. Lofton cited the 1975 DMI poll to show that the top groups owning guns solely for self-defense were blacks, the poor, and senior citizens.[22] Lofton extensively quoted pro-gun criminologist Donald B. Kates, who had himself relied on the DMI poll.[23]

Another syndicated conservative columnist, Kevin Phillips (author of *The Emerging Republican Majority*), cited Wirthlin's results for the proposition that the public was opposed to new gun controls. He did caution that the DMI poll "was commissioned by the strongly anti-gun control Second Amendment Foundation of Bellevue, Washington. Those origins must be kept in mind."[24]

Conservative outlets also sang DMI's praises. Ohio Rep. John Ashbrook   for years the most pro-gun member of the House of Representatives — wrote a short piece for *Human Events,* a conservative weekly. Ashbrook criticized the Carter administration for working with gun control groups, and cited DMI (without further

[21] Some examples: After the *Washington Post* ran its own editorial claiming that polls showed the vast majority of the public to favor gun control laws, the *Post* ran a letter to the editor from the Citizens Committee for the Right to Keep and Bear Arms, which cited the DMI poll. John Snyder, "God, Guns and Guts," *Washington Post,* (Mar. 8, 1980). Similar letters from ordinary citizens in Fardley, "Gun Opinions Aren't Truths," *Grand Rapids, Mich. Press,* (Mar. 23, 1979), circ. 125,545 — citing 1975 poll.

In April 1979, a nationally-syndicated *New York Times* story detailed how President Carter had backed down on gun control, even though "most surveys reportedly have shown that a majority of Americans support gun control legislation . . ." Letters to the editor took issue with the statement that the public backed gun control, and cited the DMI poll. Carlson, "Gun Control," *Minneapolis Trib.,* (Apr. 18, 1979).

New Orleans Times Picayune ran a series of letters on the gun control issue. The first letter touted the DMI study and disparaged the Center's study. A reply letter from Handgun Control Inc. noted that the NRA, which had paid for the DMI study, had failed to ask questions about handguns alone. The NRA was given a sur-rebutter. "Firearms Laws Are Futile," *The Times-Picayune,* (Mar. 9, 1980), written in reply to Orasin (V.P. of H.C.I.), "Controlling Guns," (Feb. 11, 1980), written in reply to letter of Jan. 12, 1980.

[22] John Lofton Jr., "Killing Not Only Purpose," *Yankton Daily Press and Dakotan,* (Jan. 20, 1978), 4, from United Feature Syndicate; Lofton, "Purpose of handguns," *Greenwich (Conn.) Times,* (Jan. 19, 1978); "Killing Is Not the Only Purpose of Handguns, And If It Were, Is All Killing Equally Deplorable?," *Battle Line (American Conservative Union)* (Mar. 1978), 23.

[23] Don B. Kates Jr., "Handgun Control: A Different View," *Field & Stream,* (May 1978), reprinted from *Inquiry.*

[24] Kevin Phillips, "Are gun control laws the answer?," *Boston Herald American,* (June 11, 1977); "New Gun Laws Opposed," *Rushville (Ind.) Republican,* (June 13, 1977).

For a non-syndicated columnist, see John Geiser, "NRA-Sponsored Survey Says Gun Control Law Not Answer," *Asbury Park (N.J.) Press,* (Mar. 25, 1979), circ. 96,092.

attribution) for the fact that 85% of Americans believe they have a right to own a gun.[25]

The Liberty Lobby, an ultra-conservative, racist organization, touted the DMI poll as confirming the results of its own poll in 1976. "The American Rifle Association" was given credit for paying for the poll, "but did not set the terms for it." The results of Harris and Gallup "Establishment polls " were ascribed to the pollsters interviewing "1,500 or fewer voters" to find the results the pollsters wanted.[26]

Anti-gun control organizations, of course, praised the DMI report.[27] And the sizeable gun hobbyist press liked it too.[28] Thus, an important fraction of the American print media reported the DMI poll results enthusiastically. Critical analysis went no further than mentioning that the polls were sponsored by anti-control groups such as the NRA and the Second Amendment Foundation.

Gun owners paint the large circulation dailies as highly biased against gun ownership. Nevertheless, some large dailies carried neutral news reports. For example, the most comprehensive DMI gun study was released to the public in April 1979. In a joint press conference, Senators Ted Stevens (R-Alaska), Dennis DeConcini (D-Ariz.), and Representatives Harold Volkmer (D-Mo.) and Steve Symms (R-Idaho) announced the results. In their press release, the author of the survey was simply "Decision Making Information of Santa Ana, California," conducting a study "Commissioned by the NRA Institute for Legislative Action."[29] Homestate newspapers for the Congressmen ran mostly neutral, factual summaries of the press release, while prominently noting the NRA's role in the poll.[30]

In other contexts also, background articles on gun control treated the pro-gun and anti-gun opinion polls with equal respect. In a general news story about upcoming gun control battles in Congress, the St. Louis Globe-Democrat noted that the NRA cited the DMI poll for the proposition that the public opposed gun control; the Globe-Democrat added that pro-control Rep. John Conyers (D-Mich.) "has just as many surveys to prove the American public favors gun control."[31] A feature story in the Arizona Republic used both DMI and Cambridge statistics in an article discussing use of firearms in self-defense.[32]

[25] John Ashbrook, "Gun Control," Human Events, (Oct. 29, 1977), 19.

[26] Herzberg, "Polls Still Find Voters Opposing Gun Controls," The Spotlight, (Mar. 26, 1979).

[27] "GAO Study Urges Congress to Impose Strong Gun Controls on Nation," The Weekly Bullet, (Feb. 13, 1978).

[28] Oliver, "Washington Report," Guns & Ammo, (June 1979).   7

[29] News Release, (Mar. 8, 1979).

[30] "NRA poll says voters would reject more gun controls," Tucson Citizen, (Mar. 30, 1979), circ. 64,788; "Paul releases poll on gun ownership," Houston Post, (Apr. 13, 1979), story on Rep. Ron Paul, who also released results, circ. 303,447.

[31] "Gun Action Expected in 1977," St. Louis Globe-Democrat, (Dec. 31, 1976), 11A.

[32] Kelly, "A Gun For Self-Defense Isn't Always Worthwhile," Arizona Republic, (Oct. 2, 1983),

Other writers, though, set out to "debunk" the DMI polls, and explain away the results. The Associated Press noted the possibility of bias, in that the survey had been paid for by the NRA, "the major lobbying group against gun control," and that the survey contradicted a General Accounting Office study from the previous year. Although Dr. Wirthlin was quoted, far more column inches were devoted to attacking the poll than to defending it.[33]

Some anti-DMI articles appeared even in smaller papers from states considered solidly pro-gun. For instance, the *Manchester (N.H.) News* (not the ultra-conservative *Union-leader*), led with the fact that the poll had been commissioned by the NRA, and closed with the fact that the NRA had paid $63,000 for the poll. Further, the story argued that the poll contrasted with seven Gallup Polls showing large majorities in favor of requiring police permits to own a gun.[34]

The *Chicago Sun-Times* also set out to attack DMI's results. The NRA was mentioned as the source of the survey in the first paragraph. The second paragraph cited gun control advocates who pointed to other polls that found Americans to favor more gun control. DMI was identified as a California-based firm; Dr. Richard Wirthlin was quoted denying that the questions had been phrased to achieve particular results. Particular questions were analyzed in detail, to argue that the poll did not really prove the public was opposed to more gun control laws. Handgun Control Inc. and the National Coalition to Ban Handguns were both quoted about their skepticism of the poll's results. In refutation of the DMI poll, the Gallup, Harris, and "Cambridge Reports Inc." studies were cited. Lastly, the article reported three questions from the survey which showed public support for gun ownership.[35]

The *Roanoke Times & World News* wrote an editorial disparaging the DMI poll, based on the *N.Y. Times* story described below. The editorial pointed out that the survey contradicted "decades" of previous research. Further, the Roanoke paper attributed the low percentage favoring more laws to public belief that laws are stricter than they actually are. (Actually, most people believe gun laws to be less strict than they actually are. Therefore a "more control needed" response to surveys does not necessarily mean the respondent favors laws stricter than the present ones.[36]) While claiming not to "reject out of hand" the DMI results, the editorial, again echoing the *New York Times*, wondered if the sample was unrepresentative.[37]

---

[33] "Survey shows Americans see no need for new firearms law." *The Daily Dispatch*, (Mar. 12, 1979).

[34] "Poll Shows No More Gun Control Laws Needed," *Manchester Sunday News*, (Mar. 18, 1979), circ. 63,518.

[35] *Chicago Sun-Times*, reprinted in, "Backers of Gun Control Open Fire on Survey Funded by Rifle Association," *The Louisville Times*, (Mar. 9, 1979), A6.

[36] Wright, et. al., "Under the Gun," 232.

[37] "A Contradictory Gun Poll," *Roanoke Times & World News*, (Mar. 17, 1979), circ. 65,412.

Three days later, a follow-up editorial quoted research from the University of Michigan's Survey Research Center to suggest that pro-control people hold their positions with more intensity than anti-control people.[38] While DMI had been chastised for violating the established wisdom, the editorial did not mention that the Michigan poll also contradicted the established wisdom (held by both sides of the gun control debate) that the minority against gun control gets its way because it is so much more passionate than the majority.[39]

The New York Times made its skepticism about the poll clear. The headline ran: "Rifle Association Poll Says Majority Oppose More Gun Legislation." The first sentence of the article stated that the poll "appears to conflict with decades of previous polling on the subject," and noted that the NRA had paid for the poll. DMI was, again, "a polling company in Santa Ana."

The story observed that seven Gallup polls and five surveys from the National Opinion Research Center from 1959 to 1976 had found large majorities in favor of permit requirements for handguns. In conclusion, the article stated that since the poll sample was limited to registered voters, it may not have been representative of all voters, or of the whole population.[40] The story was written by Arthur Ochs Sulzberger Jr., whose father "Punch" is a strong proponent of handgun control, and is also one of the few New Yorkers with enough political influence to have been issued a handgun carry permit.

Sulzberger Jr.'s story left much to be desired. There is no evidence that registered voters have significantly different attitudes about gun control from unregistered voters, or from the general population.[41]

Further, it was incorrect to imply that the Harris and Gallup polls on gun control were more objective than the DMI polls, since Gallup and Harris are well-known gun control advocates. Indeed, Lou Harris testified before Congress in 1975 in favor of gun controls.

Although Gallup surveys have found a large and continuous decline in the support for a handgun ban over the last 30 years, Gallup stories about its polls always emphasize the greater support found for other forms of gun control. The slant in Gallup's own stories might have been noticeable by Mr. Sulzberger during his survey of 20 years' worth of Gallup polls for the DMI article. Moreover, the *Times* article carried no response from gun advocates, not even from Dr. Wirthlin, to any of the criticisms offered by Mr. Sulzberger.

Responsible newspapers should treat a survey paid for and commissioned by the

---

[38] "Gun Control: Strong Feelings," *Roanoke Times & World News,* (Mar. 20, 1979).

[39] "Powerful Reputation Makes National Rifle Association a Top Gun in Washington," *Congressional Quarterly,* Vol. 39 (May 9, 1981), 799-803.

[40] A.O. Sulzberger Jr., "Rifle Association Poll Says Majority Oppose More Gun Legislation," *New York Times,* (Mar. 10, 1979).

[41] Wright, et. al., "Under the Gun," 220.

gun lobby skeptically. They should apply that same treatment to a survey conducted for and paid for by the anti-gun lobby. Whether they did so will be the focus of the next section.

HOW THE PRESS TREATED THE ANTI-GUN SURVEY

Most of the detailed criticism of the anti-gun Caddell poll came from pro-gun partisans.

The story in *The Weekly Bullet,* a publication for pro-gun activists, recounted the Center's study and noted Caddell's close relationship with President Carter. Anti-gun polling in general was criticized, since "the same question is not asked from year to year, even when conducted by the same polling organization." In addition, careful wording was said to be necessary to maintain objectivity. The DMI poll was mentioned in contrast, with the source of its funding disclosed.[42] A follow-up article in *The Weekly Bullet* argued that since the public is generally not aware of what the gun control laws actually are, opinion surveys in favor of "more control" are meaningless.[43]

Gun Week, another publication for pro-gun activists, reported the Cambridge story straight, except for a hostile headline, and a reminder at the end of the article that election results on gun referenda in Massachusetts and California had confounded pollsters' predictions. The rest of the article simply stated the poll's results, leading with the Center's statement that the poll indicated the American public to be strongly in favor of gun control.[44]

In the mainstream press, the most negative coverage of the Caddell poll came in Kevin Phillips' syndicated column. He faulted the wire service and other reports of the poll (detailed below) for reporting the results uncritically, and for claiming that a massive anti-gun consensus existed — without even mentioning the anti-control data in the DMI poll, as well as the landslide defeat of anti-gun propositions in Massachusetts (1976) and California (1982) referenda.[45]

The Caddell poll included some results which militated against gun control; these found their way into the press mostly through pro-gun authors' guest editorials, or through letters to the editor, or in gun sports publications. In an op-ed piece, Neal Knox, the then-director of NRA Institute for Legislative Action, quoted "the 1978 Caddell poll (commissioned by the Center for the Study and Prevention of Handgun Violence)" to show that 4.5 million handguns had been used in self-defense in

---

[42] "Carter's Pollster Issues Pro-Gun Control Poll," *The Weekly Bullet,* (June 12, 1978).

[43] "Is Congress Really in the Gun Lobby's Holster?," *Weekly Bullet,* (Oct. 28, 1980). The article's contention that the public is unfamiliar with current laws seems correct. Wright, "Under the Gun," 232.

[44] "Newest anti-gun poll shows expected stats," *Gun Week,* (June 16, 1976).

[45] Kevin Phillips, "Control Polls Are Misleading," *Human Events,* (July 8, 1978), 16; "Anti-Handgun Poll Mostly a PR Job," *San Antonio Light,* (June 18, 1978), 8-N.

America.[46] A columnist for a gun lobby magazine, writing in response to an Ann Landers column, used the DMI poll as evidence that even Americans who do not own guns believe in the right to bear arms.[47]

A *Field & Stream* editorial cited Caddell to point out that 43% of Americans owned guns, that 78% believed gun control laws would not affect criminals, that 40% believed handgun controls would be ineffective without long gun controls, and that 39% believed that licensing was a first step to firearms confiscation.[48] (Several months later, *Field & Stream* adverted to the 1975 DMI poll to show that most Americans did not believe in gun control as an answer to crime.[49])

In the mainstream press, however, the only place one could learn that 78% of Caddell's respondents believed gun control would not affect criminals was in letters to the editor.[50]

Some publications of the law enforcement hierarchy cheered news of the poll. *Crime Control Digest* gave the Center's study a long write-up.[51] The story did not mention Pat Caddell's role, and simply described the Center as a "research and educational organization." Although the article listed Nelson T. Shields as a member of the Center's Board, it did not report that Mr. Shields was Chairman of the National Council to Control Handguns.

Another publication seemed to move into the realm of deliberate distortion. The federal government's *LEAA Newsletter* announced that 84% of Americans favored registration of new handguns, and 70% a ban on Saturday Night Specials. Further, "70 percent said a stand on this issue could affect their vote on specific candidates." Actually, Caddell had found that a pro-control stance would attract 49% of voters, and repel 21%. The LEAA's revised wording gave the impression that 70% of the public would be more inclined to vote for a pro-control candidate. Additionally, the story

---

[46] Neal Knox, "Gun Control Plans Miss the Point: It's Abuse, Not Simply Possession," *San Diego Union*, (June 24, 1979), C-7. See also, "Guns Thwart Crime," *Albany (Ga.) Democrat Herald*, (July 7, 1981), in letter to editor, NRA officer cites CSPHV to show that handguns used by 4.8 million people for self-defense); M. Ayoob, *The Truth About Self Protection* 376-77 (Bantam 1983) ("A recent Pat Caudell [sic] poll indicates that, in 1981, some 3.8 million Americans has used a gun for self defense. Very few of them got shot. Very few of them had to shoot anyone else, either.") (Ayoob is author of several books on self-defense, and is director of The Lethal Force Institute, a New Hampshire school that trains police and civilians in self-defense techniques.)

[47] Jerry Ahern, "One Gun Owner's Advice to Ann Landers," *Guns & Ammo*, (Aug. 1979), 33.

[48] *Field & Stream*, (Nov. 1978).

[49] Mann, "Our Endangered Tradition," *Field & Stream*, (Jan. 1979), 12.

[50] "Gun control has two sides," *Philadelphia Inquirer*, (Feb. 21, 1979), letter to the editor. The editorial debate persisted for years. Two years later, the (New Orleans) *Times-Picayune* published a pro-gun letter which, inter alia, attacked the Center's study. In return, a supportive letter was Handgun Control Inc. was printed. "Controlling Guns," *The Times-Picayune*, (Feb. 11, 1980).

[51] "Americans Want More Effective Handgun Controls, Survey Shows," *Crime Control Digest*, (June 12, 1978), 7.

referred to "the independent firm of Cambridge Reports."[52]

UPI mentioned the Center, but not the Center's role as an anti-gun interest group. The study's author was described only as "Cambridge Reports," as if it were a disinterested group of academic experts in public opinion, rather than Pat Caddell's business. Caddell himself was nowhere in sight. The story listed three results favorable to gun control (people inclined to vote for pro-control candidates, in favor of various handgun controls, in favor of Saturday Night Special bans), but did admit "only 32% favor a ban on the future manufacture and sale of all handguns." (*Crime Control Digest* had announced that result more positively: "Although the majority of Americans oppose such a drastic step, one in three would even go so far as to favor banning the manufacture and sale of all handguns.") The next UPI paragraph contained a quote from control advocate Milton Eisenhower, and the final paragraph contained two more pro-control survey results.

Although strongly identified with gun control, the *Washington Post* only ran a short version of the UPI story, and headlined it "Poll Shows Gun Control Favored."[53] The *Christian Science Monitor* also cut the UPI article sizably.[54] The *Boston Globe* printed the UPI story in full.[55]

The AP put together a lengthier article, emphasizing that the findings showed "record support" for strict gun laws. Although the AP's piece about the Wirthlin poll had offered a pro/con debate about the survey's validity (mostly con), the Caddell poll was subjected to no critical scrutiny. None of the anti-control statistics were quoted, nor were any spokesmen for opposing views questioned. The article did disclose the source of the data more fully than most papers did, "the Center for the Study and Prevention of Handgun Violence." AP also identified "Pat Caddell, President Carter's pollster."[56]

The Caddell survey received a friendlier welcome at the *New York Times* than the Wirthlin survey had. The headline ran "Most Americans Support Gun Control, Poll

---

52 "Around the Nation," *LEAA Newsletter*, (Aug. 1978), 5. The Law Enforcement Assistance Agency was a federal organization that provided anti-crime assistance to local police forces. It was abolished during President Reagan's first term, partly due to doubts about its efficacy.

53 "Poll Shows Gun Control Favored," *Washington Post*, (June 4, 1978).

54 "Americans favor gun control, poll finds," *Christian Science Monitor*, (June 16, 1978).

55 "U.S. Gun Control Favored in Poll," *Boston Globe*, (June 4, 1978). For other full versions of U.P.I., see "Poll: 70% Back U.S. Control of Handguns," *Baltimore News American*, (June 4, 1978); "70% favor handgun control: Poll," *The Terre Haute Tribune-Star*, (June 4, 1978).

56 "Record Support Tallied for Gun Registration," *The Virginia Pilot and the Ledger Star*, (June 4, 1978), A5. Shorter versions of the story in: "Poll: Gun Control Favored," *San Antonio Express-News*, (June 4, 1978); "Handgun Registration Favored, Says Survey," *Cincinati Enquirer*, (June 4, 1978); "Poll finds majority favor gun registration," *Baltimore Sun*, (June 4, 1978); "Poll reports huge support for gun control," *Poughkeepsie Journal.*, (June 4, 1978).

Finds," and the AP story followed.[57]

The *Washington Star* ran a shorter version, but did later print two letters critical of the poll; one letter, from the Citizen's Committee for the Right to Keep and Bear Arms, cited the DMI study.[58]

The *Philadelphia Inquirer* wrote its own article, which led with the fact that "84 percent of Americans favor stringent handgun control and registration." Of course the Caddell survey had never asked about "stringent handgun control." In fact, the only controls favored by 84% or more were those that would treat guns like automobiles; there would be a non-restrictive registration and licensing plan, under which any law-abiding sane adult could own a handgun. The *Inquirer* conclusion stated that the study was conducted by the CSPHV, which was "a non-profit educational and research group."[59]

EVALUATION OF THE PRESS COVERAGE

Small newspapers differed greatly in their approach to the gun control polls. Some offered an uncritical pro-gun perspective; some showed bias against guns; and others produced careful, incisive analysis.

The coverage of the polls in the larger papers was often flawed. To be sure, some flaws were not the result of bias. For example, it is true that pro-gun facts from the Caddell study were rarely mentioned, and that Cambridge Research/Caddell was almost never identified as a "liberal" organization. One should remember, though, that anti-gun facts from the Wirthlin study were also rarely mentioned, and that Decision Making Information's conservative slant was never detailed. While Wirthlin was never identified as a conservative pollster, Caddell *was* sometimes identified as a liberal pollster — perhaps because of his greater prominence. Given the fast-breaking pace of daily journalism, it is certainly understandable for reporters not

[57] "Most Americans Support Gun Control, Poll Finds," *New York Times,* (June 4, 1978), 33. For another headline touting a pro-control poll, see "Firearms Control Has Wide Backing: Gallup Survey Finds 67% Favor Gun Registration," *New York Times,* June 5, 1975.

The *Times* seems to engage in similar headlining tactics on other policy questions. "Contrast Real-Estate Group Poll Finds Many Support Development," *New York Times,* (Feb. 7, 1988): "A New York City real-estate trade group said last week . . ."; and "New Poll Finds Wide Support for Abortion Rights," *New York Times,* (Jan. 21, 1988), A18: "Broad public support for preserving the right of women to obtain abortions remains undiminished seven years after Ronald Reagan came to office on a strong anti-abortion platform." The actual results of the poll, however, showed that only 39% support the abortion laws as lenient as the current laws. The article also stated, "50 percent of those polled said that women under 18 years old were 'more likely' to have abortion; in fact only about one-quarter of all abortions are obtained by teenagers." But since teenagers constitute less than one-quarter of all fertile women, they are indeed more likely to have abortions.

[58] "Registration Acclaimed: Most Back Handgun Control, Survey Says," *Washington Star,* (June 4, 1978); "Polls Can Show Anything," *Washington Star,* (June 13, 1978).

[59] Holton, "New poll shows 84% favor tougher gun laws," *Philadelphia Inquirer,* (June 3, 1978).

to read the full results of an opinion survey, or to analyze the survey carefully enough to find results that contradict the sponsor's goals. Likewise, the failure to identify Cambridge Research or DMI might have sprung more from ignorance than from prejudice.

Other parts of the media coverage did seem to reflect a serious bias. The DMI survey was treated as an aberration to be explained away, with headlines such as "A Contradictory Gun Poll." The Cambridge poll was treated as an accurate reflection of real public opinion, with headlines such as "Poll Reports Huge Support for Gun Control." The Cambridge poll had been released on the eve of a major House of Representatives vote on gun registration, and many of the headlines focussed on the issue of registration. "Record Support Tallied for Gun Registration" was typical.[60]

In contrast, headlines of the DMI study often mentioned the NRA as the sponsor, as in "NRA Poll Says Voters Would Reject More Gun Controls." Only rarely did headlines even mention the Center.[61] No headline or story identified the Center as an anti-handgun interest group. In fact, the only publication that has come to my attention which identified the CSPHV as a gun control lobby was The National Journal, which discussed: ". . . one poll commissioned by the National Rifle Association and one poll by the pro-control Center for the Study and Prevention of Handgun Violence."[62] Since both polls were conducted by lobbying groups directly interested in gun control, it was wrong for the media to discuss one group's claims so much more skeptically than the other group's claims.

Perhaps the reason the NRA was treated more harshly than the Center was its greater recognition level. Reporters simply might not have known that the Center for the Study and Prevention of Handgun Violence was created in order to produce research results to justify gun control. Nevertheless, the timing of the Center's release indicated an obvious attempt to influence an upcoming vote on gun control, and the survey was conducted by a close advisor of a President whose administration had proposed the new controls.

In short, close analysis of coverage of the polls reveals a significant degree of unbalanced coverage. The next question to ask is what might have motivated the somewhat slanted treatment.

WHAT OPINION POLLS MEAN TO THE MEDIA

Despite the release of the Caddell poll and its claims that voters would support pro-control candidates, the BATF gun registration effort was crushed by a 314-80 vote in the House of Representatives.

The National Coalition to Ban Handguns newsletter explained the defeat: After "modest regulations" were proposed, the NRA launched "an unprecedented

60 It may be that the papers simply printed the story in nearly the same form that the CSPHV and Cambridge fed it to them, and that registration was featured first.

61 The only one I have found is "Center Says Public Wants Gun Control," Charleston, S.C., (June 4, 1978).

62 "Polls: Does the Gun Lobby Thwart Public Opinion?," National Journal, Vol. 39 (1981), 800.

campaign." Having misinformed its membership, the NRA created "a barrage of mail to the Department of the Treasury." Next, NRA leaders "turned to their Congressional allies," who circulated resolutions of disapproval in the Congress. "Hundreds of Congressmen co-sponsored the resolutions and dozens of Senators." The House Appropriations Committee came down on the NRA side 38-3. In the end, "eighty courageous members of Congress stood up in support of the crime controls. Three hundred fourteen members followed the NRA line and voted against them."[63] The next story in the NCCH newsletter dealt with the Caddell study, undertaken by the CSPHV, "a Philadelphia-based research and educational organization." It announced that "Public concern about handgun violence is so strong" that voters would back anti-handgun candidates by a 49-21% margin.[64] Yet somehow, concluded that article, Congress "does not reflect the feelings of its constituencies."

The mainstream press agreed with the anti-gun lobby that Congress had failed to implement the will of the people. Reuters wrote a feature which discussed a study by "Cambridge Reports" and concluded that NRA power had thwarted the will of the majority of Americans who favored gun control.[65] The *New York Post* — which almost never gives op-ed space to viewpoints with which it disagrees — ran an essay by Rep. Abner Mikva that chastised Congress for caving in to a mountain of mail in opposition to BATF's proposed regulations. Rep. Mikva cited the Center's study for the proposition that the majority of voters really did favor stricter gun controls.[66]

The *Milwaukee Journal* condemned eight members of the Wisconsin House delegation who had voted against the gun control legislation, and praised the one Wisconsin Representative who had voted in favor. "The odd thing about all this is that poll after poll finds a majority of the public — including a lot of gun owners —consistently favoring firearm control laws far more sweeping than the rules proposed by Treasury." The CSPHV and Patrick Caddell had found 49% of the public was "much more" or "somewhat more" inclined to vote for candidates who favor handgun controls." Thus, the letter-writing powers of the NRA were just "paper bullets" that might "bamboozle 314 House members (including Wisconsin's hard-ducking eight) but the public apparently isn't fooled."[67]

---

[63] "NRA Congress Vetoes Carter Crime Controls," NCCH Washington Report, (June 1978). The headline implies an interesting view of the Constitutional process, as if convincing the President to initiate a proposal should be seen as the most important step, subject only to a "veto" by Congress. Perhaps this backwards view of the Constitution stems from the fact that gun controllers can often capture the sympathy of a President or his Attorney General (as occurred in the Johnson, Ford, and Carter administrations), but can almost never command a Congressional majority.

[64] "Poll Reveals Overwhelming Public Support for Handgun Control," NCCH Washington Report.

[65] Keirnan, "Americans Firmly Attached to Their 'Shootin' Irons'," *Los Angeles Times,* (July 12, 1978), 2.

[66] Abner Mikva, "How the gun lobby shot down the latest bid to curb crime," *New York Post,* (Oct. 18, 1978).

[67] "Chickening Out on Handguns," *Milwaukee Journal,* (June 12, 1978), circ. 338,597.

The *Louisville Courier-Journal* warned: "Gun Lobby's Fanaticism May Backfire." It explained: "a large constituency exists among the victims of handgun violence. Because their lives have been directly affected by these guns, they should have the zeal and commitment equal to that of the gun lobby."[68] Similarly *The Tennessean* cited the Cambridge poll in an editorial urging President Carter to go over the head of Congress, and appeal directly to the American people for stronger gun controls.[69] An op-ed piece in the *Philadelphia Daily News* made the same point.[70]

Did the NRA extremism backfire? Did the public strike back at its unrepresentative representatives in the next election? In 1980, a life member of the NRA was elected President. *After* a handgun assassination attempt against him, that President signed into law the most significant relaxation of federal gun control in history, the McClure-Volkmer Firearm Owners Protection Act.[71] That legislation was enacted in part because the NRA membership had ousted officers considered too accommodating and had elected a more "extreme" anti-control leadership, dedicated to rollback rather than containment.[72] Although the Caddell study had "proved" — and the press had agreed — that the voting public was ready to elect pro-control candidates, just the opposite happened.

One explanation why events confounded the Caddell/press prediction may be the way the Caddell survey was conducted. Questions about voting for pro-control candidates were posed only after a long series of preparatory questions discussing the horrors of gun accidents and domestic shootings. It may be that once citizens are emotionally energized about the dangers of handguns, they will adopt an active pro-control position, as the Caddell respondents did. Most voters, though, are not so energized.

Given the real-world facts of handgun death, the attitude of most voters is understandable. Drowning claims far more lives than do handguns. Bicycles kill many more children than guns do.[73] A sizable fraction of the people who are shot by handguns in domestic/acquaintance quarrels are themselves felons, hard drug

---

[68] "Gun Lobby's Fanaticism May Backfire," *The Courier-Journal*, (June 8, 1978).

[69] "Politics of Gun Control," *The Tennessean*, (Apr. 17, 1979).

[70] Leon Katz, "Wanted: Strict Gun Laws," *Philadelphia Daily News*, (July 26, 1979).

[71] Significant pro-gun action was also taken by the U.S. Senate Subcommittee on the Constitution, which, in a bipartisan report, adopted the NRA's view of the historical record and concluded that the second amendment's original intent was the protection of the individual's right to bear arms. U.S. Senate Subcommittee on the Constitution, The Right to Keep and Bear Arms, 97th Cong., 2d sess. (D.C.: G.P.O., 1982).

[72] "The Gun Lobby," *Congressional Quarterly Weekly Report*, Vol. 39 (May 9, 1981), 781, 801. According to an NRA board member, "The membership did not want to be 'reasonable' anymore." Three of the NRA's top five lobbyists resigned, because the new leaders "don't feel you have to compromise on anything."

[73] National Safety Council, *Accident Facts 1986 Edition* 12 (Washington Government Printing Office); David B. Kopel, *Trust the People: The Case Against Gun Control* (Washington: Cato Institute, 1988).

abusers, or others on the very fringes of society — not regular voters.[74] Thus, despite optimistic claims about a large constituency of politically active handgun victims, such a group is very small. It is dwarfed by the number of people who enjoy guns for sport, or who believe that their guns protect them. Further, a poll taken before a gun control referendum in Maryland in 1988 found handgun victims were *less* supportive of gun control than was the general public.

Incumbent politicians — like 8/9 of the Wisconsin delegation — know more about getting elected than do editorial writers. Congressmen read their mail, and they follow the election returns of their pro and anti-gun colleagues. When they look at direct election results, they see Massachusetts and California defeating anti-handgun bills by landslides. In addition, since 1978, several states have added a "right to keep and bear arms" to their own state constitutions, always by a vote of at least 70%. The only place anti-gun laws have won at the polls have been in very small jurisdictions like Oak Park, Illinois, and in Maryland in 1988. In Maryland, the proponents of control successful portrayed their bill as a ban only on "Saturday Night Specials," and not as a general attack on handgun ownership.

Notwithstanding the claims of the Caddell poll and the press, the pro-gun stance seems to gain many more actual votes than does a pro-control stance — except on fringe issues like Saturday Night Specials. In the real world, polling booths matter; polling organizations do not. As Harry Truman put it: "I think the best poll there is is the count after the election."[75]

Ten years later, the large circulation press continues to write stories predicting that the NRA's "extremism" will backfire. In 1988, *Newsweek* warned that NRA would face a member revolt for opposing plastic gun legislation: "That kind of tunnel vision could damage the NRA more than any gun-control group has managed to do . . . This time the gun lobby may have shot itself in the foot."[76] A few months later, though, a

---

[74] In a study of the victims of near-fatal domestic shootings and stabbings, 78 percent of the victims volunteered a history of hard-drug use, and 16 percent admitted using heroin the day of the incident. Kirkpatrick and Walt, "The High Cost of Gunshot and Stab Wounds," *Journal of Surgical Research* Vol. 14 (1973): 261-62.

In any case, many of the domestic killings with guns involve self-defense. In Detroit, for example, 75 percent of wives who shot and killed their husbands were not prosecuted, because the wives were defending themselves or their children against attack. M. Daly and M. Wilson, *Homicide* (New York: Aldine, 1988), pp. 15, 200 (table p. 1).

[75] Quoted in Arthur M. Schlesinger Jr., "A Critique of the Scientific Hope," reprinted in Robert Allen Skotheim (ed.), *The Historian and the Climate of Opinion* (Reading, Mass.: Addison-Wesley, 1969), p. 192.

[76] "Battle Over the Plastic Gun," *Newsweek,* (June 1, 1987), 31. The article also stated: "The NRA last year lost the fight over the armor-piercing slugs, as well as its effort to permit private ownership of machine guns." In fact, the NRA helped draft the current armor-piercing bullet legislation (after defeating a broader bill that would have outlawed hunting ammunition). Private ownership of machine guns is already legal in the United States; recent legislation merely banned the sale of new machine guns.

majority of the United States Senate adopted the NRA's "tunnel vision" and rejected plastic gun legislation.[77]

The NRA retains its extreme positions year after year, and shows little sign of losing its clout. With important exceptions, gun control proposals continue to fail in the legislatures.

Is the will of the people thwarted?

The Wirthlin and Caddell polls, like most other polls about gun control, did find a majority of Americans in favor of gun licensing and gun registration. At the same time, even larger majorities doubted that such measures would affect crime. Professors Wright, Rossi, and Daly conclude that licensing and registration for guns are favored for the same reason that licensing and registration are favored for cars. There is no expectation that criminals will have less access to automobiles or guns, but it just seems sensible to have some regulation for deadly tools like automobiles and guns. At the same time, the public opposes laws which would make guns more difficult to obtain than cars, such as laws giving the police discretion about who may own a gun.[78]

Wright's hypothesis helps explain why the mail count for letters to elected officials is so overwhelmingly and consistently pro-gun. After all, if cars were not registered, few people would care enough to write their elected representatives demanding automobile registration. But car-owners, if they feared registration as a prelude to confiscation, would be highly active politically.

Moreover, the reluctance of the majority of the public to do something about gun control may be exacerbated by the press. One unreleased section of the Caddell poll asked if particular opinion leaders would actually induce respondents to follow their lead. For example, Caddell found that the respondents would be more inclined to support a gun law if the law were also backed by Martin Luther King Sr. Likewise, the Director of the FBI, the National Center to Control Handguns, local police chiefs, and the National Rifle Association would all attract more people to their side than they would repel. By speaking out, both the NCCH and the NRA would gain supporters for their point of view.

In contrast, three voices would actually make people more inclined to support the opposite view; one "anti-opinion leader" was Smith & Wesson, the handgun manufacturer. The second was "business groups." And the third was "your local paper."[79]

---

[77] Senator Metzenbaum of Ohio had proposed legislation that would have outlawed a number of small all-metal handguns which he said were not detectable. Congress adopted an NRA substitute which affected no existing guns, and required that guns made in the future contain at least a small component of metal.

[78] Wright, 236-41.

[79] Cambridge Reports, B35-B58.

Thus, there is some evidence that the majority of the public is less highly concerned about gun control than the press is. Further, press support for gun control might be counterproductive. In short, on the gun control issue, there appears to be some contradiction between the press and the people.

Pro-control polls such as Caddell's (or at least the press releases for such polls), implicitly proclaim that there is no contradiction between the press and the American people — that the public shares the big-city press' deep concern about gun control. Pro-gun polls, such as Wirthlin's, highlight the contradiction between the press and people. Perhaps that is why much of the press was receptive to Caddell, and hostile to Wirthlin.

Chapter 14

THE MEDIA AND GUN CONTROL:
A CASE STUDY IN WORLD-VIEW PUSHING

by
William R. Tonso

INTRODUCTION

Displayed prominently across the top of the full-page advertisement are the photographs of three well-known TV anchormen with their names and network affiliations identifying each of them — Peter Jennings of ABC, Dan Rather of CBS, and Tom Brokaw of NBC. Underneath the photographs printed in bold red letters a half-inch high is the question, "WOULD YOU RELY ON THEM FOR GUN NEWS?" Below this question in ordinary-sized print appears this statement: "When it comes to guns and hunting, there is no substitute for fast, accurate, authoritative news. But you won't get it from the major TV networks, from the national news weeklies or from your local newspapers." There is more, but this is the crux of the way that *Gun Week,* a weekly newspaper for gun enthusiasts, has often been advertised in its own pages. And these sentiments seem to be shared by the vast majority of gun enthusiasts who oppose the movement to bring civilian firearms ownership in the United States under stricter governmental control.

Just what is it about general-media treatment of the gun-control issue in the United States that so disturbs opponents of such controls? Is what we have here just another case of bias in the eyes of very partisan beholders, or is there substance to the charge that general-media coverage of the gun issue is heavily supportive of controls and often anti-gun? In the following pages I will attempt to demonstrate that there is indeed substance to these charges that the general media are heavily permeated by a pro-gun-control bias that can even reach all the way down to the local level in parts of the country where pro-gun anti-control sentiments are quite strong. I will also explore the nature, dimensions, and origins of this pro-control bias, provincial and otherwise.

Of course, bias is always easy to "prove" to those already inclined to believe that it exists. Skeptics, on the other hand, and those accused of bias, are inclined to locate bias in the eyes of the partisan beholder. I am well aware that I am particularly vulnerable to this charge, since I am a very strong opponent of any legislation that might conceivably threaten the right of law-abiding Americans to own rifles, shotguns, and handguns of their own choosing in accordance with the individualistic as opposed to the collectivist interpretation of the Second Amendment of the

Constitution of the United States.[1] However, I am also an extremely relativistic sociologist who views reality as a social construct in accordance with such subjectivist sociological perspectives as phenomenology and symbolic interactionism.[2] Consequently, playing my sociological role, I am quite willing and able to reflexively stand back from my personal political commitments, value stands, and interpretations of reality, accept them as social constructions, and resist the temptation to believe that I am in touch with the absolute **TRUTH** about anything. Therefore, while as a private citizen I am a strong supporter of the individualistic interpretation of the Second Amendment, as a sociologist I simply locate myself on one side of what I think might best be viewed as a clash of cultures without assuming that my side is objectively right and the other side objectively wrong. Given my sociological orientation, it is not my goal in the following pages of this sociological effort to demonstrate media bias for purposes of criticism. It is my goal to suggest how the gun issue and its treatment by the general media might best be understood by placing them in a broader sociocultural context — always keeping in mind that even social scientific efforts are social constructs.[3]

If, as the social constructionists argue, the object world must be filtered through frames of reference that we symbolically construct as we interact with each other before it has any meaning for us, bias is an unavoidable part of the human condition and it is impossible for any of us to see anything in an objective, non-culturally-contaminated manner — scientists, social and otherwise, included, as noted above. Given this perspective, it follows that those who charge the media with bias are indeed viewing the media through far from objective eyes, but so are the men and women of the media viewing the world they cover through far from objective eyes. And it seems that since the early part of this century many journalists have readily acknowledged that the "facts" they report are interpretations of reality rather than solidly and objectively out there in the real world.[4] Yet many journalists and other media folk bristle with indignation at the suggestion or accusation that the media are biased. Balance is what they allegedly strive toward, and I once heard a *Newsweek* editor claim that they feel that they have achieved balance if their coverage of a given controversial issue draws roughly the same amount of fire from one of the opposing

---

[1] The most complete presentation of the individualistic interpretation of the Second Amendment to date is by Stephen P. Halbrook, *That Every Man Be Armed: The Evolution of a Constitutional Right* (Albuquerque, New Mexico: University of New Mexico Press, 1984).

[2] For one of the most sophisticated presentations of this perspective see Peter L. Berger and Thomas Luckmann, *The Social Construction of Reality: A Treatise in the Sociology of Knowledge* (Garden City, New York: Anchor Books, 1966).

[3] Ibid. In fact, from the social constructionist perspective, even the natural sciences deal with objective reality only after it has been filtered through their social constructs. See Jack D. Douglas and Francis C. Waksler, *The Sociology of Deviance: An Introduction* (Boston: Little, Brown and Company, 1982). Ch. 12; and Thomas S. Kuhn, *The Structure of Scientific Revolutions* 2nd Edition (Chicago: University of Chicago Press, 1970).

[4] See Michael Schudson, *Discovering the News: A Social History of American Newspapers* (New York: Basic Books, Inc., 1987).

camps as it does from the other. Coverage, in other words, allegedly attempts to do justice to the biased perspectives of both sides, and a fair rendering of one extreme looks like support to the other extreme even though it has been dealt with in a similar fashion. It is believed that the public is thus kept informed, and the media, or at least the news media, can lay claim to a socially-legitimated justification for their existence. "Give light and the people will find their own way," is the motto of Scripps Howard newspapers, the chain that owns one of the local newspapers whose treatment of the gun issue will be examined in the following pages. "Truth" and "facts" may be relative, but if the citizens of a democracy are presented with opposing claims concerning "truth" and "facts" they are at least in a position to decide for themselves in an informed fashion who to believe and how to act on their beliefs — or so the ideal has it. Though the editors of the newspapers being examined may genuinely subscribe to this ideal, I hope to demonstrate through this study that they fall far short of presenting their readers with a "balanced" presentation of the conflicting views on gun controls and to consider possible reasons for their deviation from their ideal.

The Evansville Newspapers And The Tri-State Region They Serve

During the late 1970s I started collecting newspaper commentaries dealing in one way or another with guns and the gun-control issue — comic strips, cartoons, and letters to editors as well as news reports, editorials, and syndicated columns. At first, this collecting was neither systematic nor consistent, but by 1981 I was attempting to collect all gun-issue commentary from the newspapers of Evansville, Indiana, the community in which I live and profess sociology. My objective at that time was simply to document perceived imbalance in gun-issue coverage for media-critical purposes, since in 1981 I had started to react to this perceived imbalance with an invited column-length piece for one of the local newspapers followed by a continuing string of letters to the local editors.[5] Until that time my gun-related writing had consisted of my doctoral dissertation which cross-culturally and sociohistorically explored the social and existential roots of the modern attachment to firearms (since published), and two papers critiquing the orthodox sociological treatment of the gun issue in textbooks and federal commission studies, etc. (one of which has since been published in two versions).[6] Through the early 1980s, however, my writing on the

---

[5] The very anti-handgun editorial-page editor of *The Evansville Press* invited me to write an anti-control guest column for his pages after I had sent him several complaints about the almost exclusive pro-control commentaries appearing in them.

[6] William R. Tonso, *Gun and Society: The Social and Existential Roots of the American Attachment to Firearms* (Washington, D.C.: University Press of America, 1982); "Social Sciences and Sagecraft in the Debate Over Gun Control," *Law & Policy Quarterly*, Vol. 5, No. 3 (July, 1983), 325-343; and "Social Problems and Sagecraft: Gun Control as a Case in Point," in Don B. Kates, Jr. (ed.) *Firearms and Violence: Issues of Public Policy* (San Francisco: Pacific Institute for Public Policy Research, 1984), pp. 71-92.

gun issue strayed from the sociological to the sociologically-informed social critical, with several magazine and newspaper pieces critiquing the gun-control movement and/or its treatment by the media.[7] As my clipping collection grew, though, my always-present interest in reality construction and culture conflict inclined me toward a more sociological examination of the way the provincial newspapers I read every day treat the gun issue.

Evansville is located in the southwestern tip of Indiana, just across the Ohio River from Kentucky (which actually extends north of this river in some places), and some twenty air miles from my native Illinois across the Wabash River. With a population of approximately 130,000, Evansville is at least twice the size of any other community within a hundred mile radius in this farming and coal, natural gas, and oil producing tri-state region, and serves as its commercial and industrial hub, though Louisville, Kentucky falls just outside of the eastern fringe of this circle.

The Tri-State, where the Midwest and the South overlap, is hard-core, small-town and rural, bedrock America, and it is gun country where hunting, informal and formal target shooting, and gun collecting are popular activities.[8] It has been estimated that there are only 12.7 guns per one hundred persons in Chicago compared to 71.1 per hundred in the deep southern portion of Illinois, part of which qualifies for inclusion in the Tri-State, and there is no reason to suspect that this figure differs significantly in the Indiana and Kentucky portions of the region.[9] The regional gun-related crime rate has not been such as to generate even media criticism of existing gun controls, which vary considerably in each of the three states that come together here. Indiana has a seven-day waiting period for handgun purchases except for those individuals with clean records possessing easy-to-get carry permits. Kentucky does not allow concealed carry of handguns, but does allow open carry without permits. Illinois requires owners of all firearms to possess a police-cleared Firearms Owners Identification Card, and does not allow concealed carry of handguns.

As anyone familiar with the gun culture of the Tri-State knows, even otherwise law-abiding individuals can with clear consciences violate existing gun laws. And as politicians know, opposition to further attempts to regulate civilian firearms possession is strong in this region. Frank McCloskey, the United States representative

[7] See William R. Tonso, "Media Culture and Guns," The Quill (March, 1983), 17-20; "Calling the Shots," Reason (March, 1985), 42-47; "Gun Control: White Man's Law," Reason (December, 1985), 22-25; and "Guns and the Media," American Rifleman (April, 1986), 42-43, 78-79.

[8] See Joycelyn Winnecke, "People around here would rather hunt, fish, read Bible or watch the tube," Sunday Courier (September 17, 1989), IA. This story summarizes what The Lifestyle Market Analyst (Chicago: Standard Rate & Data Service, 1989) has to say about the Evansville region.

[9] David J. Bordua, "Firearms Ownership and Violent Crime: A Comparison of Illinois Counties," in James M. Byrne and Robert J. Sampson, The Social Ecology of Crime (New York: Springer-Verlag, 1986), p. 180.

from southern Indiana, placed a large campaign advertisement in the Evansville newspapers just prior to the 1984 elections to quell accusations by his Republican opponent that he supported gun controls. Democrat McCloskey pointed out his support for National Rifle Association of America (NRA) efforts and that organization's support of him.[10] Democratic representative Kenneth Gray of my native Illinois district voted against the national handgun-purchase waiting period that he personally supported because he felt obliged not to go against strong anti-gun-control and pro-NRA feelings among his constituents.[11] Gun control cropped up again during the 1988 presidential campaign when the Democratic vice presidential candidate, Senator Lloyd Bentsen of Texas, speaking in nearby Owensboro, Kentucky, was put on the defensive due to the strong pro-gun-control stand long taken, but later denied, by his presidential running mate, Massachusetts Governor Michael Dukakis.[12] And indeed, NRA stickers on vehicle windshields are quite common all through the Tri-State.

Until October 27, 1986, Evansville was served by three newspapers. The Evansville Courier, the morning newspaper with a circulation of 64,000, was established in 1845 and was locally owned. The Evansville Press, the evening newspaper with a circulation of 40,500, was established in 1906 by the Scripps Howard newspaper chain headquartered in Cincinnati, Ohio. Both of these newspapers were published six days a week by the Evansville Printing Corporation in which they were equal partners, and on Sundays they combined to produce The Evansville Sunday Courier and Press, which had a circulation of 115,000. While the Sunday newspaper had its own editor as well as several features of its own, including an editorial page (generally commenting on rather mundane local issues), an entertainment section, and Parade Magazine, it also carried an editorial page from The Courier and one from The Press, and the comic section was composed almost entirely of the strips regularly carried in the two dailies. All of this changed, however, when Scripps Howard sold The Press to a retiring vice president, purchased The Courier, and took over full control of the Sunday newspaper. Slightly over two months before the end of 1986, when I had planned to finally stop collecting what had become the basis for this study, The Courier became a seven-day-a-week chain newspaper, The Press became a six-day-a-week independent newspaper, and The Sunday Courier and Press became defunct. Since I was interested not only in documenting pro-control bias in the coverage of the gun issue by the local newspapers, but in determining if there was any basis to my suspicion that the

---

10 This issue was raised in Kit Wagar, "McCloskey masters the balancing act in diverse district," The Evansville Courier (Thursday, November 1, 1984), 13. The advertisement appeared in the same newspaper on November 4.

11 See Larry Margasak, "NRA shows firepower against gun control," The Sunday Courier (Sunday, September 16, 1988), A6.

12 See Terri Likens and Barry Rose, "Bentsen claims Demos are gaining momentum," The Evansville Courier (November 2, 1988), 3.

independently-owned morning newspaper was less biased along these lines than the chain-owned evening newspaper, I could not ignore these ownership changes. Consequently, the period covered by the original version of this study presented in skeletal form at the 1987 meetings of the Popular Culture and American Culture Associations in Montreal, fell two months short of six years and I had no intention of going further with it beyond putting it into publishable form. However, for various partly-anticipated methodological reasons this publishable form continued to evade me until I decided to shift the emphasis of this study from the too-broadly defined categories and too-loosely defined subjects I used in my original effort to a narrow focus on the local treatment of what might well be the most heated gun-control battle of the second half of the 20th century — the ongoing effort to regulate possession of "assault weapons" that became a national issue in January, 1989.

To help the reader to keep track of each newspaper's place in the local media scene, from this point on I will refer to *The Courier* as *Morning & Sunday-Chain* and *The Press* as *Evening-Private* for the period beginning with the transfer of ownership in late October, 1986 to the present time. For the period before the transfer, *The Courier* will be referred to as *Morning-Local, The Press* as *Evening-Chain,* and *The Sunday Courier and Press* as *Sunday-LC,* denoting combined local and chain ownership.

PERSPECTIVES ON GUN CONTROL AND METHODS OF THIS STUDY

The position of the NRA and other anti-control organizations commonly referred to in the general media as the "gun lobby," can accurately be described as pro-gun and anti-any kind of regulation of civilian gun ownership that *might* in any way undermine what they see as the Second Amendment-guaranteed right of all law-abiding American citizens to keep and bear not only sporting and self-defense guns but militarily-effective small arms.[13] People on this side of the gun debate are not only gun enthusiasts in that they like guns and enjoy their legal sporting and recreational uses. These enthusiasts also are convinced that the possession of guns and gun-handling skills by law-abiding Americans are useful for self-, community-, and national-defense purposes, and that they can deter the establishment of domestic tyrannies at local, state, and/or federal levels of government. Indeed, it is this rather libertarian uneasiness about government and its police powers that marks off the hard-core anti-control position of the "gun lobby" from the other side of the gun debate, which ranges from perspectives that could be described as pro-gun pro-control all the way out to the vehemently anti-gun pro-control.

While no clear-cut line of demarcation exists between the pro-gun anti-controllers

---

13 See Bill R. Davidson, *To Keep and Bear Arms* (New Rochelle, New York: Arlington House, 1969); Neal Knox, "Lessons From Tiananmen Square," *Guns & Ammo* (September, 1989), 32; and Sue Wimmershoff-Caplan. "The Founders and the AK-47," *The Washington Post* (July 6, 1989), A17 for strong statements of the pro-gun anti-control position.

and the pro-gun pro-controllers, the former position blends into the latter as trust increases that politicians and the police they control will not take advantage of such apparently reasonable and nonthreatening measures as gun registration, waiting periods for purchase, and police background checks of purchasers to keep law-abiding citizens from acquiring and possessing guns. Such trust in government was reflected in the comments of an outdoors writer for *Morning & Sunday-Chain* (May 7, 1989) who, fearful of the fallout of efforts to ban "assault weapons," called on fellow sportsmen to act to protect their cherished and responsibly used sporting guns. "Why can't some group do something revolutionary and pioneer a movement to license all firearms — not just handguns — in the United States?" he asked. In an accompanying Scripps Howard piece, a writer claiming 40 years' involvement in the shooting sports took the NRA, the gun industry, and the gun press to task for putting the shooting sports in jeopardy by promoting and defending the civilian ownership of "assault rifles." Neither of these writers expressed any concern for the individualistic interpretation of the Second Amendment nor awareness that Americans might ever need militarily-effective guns to protect themselves from some level or other of their own government. The local writer was primarily concerned about protecting civilian ownership of sporting guns, while the Scripps Howard writer was not only pro-sporting gun but anti-"assault rifle." At the point where some guns are accepted for civilian possession, though possibly subject to permits, etc., while others are not, the pro-gun pro-control position begins to merge imperceptibly with the anti-gun pro-control position.

For example, Handgun Control, Incorporated claims to take a centrist position on gun controls, supporting waiting periods, background checks, and police permits aimed at keeping handguns out of the "wrong hands," rather than advocating a ban on their ownership by civilians. However, HCI has expressed approval of handgun bans wherever they have been enacted, and has been the prime mover behind attempts to ban "Saturday Night Specials," "cop-killer" bullets, "plastic" guns, and "assault weapons," all defined so vaguely as to conceivably include many common guns and bullets.[14] The National Coalition to Ban Handguns, of course, makes no attempt to disguise its position on handguns, but NCBH also has supported bans on the previously listed and vaguely-defined items on the HCI list.

While no well-publicized, pro-control organization openly advocates banning the civilian possession of all guns in the United States, such sentiments have long existed in influential circles. Morris Janowitz was quoted as follows in a 1968 *Time* article: "I see no reason ... why anyone in a democracy should own a weapon."[15] A few issues later, the same magazine published a letter to the editor from Marvin E. Wolfgang expressing identical sentiments: "My personal choice for legislation is to remove all guns from private possession. I would favor statutory provisions that require all guns

---

[14] See the Spring, 1989 solicitation and membership appeal from Handgun Control, Inc.
[15] In "The Gun Under Fire," *Time* (June 21, 1968), 17.

to be turned in to public authorities."[16] Both of these prominent sociologists were associated with Milton Eisenhower's federal commission which investigated the causes and prevention of violence and ended up recommending somewhat less restrictive gun controls.[17]

With this extreme gun-control position, trust in government and its police powers obviously is complete, and the state's monopoly of weaponry is not perceived as posing any threat to the civil liberties of law-abiding citizens. Law-abiding citizens cannot be trusted with guns, instruments that the anti-gun pro-controllers associate so exclusively with crime, violence, and barbarism in general that, as Kates and Varzos note in Chapter 8, a private citizen's interest in them is considered to be psychiatrically suspect. While even middle-range pro-gun pro-controllers seem inclined to view the Second Amendment as either outdated or as guaranteeing no more than a National Guard-like militia's right to keep and bear arms, such views of this amendment are accepted as articles of faith by anti-gun pro-controllers from HCI and NCBH to those who openly advocate complete civilian disarmament.

The pro-gun pro-control position that overlaps the pro-gun anti-control position at one extreme and the anti-gun pro-control position at the other extreme thwarted my initial examination of local newspaper treatment of the gun issue because I ignored its implications. From the standpoint of the pro-gun anti-controllers, the right to keep and bear arms that they are convinced that the Second Amendment guarantees them is no less threatened by the vociferous pro-gun pro-controllers than it is by the anti-gun pro-controllers, and there is widespread suspicion among pro-gun anti-controllers that many pro-gun pro-controllers are actually anti-gun pro-controllers.[18] As shall be seen, these suspicions have hardly been put to rest by the efforts of the pro-control organizations and general-media treatment of these efforts. Therefore, though three distinct (if overlapping) perspectives on guns and their control in the United States can be identified, most parties involved and the media covering the battle between them tend to blur the distinction between the pro-gun pro-controllers and the anti-gun pro-controllers in many ways. Consequently, the ongoing battle is basically between those who do not trust the government to regulate the acquisition and possession of firearms by law-abiding citizens, and those who do trust the government with such regulatory powers, regardless of how these trusters of government feel about guns. Since it is the government-suspecting pro-gun anti-controllers who claim that general media coverage of the gun issue favors the government-trusting pro-controllers, and since I am attempting to demonstrate that this claim is far from groundless, in the following pages I have classified gun-issue items from each of the local newspapers commenting on attempts to regulate

---

[16] Marvin E. Wolfgang, "Letters to the Editor," *Time* (July 5, 1968), 6.

[17] This commission's gun-control recommendations were presented in George D. Newton and Franklin E. Zimring, *Firearms and Violence in American Life,* a staff report to the National Commission on the Causes and Prevention of Violence (Washington, D.C.: Government Printing Office, 1969).

[18] See Alan Gottlieb, *The Gun Grabbers* (Bellevue, Washington: Merril Press, 1986).

possession of "assault weapons" as either pro-control, conventional, unconventional, or anti-control. And I have not only examined how the local newspapers compared with each other in their treatment of this gun-control effort, but how several different features of each newspaper have treated this effort: (1) news service stories, (2) local stories, (3) syndicated columns, (4) local columnists, guests included, (5) syndicated and local political cartoons appearing on the editorial pages, (6) comic strips, and (7) letters to the editors. In other words, I am interested in all of the messages concerning this issue that have been transmitted through the local newspapers, not only their news messages, the manifest objectives of which are to keep the public informed. And I also wanted to document as best I could the origins of these various messages. The period covered by this study extends from January 18, 1989 through July 17, 1989, the first six months after "assault weapons" became a national issue.

Criteria for classifying items as pro-control, conventional, unconventional, and anti-control are as follows: Pro-control items are columns, editorials, cartoons, comic strips, or letters blatantly supportive of the regulation of the civilian possession of whatever guns are classified as "assault weapons," and/or that attack these weapons or those who oppose regulating them. Conventional items are generally news stories, though they also include columns and so forth that do not openly support "assault weapon" regulation. But even when such items report reasonably accurately on the issue and include comments from the opposition, they are more or less permeated by the unexamined assumptions of the pro-controllers concerning the uniqueness of the weapons themselves, widespread police and public support for their regulation, NRA money power as the chief obstacle to regulation, and so forth. Unconventional items are also generally news stories, though they also include items of the other kinds that do not oppose "assault weapon" regulation, but that are not permeated by the unexamined assumptions of the pro-controllers and may even undermine them. Anti-control items are columns, editorials, cartoons, comic strips, or letters blatantly opposed to the regulation of "assault weapons" and/or to those who support such regulations.

Of course , as a social constructionist, I would be the first to acknowledge that establishing criteria and applying them are far from the same thing, since criteria are defined into existence while determining what meets them is a matter of judgment. The newspaper items that I examined for this study did not automatically and objectively sort themselves out as pro-control, conventional, unconventional, or anti-control. I sorted these items, and the reader should keep this in mind. However, the reader might also keep in mind that my sorting effort was informed by a lifetime of insider familiarity with the world of guns, a long-time familiarity with the reality of that world as it has been projected through the gun press, 30 years' familiarity with the reality of that world as it has been projected through the general media, and 20 years' familiarity with it as it has been projected through scholarly publications. Still, the subjectivity of my effort cannot be escaped.

Actually, I had no problem classifying the vast majority of these items. Pro-control items were blatantly so, as were almost all of the anti-control items. However, a few of the conventional and unconventional items were labeled with less confidence. The most difficult judgment calls I had to make, though, concerned which items were relevant to the "assault-weapon" controversy and which were not. Several columns and comic strips lambasting the NRA but not mentioning "assault weapons" seemed relevant, since the NRA was being attacked at the time primarily for supporting civilian ownership of such weapons. I classified these items as pro-control. I excluded several other comic strips with more ambiguous anti-gun or pro-control messages. I excluded one blatant anti-control column by a prominent anti-control activist because it opposed waiting periods for handgun purchases and completely ignored the "assault-weapon" issue, but I also excluded several pro-control and conventional items that focused completely on other than "assault weapons." On the one hand, I am uneasy about not including every gun-related item carried in the local newspapers during the six-month period covered by this study. On the other hand, however, my previous attempts to measure meaningfully the pro-control bias in these newspapers have taught me that trying to include everything tends to encourage cumbersome conceptualization and to shift the focus of the effort to their treatment of guns and away from their treatment of gun controls. I have, therefore, tried to exclude all gun-related items that cannot be readily related to the rather clear-cut "assault-weapon" controversy. And since most of the excluded items were classifiable as pro-control or conventional, the effect of their exclusion has not been to increase the appearance of bias in favor of controls. I mention the preceding judgment calls in order to remind the reader of the very subjective grounding of the numerically-precise item and line counts and percentages that I will present in the following pages. Due to my social-constructionist outlook, I am very suspicious of numbers; consequently, I feel obliged to remind others that even those numbers that I generate are not as objective as they may appear to be.

Comparisons of the pro-control, conventional, unconventional, and anti-control items between newspapers and between features of newspapers will be made in terms of units, with each full or partial story, editorial, and so forth counting as one item, and for all items except cartoons and comic strips, line count, with half lines and over counting as full lines (including headlines) and less than half lines not counted. In the following section, these items have been documented, classified, quantified, and commented on according to the seven types of features mentioned above (news-service stories, etc.) for each of the local newspapers.

SIX MONTHS OF "ASSAULT-WEAPON" COVERAGE

News-Service Stories: On January 17, 1989, a young man with a history of emotional problems walked into a Stockton, California schoolyard crowded with Asian-American children and opened fire on them with a Chinese-made semi-automatic variation of a Soviet AK-47 assault rifle. The gunman killed 5 children and wounded 30 other adults and children before he took his own life with a handgun. The gunman's semi-automatic rifle had been purchased in Oregon, and the Associated Press story of this tragic event carried in *Morning & Sunday-Chain* on January 18 ended with the following comments:

A semiautomatic rifle can be purchased easily in Oregon, without even the five-day waiting period required for a handgun, if the buyer signs a federal form stating he has never been convicted of a serious crime or indicted, among other requirements, said Bob Imel, a Salem, Oregon, gun shop owner.

"You use it for one purpose and one purpose only — to kill a human being," said Los Angeles Police Lt. Fred Nixon.

Though part of an allegedly neutral news-service story of a crime, the preceding comments suggest that semi-automatic rifles in general are too easy to acquire in Oregon, and that civilians have no business owning them — debatable points that were left undebated. These comments served as previews of things to come, and this portion of the longer news story serves as a prime example of allegedly unbiased news reportage of the sort that I have classified as conventional.

In the days and weeks that followed the shooting, pro-gun anti-controllers and the gun press tried in vain to keep public and media attention focused on the killer, the shortcomings of the criminal justice system that had allowed him to roam free, and the failure of existing gun controls (including waiting periods) to keep him from acquiring his weapons. It seems that this young man had been in trouble with the law frequently, but that his felony offenses had been plea-bargained down to misdemeanors; that a psychiatrist had considered him to be a danger to himself and others and that he was drawing $682 monthly from the Social Security Administration as a result of his officially-diagnosed emotional problems; and yet he had been able to buy five handguns in California in spite of that state's 15-day waiting period and background check.[19] He had acquired the handgun he used to kill himself only a few days before he went on his shooting rampage. However, hardly a day had passed after the shooting before the national media lost interest in the killer and focused attention on his gun and the efforts of those trying to regulate or ban civilian possession of "assault rifles." Actually, efforts to regulate or ban civilian possession of semi-automatic weapons misleadingly labeled "assault rifles" were already well underway in California, and the schoolyard shooting simply got them the media attention they needed to go national.[20]

---

[19] From Neal Knox's testimony before the Subcommittee on the Constitution of the U.S. Senate Judiciary Committee on February 10, 1989, reported in "Semi-Auto Hearing: Logic Against Emotion," *The New Gun Week* Vol. 24, Issue 1145 (Friday, March 10, 1989), 3.

[20] See "California Agencies Push Anti-Gun Bill," *The New Gun Week* Vol. 24, Issue 1138 (Friday, January 20, 1989), 1. Though dated after the California shooting, this issue was printed and mailed before that event and this report is on "assault-weapon" legislation.

To those who know firearms, the label "assault rifle" is properly applied to only relatively short rifles (carbines) capable of being fired full automatic (firing continues as long as the trigger is held back) as well as semi-automatic (one trigger pull per shot), and chambered for cartridges considerably less powerful than those used in the battle rifles of the two world wars. Civilian possession of full-automatic weapons has been federally regulated since 1934, and a number of states ban their possession by civilians; therefore, possession of true assault rifles has long been regulated. But purposely or otherwise, the distinction between full-automatics and semi-automatics is lost on some pro-controllers, while others claim that semi-automatic versions of assault rifles can be converted to full-automatics so easily that for all practical purposes they are the same.[21] Pro-controllers also argue that these semi-automatic rifles are too powerful and/or have magazine capacities too great for sporting uses, and that they are being bought in legitimate gun shops by criminals for use in urban drug wars. Therefore, it is claimed, such guns are particularly troublesome to the nation's police and jeopardize the lives of innocent bystanders. And it is this pro-control version of the "reality" of "assault rifles" that permeates practically all of the major-media news coverage of efforts to regulate civilian possession of such weapons, and that filters down to provincial newspapers via the news services.

The most complete presentation of this "reality" in a news-service story to appear in a local newspaper during the period covered by this study came from the the *New York Times* News Service and appeared in the February 2, 1989 edition of *Morning & Sunday-Chain* under the headline "Weapons of drug wars force war time medical techniques." "The medical techniques used in the Vietnam War are now being used in civilian life," an assistant professor of medicine at the University of California at Davis who once served as the medical director of a Cambodian refugee camp is quoted as saying. And the article goes on to state that this doctor's "comparison to Vietnam was echoed in interviews with more than a dozen other doctors and paramedics across the nation, who described exploded organs and pulverized bones, the flood of internal bleeding and bodies riddled with holes from high-velocity, rapid-fire assault rifles." This news story carried no opposing comments and though conventional, an editorialist would be hard pressed to write a more partisan piece in support of the strictest regulation of civilian possession of weapons referred to in the article as either "assault rifles" or "automatics." And without opposing comments, this and similar conventional "news reports" may impact heavily and negatively on the definition of "assault-rifle" reality held by ordinary people, including non-politically-involved gun owners, across the United States. From the perspective of the informed pro-gun anti-controllers, however, the anti-"assault-rifle" position is either incredibly uninformed about firearms at best or outrageously dishonest at worst, and can easily be rebutted on all counts. And since this perspective has hardly been mentioned in general-media news and commentary, I will briefly summarize it below.

---

[21] See Tom Morganthau, et. al., "Machine Gun U.S.A." *Newsweek* (October 14, 1985), 46-51.

From the perspective of the pro-gun anti-controllers it is completely irrelevant whether or not semi-automatic versions of the Soviet AK-47, our own M-16, and other true assault rifles, or of the Israeli Uzi and other submachine guns, or any of the semi-automatic or slide-action shotguns and many other weapons that have come to be labeled "assault weapons" have any sporting uses at all. The Second Amendment, from this perspective (or any other perspective that I know of) has nothing to do with sporting weapons — it is believed to guarantee Americans the right to possess militarily-effective small arms as members of a militia to which all able-bodied males between the ages of 17 and 45 belong.[22] Of course, given the symbolic and politicized nature of this issue, it is extremely doubtful that what the Second Amendment really guarantees will ever be agreed upon by the opposing factions in the battle over gun controls, though in recent years the individual-right interpretation of this amendment has received some rather impressive scholarly support.[23] Those who claim that if this interpretation of the Second Amendment is what the Founding Fathers actually intended, it has long been outdated might consider how various minorities in this country have on occasion been treated by their governments and police forces, local, state, and/or federal, as Salter has done in Chapter 2. And it would seem that the Director of Civilian Marksmanship, which was established under the National Defense Act in 1916, is based on a philosophy opposed to the one accepted by those who claim that American civilians have no business possessing small arms created expressly for battlefield use. The DCM has at bargain-basement prices sold literally millions of surplus American military rifles and handguns, including semi-automatic M-1 Garand rifles and M-1 carbines, to NRA members and others over the years in connection with its official objective of promoting military preparedness among the civilian populace.

However, to point out that pro-gun anti-controllers do not oppose "assault-weapon" legislation primarily on the grounds that such weapons are useful for sport is not to accept the claim that such weapons actually are not useful for sport because of their power or magazine capacities. As I have noted previously, true assault rifles are less powerful than the battle rifles of the two world wars. The semi-automatic military lookalikes are chambered for the same cartridges as the military full-

[22] 10 United States Code section 311 (a).

[23] See Halbrook; Don B. Kates, Jr., "Handgun Prohibition and the Original Meaning of the Second Amendment," *Michigan Law Review* 82 (1983), 1701-1770; Kates (ed.) *Firearms and Violence,* Part VII; Robert E. Shalhope, "The Armed Citizen in the Early Republic," Kates, "The Second Amendment: A Dialogue," and Halbrook, "What the Framers Intended: A Linguistics Analysis of the Right to 'Bear Arms,' " all in *Law and Contemporary Problems* Vol. 49, No. 1 (Winter, 1986); David I. Caplain, "The Right of the Individual To Bear Arms: A Recent Judicial Trend," *Detroit College of Law Review* Vol. 1982, Issue 4 (Winter); and James B. Whisker, *Our Vanishing Freedom: The Right to Keep and Bear Arms,* 2nd Edition (Skokie, Illinois: Publisher's Development Corporation, 1972).

automatics, and the more powerful cartridges used in the old battle rifles, such as our own .30-06, are among the favorite, but hardly the most powerful, cartridges used for big game hunting. Ex-police lieutenant and nationally-known firearms and self-defense authority Massad Ayoob, has noted that on paper the performance of the 7.62X39mm AK-47 round appears to be similar to that of the modest performance of the .30-30, a long-time favorite of American hunters, but that it is actually a less potent round than the .30-30.[24] And Colonel Martin Fackler, once a combat surgeon who treated AK-47 wounds in Vietnam and who is now head of the Army's Wound Ballistics Laboratory in San Francisco, told a *Washington Post* reporter that the AK-47 is the "mildest-wounding assault rifle in existence."[25] As horrible as the casualties in the schoolyard shooting were, the fact that only 5 of 35 people hit were killed bears out the colonel's claim, especially when we consider that most of those people were children. In a *Gun Week* interview, this same veteran medical officer stated: "The AK-47 bullet is designed more to wound than to kill because a wounded man ties up other personnel who have to aid him."[26]

Aware of the power limitations of the AK-47 round, Fackler was suspicious of the demonstrations of that weapon's destructiveness filmed by a California TV crew and shown to national as well as local audiences. Checking with law-enforcement sources, this military medical doctor claimed that he was told that the melon shown supposedly being blasted apart by an AK-47 slug had actually been shot with a 9mm expanding *hollow-point slug* from the far less powerful handgun of a member of the Los Angeles County Sheriff's Department. When the AK-47 being used for the demonstration produced only a large neat hole in a melon, the TV crew asked for something more spectacular, so the obliging lawman shot a melon with his 9mm, a cartridge that many American authorities consider barely, if at all, adequate for military or police use, and that is used in both full- and semi-automatic Uzis. The hollow-point-splattered melon was then credited to the AK-47. When *Gun Week* staffers conducted their own experiment using a .30-06 rifle, a 9mm pistol *using hollow-points,* a semi-automatic version of our own .223 assault rifle, and a semi-automatic version of the AK-47, the last was the only gun that did not blow the honeydew melon targets apart. The .223, which is also used in semi-automatic sporting rifles, was less destructive than the 9mm hollow-point (which does not prove that this pistol is more powerful than the rifle), and the old military .30-06 blew the melon to smithereens.[27] Colonel Fackler also commented on other suspect TV demonstrations of AK-47 destructiveness and summed up the situation as follows: "I didn't mean to take sides in the gun-law controversy but that assault-rifle fiasco on TV brings to light a far more serious problem: who is to protect the public from an overzealous media whose causes take them beyond falsehood to fabriction?"[28] The general media have not seen fit to mention Fackler's concerns.

[24] Massad Ayoob, "In Defense of the Assault Rifle," *Guns* (July, 1989), 71.

[25] Henry Allen, "The Mystique of Guns," *The Washington Post* (April 19, 1989), D1-3.

[26] Marshall J. Brown, "Wound Ballistics Expert Exposes Media AK Fakery," *The New Gun Week* Vol. 24, Issue 1153 (Friday, May 5, 1989), 1.

[27] Ibid.

[28] Ibid.

Lest the preceding comments be misconstrued, I am not trying to make the case for opposing the regulation of the civilian possession of any of the increasingly broad range of guns that as a result of enacted or proposed legislation has become potentially classifiable as "assault weapons." My objective is to point out some of what would seem to be relevant information concerning the basis of opposition to such legislation that the news services have not seen fit to pass on to the local newspapers, or that these newspapers have not seen fit to print. In examining "media bias" it is at least as important to consider what the media do not mention as it is to consider what they mention and how they mention it. As much importance as opponents of "assault-weapon" legislation attach to Second Amendment guarantees of their right to own such weapons, out of the 35 news-service stories related to this issue that have appeared in the two local newspapers, 18 in *Morning & Sunday-Chain* and 17 in *Evening Private*, only two pieces, both in *Evening Private* a United Press International story on February 8 and a reprint from *The Baltimore Sun* on July 8, briefly mentioned the constitutional issue. On the other hand, 16 news stories in these newspapers, 8 in *Morning & Sunday-Chain* and 8 in *Evening-Private*, mentioned the legitimate-sporting-use criteria for justifying the ownership of "assault weapons" — criteria that pro-gun anti-controllers reject.

News-service reportage on "assault weapons" themselves in the local newspapers is difficult to briefly summarize, but can best be described as confused. This confusion is certainly understandable since once the "assault" label is applied to weapons other than the selective-fire (full- and semi-automatic) rifles used by the military, there is no generally accepted way to identify which weapons should be so labeled. While these reports have covered the attempts of lawmakers to define "assault weapons" in terms of the number of rounds their magazines will hold, no news-service story in a local newspaper has yet to point out that any gun capable of using a detachable magazine can use any magazine of greater capacity fitted for it. Thus, any magazine-equipped weapon from a .22-caliber pistol on up would be classifiable as an "assault weapon."

Though one *Morning & Sunday Chain* story from the *New York Times* News Service that accompanied the same-source story comparing the drug wars to Vietnam did an acceptable job of explaining the difference between full- and semi-automatics, and there were other brief but accurate attempts to do the same, confusion between full- and semi-automatics was common at the beginning of the heavy coverage of efforts to control such weapons and it can still be found. As late as April 20, three months after the schoolyard shooting, an *Evening-Private* story from Knight-Ridder Newspapers under the headline "Tragedy prompts action against assault weapons across U.S." referred to the McDonald's shooting, "when a man in San Ysidro, Calif., killed 21 people and wounded 19 others with an Uzi submachine gun." Actually, a shotgun and a handgun were also used in that shooting, but more to the point here, the Uzi used was a semi-automatic rather than a submachine gun — a misleading blurring of full- and semi-automatics that Handgun Control, Inc. also uses when referring to that shooting in its pro-control mailings.[29] Even later, on July 17, an Associated Press story in *Morning & Sunday-Chain* correctly identified the gun used in the McDonald's shooting as a semi-automatic, but then went on to report that the more recent schoolyard shooting had "spurred a rash of legislation to limit private use of automatic weapons." Again, the blurred distinction. The impression one gets from many of these stories is that the reporters and/or editors responsible for them have never heard of semi-automatic firearms, even though civilians have used them for sport and protection since the turn of the century.

Though as I have noted above, firearms authorities consider the AK-47 cartridge, and even those of more potent assault rifles such as our own M-16, to be mild relative to cartridges used by older military rifles and mid-range big-game rifles, and any magazine-equipped gun can be equipped with a larger-capacity magazine, not one of the news-service stories carried by the local newspapers passed this information on to the public. When not mentioned specifically, the alleged extraordinary destructive potential of these semi-automatic military lookalikes was implied by many of the stories reporting attempts to regulate them. Both local newspapers carried Associated Press pieces about the 400,000 "military-style assault weapons" the importation of which the Bureau of Alcohol, Tobacco, and Firearms had stopped at our borders *(Morning & Sunday-Chain,* March 25 and *Evening-Private,* April 12) as if an invasion of killer bees had been halted. Another AP story in *Morning & Sunday-Chain* on February 11, under the headline "Nation's police urging Congress to ban assault rifles," quoted Los Angeles Police Chief Daryl F. Gates as telling a Senate Judiciary subcommittee, "The police of America are pleading with you." No evidence was presented that Gates' fears were shared by the nation's police, and the story did not mention that Edward D. Conroy, acting deputy associate director of enforcement for the Bureau of Alcohol, Tobacco, and Firearms, testified before the same subcommittee that technical distinctions between semi-automatic "assault rifles" and many semi-automatic hunting rifles would be difficult if not impossible to make.[30] Such weapons are claimed to be favored by the drug gangs, and one AP writer in a story about Washington, D.C.'s murder rate carried by *Morning & Sunday Chain,* while not mentioning "assault weapons," did see fit to state the

---

[29] See HCI's Spring, 1989 solicitation. A position paper entitled "Assault Weapons and Accessories in America," published by The Education Fund to End Handgun Violence and dated September, 1988, openly encouraged taking advantage of the public's ignorance of the difference between full- and semi-automatics to gain public support for regulation of the latter. The ease with which such organizations can utilize the media to further their efforts is indicated by the fact that the *Associated Press Stylebook and Libel Manual* has defined "submachine gun" as any "lightweight automatic or semi-automatic gun." If journalists do not know the difference between these weapons, they are in no position to critically examine the claims of the pro-controllers.

[30] From Edward D. Conroy's testimony before the previously mentioned subcommittee, reported in "Semi-Auto Hearings."

following: "Ten to 20 years ago, high school students might have carried pen knives as protection. Today, said a city officer, protection is a handgun, often an automatic." Here again, attention was drawn to the sinister "automatic," as semi-automatic pistols are often misleadingly referred to even by knowledgeable gun people. Semi-automatic pistols have been in common use since the turn of the century, but now their use is noteworthy because "automatic" has become synonymous with "assault weapon."

Very rarely a news-service story undermined claims that "assault weapons" are becoming ever more troublesome to the police, or that enacted or proposed legislation will effectively keep such weapons out of the hands of drug gangs or other troublemakers. On April 3, *Morning & Sunday-Chain* carried a story from the *New York Times* News Service that noted that "Several urban police chiefs and executives of police organizations support a ban on military-style semi-automatic rifles," but went on to point out that while record-keeping on such matters is incomplete, only a small percentage of the guns seized by the police across the nation fits this category. And an AP story of a Washington, D.C. teenager's testimony before the House Select Committee on Children, Youth and Families that appeared in *Evening-Private* on June 16 reported that the girl claimed that youngsters generally "get their guns from drug traffickers for whom they work." How will laws regulating "assault weapon" possession by ordinary Americans keep such weapons out of the hands of traffickers who can smuggle in guns with their drugs? Such unconventional stories were rare indeed, though there is an abundance of what would seem to be relevant subject matter for them.

On September 18, 1988, before the period covered by this study, the Sunday edition of *Morning & Sunday-Chain* carried an AP story under the headline "NRA shows firepower against gun control measure." This otherwise conventional story briefly mentioned that the NRA had countered HCI's claim that law enforcement unanimously supported the handgun waiting period about to be voted on by the House of Representatives by bringing police from across the nation who opposed this measure to Washington to visit congressmen. This AP story is the only news-service report I have found in the local newspapers since I have been systematically collecting such items that has mentioned police opposition to any gun-control measure, even though such opposition may be considerable. According to *Gun Week:* "On June 6, 225 law enforcement officers from 49 states demonstrated on Capitol Hill in Washington, D.C. against legislative proposals for semi-automatic firearms bans and then fanned out in smaller groups to lobby individual Senators and Representatives against the proposals."[31] The same issue of this gun publication reported on the founding of a new national police organization called Law

---

[31] "Police Capital Rally Opposes Ban," *The New Gun Week,* Vol. 24, Issue 1160 (Friday, June 30, 1989), 1, 3.

Enforcement for the Preservation of the Second Amendment (LEPSA), that includes the following statement in the recruiting letter that it is sending to police personnel across the country: "Traditional law enforcement groups, comprised mainly of politically appointed bureaucrats, have misrepresented the mainstream views of you, the front-line officer, to the general public, the media, and lawmakers."[32] I have yet to see a news-service story in the local newspapers mentioning or questioning these events, though they would seem to be significant developments related to an ongoing and very heated controversy. *If anyone has expressed any concern over what role the police should play in determining public policy, that concern has not been passed on to the public.* Nor have I seen any mention of the 3,000 Texans who reportedly demonstrated against "assault-weapon" legislation in Austin on April 1, or of the even larger anti-control demonstration (7,500 according to media estimates, 22,000 according to police estimates) reportedly carried out in Columbus, Ohio on May 20.[33]

The preceding examples are hardly exhaustive, but they are typical of the sorts of things that for reasons to be considered later are not compatible with the "reality" of guns and their control apparently widely shared in media circles; therefore, they are seldom transmitted to the public through the general media. And as I have already noted, what is not covered by the media is at least as important as what is covered and how it is covered. However, what is not covered defies measurement.

The conventional news-service stories in these newspapers ranged from a few that did everything but openly take a stand in support of "assault-weapon" legislation, to the majority that simply took for granted the power and uniqueness of semi-automatic versions of military weapons or other questionable matters of the sort mentioned above. An example of a near-editorial conventional piece was the already-mentioned 32-line AP story carried by *Morning & Sunday-Chain* on February 11, that, presenting no opposing views, misleadingly gave the impression that the nation's police are unanimously behind "assault-weapon" legislation. An example of a very mild conventional story was another AP piece (44 lines) that appeared in this same newspaper on May 12 titled "Ban on assault-type weapons to be permanent," which, not recognizing the principled opposition to the banning of these guns themselves, stated that this opposition was based on the fear that anti-

[32] John M. Snyder, "HCI Rapes Law Enforcement Says LEPSA Police Founder," *The New Gun Week*, Vol. 24, Issue 1160 (Friday, June 30, 1989), 5. It should also be noted that Gerald S. Arenberg, Executive Director of the National Association of Chiefs of Police (10,000 members), Dennis Ray Martin, National President of the American Federation of Police (78,000 members), and Robert Kliesmet, President of the International Union of Police Associations AFL-CIO, have all taken public stands in support of NRA positions on gun control.

[33] Ken Carter, "3,000 Texas Gun Owners Attend Freedom Rally," *The New Gun Week*, Vol. 24, Issue 1151 (Friday, April 21, 1989), 1, 11; and Jim Schneider, "Ohio Holds Largest Ever Pro-Gun Rally," *The New Gun Week*, Vol. 24, 1157 (Friday, June 9, 1989), 1, 7.

gunners would use this ban "to push for stiffer restrictions on all types of guns." This story was straightforward and I do not suggest that it was partisan in any way, but its reading of the pro-gun anti-control position was still very superficial and as usual completely ignored Second Amendment concerns.

The unconventional stories included the 106-line *New York Times News Service* story carried by *Morning & Sunday-Chain* on April 12 that pointed out that police apparently are not running across many "assault weapons," and the 82-line AP story carried by *Evening-Private* on June 16 that noted that young people involved in the drug wars get their guns from the drug traffickers. The 51-line February 21 *New York Times* News Service story in *Morning & Sunday-Chain* that did a good job of explaining the differences between full- and semi-automatics also seemed to fit the unconventional criteria, given the general-media confusion over such things. And the remaining four unconventional news-service stories, one in *Morning & Sunday-Chain* and three in *Evening-Private,* were all straightforward pieces relatively unpermeated by pro-control assumptions.

By way of summary, few news-service stories carried in the local newspapers that touched on the "assault-weapon" controversy exhibited even the most basic familiarity with firearms, and most of them were permeated by pro-control assumptions concerning guns and their control. Exactly how many of these items and lines fitted the categories established above are detailed in Table 1.

Table 1: News-Service Stories

	Morning & Sunday-Chain		Evening-Private	
Total Items	18		17	
Pro-control	0	(0%)	0	(0%)
Conventional	15	(83.3%)	13	(76.5%)
Unconventional	3	(16.7%)	4	(23.5%)
Anti-control	0	(0%)	0	(0%)
Total Lines	988		1154	
Pro-control	0	(0%)	0	(0%)
Conventional	777	(78.6%)	1025	(88.8%)
Unconventional	211	(21.4%)	129	(11.2%)
Anti-control	0	(0%)	0	(0%)

Local News Stories: Only six "locally-written" news stories touching on the "assault-weapon" issue appeared in the local newspapers during the six-month period covered by this study. Actually, one of these stories was done by *Morning & Sunday-Chain's* Indianapolis bureau, and a second combined the efforts of that newspaper's staff with wire reports. These two stories were the only ones that explored reactions to this issue beyond the Tri-State.

One of the conventional stories (66 lines) was carried in *Morning & Sunday-Chain* on February 23, and dealt with the failure of a local state representative to gain support for his proposal to ban the sale of guns that were referred to some times as "semi-automatic assault weapons" and other times simply as "semi-automatics." The other conventional story (84 lines) appeared in the same newspaper on March 6, and reported the results of a locally-conducted telephone poll of 155 Tri-State residents that indicated that 59% of the respondents did not consider "semi-automatic assault weapons" useful for sporting purposes (again, the questionable criteria), 86% believed that such weapons should not be sold to convicted felons (it is already illegal under federal law for most felons to buy guns), 65% believed that such weapons should not be sold to the general public, and 65% believed that bans or restrictions would reduce the number of crimes committed with such weapons. The poll itself and the discussion of its findings were heavily permeated by pro-control assumptions of the sort that I have mentioned in the previous section on news-service stories, and sampling problems combined with the contaminating effect of these assumptions and the ongoing general-media treatment of this issue undermine the meaningfulness of these findings.

Of the four unconventional stories (two in each newspaper) one in each newspaper was primarily devoted to reporting the anti-"assault-weapon"-regulation efforts of area pro-gun anti-controllers that resulted in their placing purchased 121-line pieces presenting their side of the issue in each of the local newspapers, including the Sunday edition of *Morning & Sunday-Chain.* The *Morning & Sunday-Chain* story (63 lines) appeared in its Sunday edition on March 19, while the *Evening-Private* version (99 lines) appeared on March 20. The other two pieces (*Morning & Sunday-Chain,* 78 lines on March 17, and *Evening-Private,* 77 lines on May 3) examined the effects regulation attempts had had on the prices, availability, and desirability of semi-automatic versions of military assault rifles.

It would certainly seem that unconventional pieces on the "assault-weapon" issue are more common than conventional pieces at the local news-story level. Of course, six items provide little to judge by, but other locally-written gun-issue stories all the way back to 1981, including two interviews with me and several other stories that have mentioned my involvement in debates, indicate that such unconventional coverage of the gun issue has not been limited to "assault weapons" or any of the local newspapers before or after the ownership changes. The item and line counts for local news stories are presented in Table 2.

Table 2: Local News Stories

	Morning & Sunday-Chain		Evening-Private	
Total Items	4		2	
Pro-control	0	(0%)	0	(0%)
Conventional	2	(50%)	0	(0%)
Unconventional	2	(50%)	2	(100%)
Anti-control	0	(0%)	0	(0%)
Total Lines	291		176	
Pro-control	0	(0%)	0	(0%)
Conventional	150	(51.5%)	0	(0%)
Unconventional	141	(48.5%)	176	(100%)
Anti-control	0	(0%)	0	(0%)

Syndicated Columns and "Local" Editorials: The first syndicated column dealing with the "assault-weapon" issue to appear in a local newspaper after the January 17 schoolyard shooting was carried by *Morning & Sunday-Chain* on January 25. The piece was written by long-time anti-gun pro-controller Mike Royko of the *Chicago Tribune*. This 140-line cartoon-accompanied column lambasted AK-47s, the NRA, the lack of waiting-periods (which had not stopped the killer from buying 5 handguns in California), and so forth, in Royko's satirical fashion, and near its end stated: "The children died for your right and my right to own an AK-47, the NRA's rights, the right of congressmen and other lawmakers to pick up fat contributions. They died for the right of gunmakers, gun importers, gun dealers, the ammo manufacturers."

The second post-shooting syndicated column on these weapons appeared in *Evening-Private* on February 2. Printed in the "Insight" section of the editorial page, this 96-line column was written by Glenn McNatt of *The Baltimore Sun*, who in a calm non-satirical fashion questioned the wisdom of allowing civilians to possess "military-type assault weapons." McNatt also unknowingly demonstrated the tremendous gap between the "reality" of guns experienced by convinced controllers and the "reality" of guns experienced by pro-gun anti-controllers through comments so numerous that samples will have to suffice. According to McNatt: "Most assault weapons fire large-caliber, high-velocity military ammunition that makes them of limited use for sportsmen." Again, the sporting justification for gun ownership that anti-controllers reject, and the unsupportable claim that these weapons are more powerful than sporting guns. And McNatt also stated: "In fact, the United States is probably the only country in the world that allows private citizens to own what are essentially military weapons." Even if he was referring only to modern semi-automatic weapons, McNatt ignored peaceful Switzerland where practically every able-bodied male is issued a *full-automatic assault rifle* by his government, such weapons and ammunition for them being kept in individual homes. McNatt's comments were typical and not surprising to anyone who has closely followed syndicated-column treatment of any gun-control effort in these and many other newspapers.

Of the pro-control columnists regularly appearing in *Morning & Sunday-Chain,* Richard Cohen of the *Washington Post* provided 3 "assault-weapon" columns and mentioned these guns briefly in two others for a total of 353 lines; Mike Royko devoted three columns and a large part of a fourth to "assault weapons" for 457 lines; and Ann McFeatters (an Evansville native) of Scripps Howard devoted one column, a large part of a second, and brief mentions in two others to these weapons for a total of 136 lines. But the line championship, 539, went to non-regular Andrew Malcolm for a single effort that came to the Sunday edition's "Insight" column on April 30 via the *New York Times* News Service. Entitled "Anatomy of Gun Murders: Ten deaths, one city, one month," Malcolm's was an anti-gun piece that touched here and there on "assault rifles," unquestioningly cited standard HCI claims concerning the danger of guns in the home as if these claims were based on careful non-partisan research, and related how several gun-related killings occurred in San Jose, California. No mention was made of the fact that San Jose Police Chief Joseph McNamara, who was quoted in the piece, is a nationally-known pro-gun-control activist who has appeared in uniform in HCI pro-control advertisements while forbidding members of his department who oppose controls to actively support the NRA.[34] Actually, 11 rather than 10 shooting deaths were described, but one was a suicide, three were carried out by police (one of whom used an assault weapon) and were not considered murders, and two were murders of policemen accomplished with a gun taken from one of them rather than with a privately-owned gun. Therefore, only 5 of the killings described that were carried out with privately-owned weapons, one of which was a shotgun, could properly be labeled murders.

Of the pro-control columnists regularly appearing in *Evening-Private,* Art Buchwald of the *Los Angeles Times* Syndicate provided 5 "assault weapon" columns for a total of 344 lines; Sandy Grady of Knight-Ridder Newspapers devoted 3 columns and a brief comment in a fourth to "assault weapons" for 298 lines; and Lewis Grizzard of the *Atlanta Constitution* devoted 3 columns and brief comments in three others to these weapons or the NRA for 220 lines. *Evening-Private* carried no single column even approaching in length the 539-line *Morning & Sunday-Chain* "Insight" column described above.

As with the Royko, McNatt, and Malcolm commentaries mentioned above, most of the other pro-control columnists rarely demonstrated even the slightest familiarity with firearms or current firearms controls. In a 119-line February 23 column

---

[34] Chief McNamara's treatment of Officer Leoy Pyle, a member of his department who is an outspoken opponent of gun controls, has received considerable publicity in the gun press but has been ignored by the major media. See Ronald L. Cameron, "Police Say No To More Gun Laws," *Guns & Ammo* (June, 1988), 31-32; "Police Officer Harassed For His Pro-Gun Testimony," *American Rifleman* (June, 1989) and David Kopel, "A Victim of Truth," *Gun World* (September, 1989), 19-20.

appearing in *Morning & Sunday-Chain*, A. M. Rosenthal of the *New York Times* railed against "hand-held machine guns, complete with bullets" being sold over the counter, and against President George Bush's refusal "to support federal legislation against street-spraying automatic weapons. . . ." As I have mentioned, the legal possession of full-automatic weapons by civilians has been federally regulated since 1934 and a number of states have long banned the civilian possession of such weapons. In the March 27 edition of the same newspaper, Leonard Larsen of the Scripps Howard News Service attacked the NRA and Bush's position on gun controls in an 87-line column. "Ordinarily only gun-nut simpletons, NRA propagandists and tinhorn members of Congress striving for careers at the public trough defend against gun controls on constitutional grounds," according to Larsen. As I have indicated above, the opposing factions in the battle over gun controls will probably never agree on the "true" meaning of the Second Amendment; however, such students of that amendment as Don B. Kates, Jr., Stephen P. Halbrook, Joyce Lee Malcolm, William Marina, Robert E. Shalhope, David I. Caplan, and James Whisker, who have defended against gun controls on constitutional grounds are likely to be dismissed as "gun-nut simpletons" or "NRA propagandists" only by those unfamiliar with their works.[35] Art Buchwald, in the first of his five "assault-weapon" columns (February 7, 71 lines), kept referring to "semi-automatic machine guns," and in columns two (March 6, 68 lines) and three (March 21, 76 lines) alternately referred to them as "semi-automatics" and "machine guns," thus blurring the distinction between a type of firearm the civilian possession of which has long been federally regulated and a type that has been used by civilians for sport and self-protection since the turn of the century. Sandy Grady commented on AK-47s in passing (11 lines) in a May 25 column: "It's ironic that Washington politicians, including Bush, are suddenly concerned about AK-47 rifles; their interest piqued by 115 murders in the U.S. capital." But according to the unconventional *New York Times* story previously mentioned, "George Wilson, head of the Firearms Examination Division of the Washington, D.C. police force, said in 1988 the department had 'not recovered any' of the rifles covered by last month's importation ban" — a ban aimed at AK-47s and other such weapons. And the sentiments of these and other pro-control syndicated columnists concerning the NRA seem to have been summed up by a 3-line comment in a May 19 Lewis Grizzard column that suggested that the controversial "Iron Gate" figure, Colonel Oliver North, "go to work for the National Rifle Association, which is about as squirrely and stubborn and dangerous as Iran." Though Grizzard did not mention "assault weapons" in this column, his comments came during the period when he and other columnists were berating the NRA for opposing the regulation of such weapons.

Two columns from *Washington Post* writers supportive of controls, one in *Morning & Sunday-Chain* and the other in *Evening-Private*, demonstrated some

---

[35] See footnotes 1 and 20.

slight gun sophistication. Richard Cohen, in an April 4, 145-line column in the former newspaper, acknowledged the fuzziness of "Saturday Night Special" and "assault-rifle" labels, but then suggested that the civilian possession of all firearms be restricted. George Will, on the other hand, extensively citing pro-gun advocate Don B. Kates, Jr., actually criticized the position taken by the National Coalition to Ban Handguns (a media rarity, indeed) in a March 23, 110-line column in the latter newspaper. Will noted the "class bias in the gun-control argument," and that many Americans need handguns because they live in urban areas "where government cannot, or will not, enforce its proper monopoly on the use of force." But after demonstrating more familiarity with the scholarly support for the other side of the gun controversy than any other pro-control columnist of whom I am aware, Will claimed that "assault rifles" are different and the general public has no business having access to them. Will obviously does not accept the individual interpretation of the Second Amendment or believes that such an interpretation has outlived its usefulness, as his support of the state's monopoly of the use of force suggests.

Interestingly enough, of the total of four anti-control columns that came to the local newspapers regarding this issue, only one of them was written by a regular syndicated columnist, James Kilpatrick of Universal Press. The other three pieces opposing "assault-weapon" legislation included one by Paul Craig Roberts, "the William E. Simon professor of political economy at the Center for Strategic Studies in Washington and . . . a former assistant secretary of the U.S. Treasury," provided to *Morning & Sunday-Chain,* the same newspaper that carried Kilpatrick's column, by Scripps Howard News Service. *Evening-Private* carried the remaining two columns opposing "assault-weapon" regulation, one by popular novelist Tom Clancy via the *Washington Post,* and the other by Rudy D'Angelo, "a private detective who lives in Farmington, Connecticut," via the *Hartford Courant.*

Kilpatrick, a conservative columnist who generally opposes gun controls, but who has also been critical of the "gun lobby," presented the most sophisticated anti-regulation argument through his 123-line, April 25 column. He noted the shift in blame from the schoolyard killer to his gun, the problems associated with legislative proposals that ignore the fact that semi-automatic "assault weapons" operate the same as semi-automatics long used by civilians, and that the Second Amendment may guarantee the right to own military-type weapons, though he also claimed that any right conferred by that amendment is not absolute. Roberts (May 5, 96 lines) noted that government efforts to increase automobile gas mileage have reduced car size,thereby significantly increasing the number of highway deaths, at the same time that that same government paradoxically tries to regulate rifles of a sort that are involved in less than one percent of all homicides. Tom Clancy (April 10, 153 lines) noted that the heavily-armed Swiss and Israeli citizenries and his heavily-armed rural Chesapeake Bay neighbors cause no problems with their guns, and that in his numerous contacts with police officers and FBI agents he has "yet to meet a single law-enforcement officer who thinks that confiscating firearms from the general public will do any good at all concerning crime in the United States — not one." And D'Angelo (May 4, 135 lines), beginning with a reference to the California gun-control effort, claimed that strict Italian gun laws have left law-abiding Italians at the mercy of armed military and police forces on one side and armed criminals on the other, though his claims might be disputed on the grounds that there is no reason to believe that ordinary Italians have complied with their nation's strict gun laws.

Due to the fact that *Morning & Sunday-Chain* carried 21 *clearly-identified non-local commentaries* supportive of "assault-weapon" regulation, and *Evening-Chain* carried 19 such pieces, I have mentioned only a select few to serve as examples of the messages transmitted to the local reading public through them. On the other hand, since these newspapers carried only 4 such commentaries opposing such regulations, I have briefly summarized each of these. A two-newspaper total of five other syndicated columns very briefly touched on "assault weapons" in ways that I have classified as conventional, 2 items of one line each in *Evening-Private*, or unconventional, one item of 16 lines in *Morning & Sunday-Chain* and one item of 5 lines in *Evening-Private* — hardly worth further discussion. However, the outside commentary on this issue went beyond the already-mentioned syndicated columns.

Having no insider sophistication concerning the operation of newspapers, I had long assumed that the non byline items presented as editorials on the editorial pages of local newspapers were written by members of the editorial staffs of these newspapers — an apparently widely-shared assumption on the part of the general public. I had already begun to suspect that this was not the case when I read an enlightening, if partisan, article by Paul Blackman of the NRA in that organization's magazine that mentioned that such editorials are often not the work of local editors.[36] Since that time, I have been told by the editorial page editor of *Morning & Sunday-Chain* that their editorials on other than local matters are written by three Washington, D.C.-based Scripps Howard editorialists. Before this newspaper was taken over by Scripps Howard, such editorials were purchased in packages of such pieces dealing with various subjects. Now, according to the editor of *Evening-Private*, his newspaper uses these "canned' editorials. Therefore, these "local" editorials are not written by locals for either local newspaper, though the *Evening-Private* editor told me that he often alters these "canned" pieces to suit himself. Since each local newspaper has published these local-appearing editorials on the "assault weapon" issue, all supportive of regulation, 3 totaling 100 lines in *Morning & Sunday-Chain* and 4 totaling 150 lines for *Evening-Private*, they add to the outside pro-control input

---

[36] Paul H. Blackman, "Mugged by the media," *American Rifleman* (June, 1987), 34-36, 80-81. Accoding to Blackman, "National Enterprises Ass'n . . . often writes and syndicates anti-gun editorials that are printed in local newspapers as if written locally."

reaching the local public. In fact, these editorials were the first local or outside commentaries (though not labeled as such) to reach Tri-State readers through these newspapers — January 21 for *Evening-Private* and January 22 for *Morning & Sunday-Chain*. The item and line counts for syndicated columns and "local" editorial are presented in Table 3.

Table 3: Syndicated Columns and "Local" Editorials

	Morning & Sunday-Chain		Evening-Private	
Total Items	27		28	
Pro-control	24	(88.9%)	23	(82.1%)
Conventional	0	(0%)	2	(7.1%)
Unconventional	1	(3.7%)	1	(3.6%)
Anti-control	2	(7.4%)	2	(7.1%)
Total Lines	2330		1588	
Pro-control	2095	(89.9%)	1293	(81.4%)
Conventional	0	(0%)	2	(.1%)
Unconventional	16	(.7%)	5	(.3%)
Anti-control	219	(9.4%)	288	(18.1%)

Locally-Written Columns: In the six months after the schoolyard shooting, only four truly locally-written columns dealing with "assault weapons" appeared in the local newspapers, and two of these pieces were written by guest non-journalists while the other two were written by persons employed by these newspapers. Of these four columns, three, including the column by the local outdoors writer (May 5, 101 lines) that I have already mentioned, and the two guest columns, appeared in *Morning & Sunday-Chain*. The outdoors writer's column was supportive not only of "assault-weapon" control but of the licensing of all firearms in the United States. I wrote a 135-line column that was published on March 9 and that criticized media coverage of the "assault-weapon" issue, covered the differences between full- and semi-automatics, and mentioned already-existing legislation regulating the civilian possession of the former. The other guest column (April 6, 190 lines) was written by a local attorney in response to Scripps Howard-columnist Leonard Larsen's previously mentioned April 27 column ridiculing those who believe that the Second Amendment guarantees individual Americans the right to possess firearms. The single locally-written *Evening-Private* column dealing with "assault weapons" was written by a columnist employed by that newspaper (March 17, 106 lines) and argued that like it or not (and he made it clear that he did not like it) both the Second Amendment and the Indiana Constitution support the individual's right to possess firearms. I classified this piece as unconventional. The item and line counts for locally-written columns are presented in Table 4.

Table 4: Locally-Written Columns

	Morning & Sunday-Chain		Evening-Private	
Total Items	3		1	
Pro-control	1	(33.3%)	0	(0%)
Conventional	0	(0%	0	(0%)
Unconventional	0	(0%)	1	(100%)
Anti-control	2	(66.6%)	0	(0%)
Total Lines	426		106	
Pro-control	101	(23.7%)	0	(0%)
Conventional	0	(0%)	0	(0%)
Unconventional	0	(0%)	106	(100%)
Anti-control	325	(76.3%)	0	(0%)

Cartoons — Syndicated and Local: The first political cartoon dealing with "assault weapons" to be carried by a local newspaper after the January 17 shooting appeared in *Evening-Private* on January 24, and the second appeared in *Morning & Sunday-Chain* on January 25. Five cartoons in *Morning & Sunday-Chain* and seven in *Evening-Private* were blatantly anti-"assault weapon." Most of these pro-control cartoons ridiculed the straw-man position that civilians need such weapons for sporting purposes. On April 24, for example, "Berry's World" a regular feature in *Evening-Private* editorial pages, depicted a Rambo-like character surrounded by spent cartridges looking at a crater that he had just created with the smoking assault rifle he was holding. The cartoon carried the caption "THE RABBIT HUNTER." Such pro-control cartoons generally depicted these weapons as being incredibly powerful and destructive, and several made an issue of their being semi-automatic as if this feature in itself disqualified them for sporting use. Only 3 of the 12 pro-control cartoons related these weapons to the schoolyard shooting, though a fourth, *Evening-Private's* initial January 24 offering, depicted a wild-eyed individual loaded down with a handgun, an assault rifle, and what looked like a submachine gun walking away from a gun shop posted with "semi-automatic special" and "no wait for rifles" advertisements as the owner reminded him that his purchases were for "target practice only."

I classified two *Evening-Private* and one *Morning & Sunday-Chain* cartoons as conventional because they helped to perpetuate the questionable assumption that "assault weapons" are the "weapons of choice" of the urban drug gangs. One of these cartoons was carried in the April 22 edition of *Evening-Private* and showed a couple dashing for cover with their two young children as police and criminals, several of the latter armed with "assault weapons," engaged in a gun battle. The wife complained to her husband: "We could've been in the Bahamas or Bermuda ... but, nooo ... I had to listen to Mr. 'Washington-is-beautiful-in-the-spring.'" The conventional *Morning & Sunday-Chain* cartoon (March 20) was based on the same theme. The second conventional *Evening-Private* cartoon (May 2) showed two people standing in front of the Lincoln Memorial with the Washington Monument in the background. In the first panel, the person holding a D.C. guidebook said that she was going to visit the Jefferson Memorial, and in the second panel she asked her companion, who was holding an "assault rifle," to cover her. Admittedly, an argument could be made for classifying this cartoon as unconventional. However, I did not hesitate to classify a *Morning & Sunday-Chain* cartoon (April 3) as unconventional. It showed a demonstrator carrying an anti-NRA placard shouting "Save the children! Ban assault weapons!" while a black man sitting nearby said "Amen, brother!" But in the second panel, the black man went on to say that after that was accomplished "we'll attack the roots of drug violence,-- the disintegration of the black family, the lack of prison space, and the failure of the criminal justice system!" In the third panel the demonstrator frowned without saying a word, and in the final panel he moved on repeating his anti-assault-weapon refrain.

Not only "Berry's World," but all of the rest of these cartoons came to the local editorial pages from Scripps Howard or other newspapers via syndication. Only one cartoon that might be considered related to the "assault-weapon" issue took a strong pro-Second Amendment stand, and this cartoon was drawn by a local cartoonist for *Morning & Sunday-Chain* (June 7) after the Chinese slaughter of student demonstrators. In the first panel, two Chinese students, one carrying a "Democracy now" placard, listened to a third student saying, "then we're agreed . . . freedom of speech . . . freedom of the press . . . the right to assemble." In the second panel, having been mowed down by automatic-weapons fire, one of the fallen students gasped an addition: "er . . . the right to keep and bear arms." The item count for syndicated and local cartoons is presented in Table 5.

Table 5: Syndicated Cartoons

	Morning & Sunday-Chain		Evening-Private	
Total Items	7		9	
Pro-control	5	(71.4%)	7	(77.8%)
Conventional	1	(14.3%)	2	(22.2%)
Unconventional	1	(14.3%)	0	(0%)
Anti-control	0	(0%)	0	(0%)

	Local Cartoon	
Anti-control	1	(100%)

Comic Strips: Much editorializing, moralizing, and propagandizing, some subtle and some anything but subtle, is aimed at the public through newspaper comic strips; consequently, it should not be surprising that the gun-control controversy has reached the comic pages. "Doonesbury's" creator, Garry Trudeau, has on numerous occasions over the years ridiculed the NRA and gun enthusiasts in general through his strip. In fact, Duke, possibly the sleaziest, most disreputable character in this strip, a heavy user of alcohol and other drugs who cares for no one but himself and is always open to a "fast-buck" scheme, is also a gun enthusiast and avid NRA supporter, as established by a 12-episode series carried by *Morning-Local* in February and March of 1979 and many episodes since then. However, in the only "Doonesbury" episode dealing with "assault weapons" thus far (in the Sunday edition of *Morning & Sunday-Chain* of May 7), Trudeau had an NRA spokesman on a radio talk show defending the sporting use of these weapons. Then, in the last panel, a hunter holding a smoking "assault rifle" displayed a small antler fragment to his camera-wielding companion who asked, "Um . . . can't you find a bigger piece?" The reply was, "How about a hoof?" Again, the straw-man sporting-use theme, and the perpetuation of the notion that such weapons are incredibly powerful and destructive.

Other *Morning & Sunday-Chain* comic strips that attacked "assault weapons" and/or the NRA, were the revived "Pogo" (April 24, 25, 27, 28, and May 20), "Bloom County" (Sunday edition, May 14), and "John Darling" (May 25). The four linked "Pogo" episodes made the point that "crackpots" can acquire guns too easily, and the first episode included a poster that stated, "The NRA is working to make guns a part of your life." The single May episode has Pogo mentioning the honoring of our various armed forces to his companion. The companion then goes on to state: "Then, on the B list, we got hunters, insecurity guards, robbers, mobsters, gun enthusiastics, drug lords, the NRA an' other gang members." "John Darling" presented its own variation on the non-sporting-use theme, and "Bloom County's" shot at "assault weapons" and the NRA was too contrived to summarize briefly.

Only three *Evening-Private* comic strips were relevant to the "assault-weapon" issue. "Bloom County" (March 3), which is carried by this newspaper on week days, had one of its main characters defending a concocted "constitutional right," and when challenged to point out where that right is specified replied, "Uh . . . probably not far from the part about the right to stockpile assault guns and 'cop-killer' bullets." "D.C." (June 5) had one character saying that he was going to be sworn in as chairman of the ethics committee the next day, and his female companion suggested that he wear "that nice tie the NRA gave you last year" — no mention of "assault weapons," but an attack on the NRA during the period when that organization was under fire for its opposition to stricter regulations of these weapons. Similarly, "Herman" (June 1) did not touch on "assault weapons," but did have a revolver- and shotgun-armed character in a camouflaged outfit asking the person who had just opened the door to him, "What do you think of gun controls?" "Assault weapons" were not specified, though the stereotype of opponents of gun laws was perpetuated during the period when such weapons were the issue.

Only one locally-carried comic strip dealing with "assault weapons" *might* have been considered anything other than supportive of their regulation or banning.

"Zippy," carried by *Morning & Sunday-Chain,* is to say the least, a very unconventional satirical critique of our popular culture, and as a whole or as individual episodes defies brief description that would make sense to the uninitiated. In its July 10 episode, one character mentioned to another that he had heard that the bad-tempered Mr. Toad had gone on the Oprah Winfrey diet. The other character confirmed Toad's diet, but went on to say that unfortunately he had bought an "automatic-weapon" before starting it. The character then commented that a good lawyer would probably get Toad "off with a stern lecture," his victim having been his bathroom scale. I very charitably classified this episode as unconventional for reasons hardly worth spending the time and space to justify. The item count for comic strips is presented in Table 6.

Table 6: Comic Strips

	Morning & Sunday-Chain		Evening-Private	
Total Items	9		3	
Pro-control	8	(88.9%)	3	(100%)
Conventional	0	(0%)	0	(0%)
Unconventional	1	(11.1%)	0	(0%)
Anti-control	0	(0%)	0	(0%)

Letters to the Editor: Since I began systematically collecting gun-issue items from the local newspapers in 1981, the local-newspaper coverage of no other gun-control effort has generated so much reader response through letters to the editors as has the current effort to regulate or ban the civilian possession of "assault weapons." Not having considered letters to editors reflective of media perspectives on the gun issue when I first started collecting, I may have allowed three or four letters to go unrecorded in early 1981, but my total count for the old *Morning-Local, Evening-Chain,* and *Sunday LC* newspapers for the period beginning in January of that year and continuing through October of 1986 was 66 — 11 per year. However, 23 of those letters were mine, leaving only 43, or 7.2 per year, from the rest of the Tri-State readership. During the six months after the schoolyard shooting, the two remaining and realigned newspapers have published a total of 41 letters on the "assault-weapon" issue, for a projected rate of 82 letters per year. Since only 3 of these letters have been mine, the Tri-State readership has supplied letters at a rate of 76 per year. And these letters taken as a whole were as overwhelmingly opposed to "assault-weapon" regulation as the columns and cartoons that prompted them taken as a whole were overwhelmingly supportive of such regulations.

To the extent that Tri-State readers have been exposed to the most complete pro-gun anti-control perspective on "assault weapons," they have received it from these letters to the local editors, the two locally-written guest columns mentioned above, and the purchased column to be discussed in the next section. Many of these anti-control letter writers complained about media bias in the coverage of this and other gun-control efforts; many commented on technically, historically, and/or legally, debatable comments made by columnists; many pointed out that the Second Amendment ignored by columnists and others is central to the "assault-weapon" debate, not the sporting utility of such weapons; many pointed out the draconian aspects of proposed legislation, and so forth. Since most of these letter writers were articulate, they could not easily be dismissed as "redneck gun nuts." I have no way of knowing how much of this outpouring of anti-control letters was spontaneously generated by the perceived threatening nature of proposed and enacted legislation, and how much was prompted by anti-control activists in local gun clubs. I made one such plea for action myself.

Those few letter writers who supported "assault-weapon" regulations did so for reasons identical to those articulated by the syndicated columnists and cartoonists who supported such measures. And one two-line comment referring to the possible need for gun laws to solve Washington, D.C.'s problems was of questionable relevance, but I included it and classified it as conventional. The item and line counts for letters to the editors are presented in Table 7.

Table 7: Letters to the Editor

	Morning & Sunday-Chain		Evening-Private	
Total Items	23		18	
Pro-control	4	(17.4%)	2	(11%)
Conventional	0	(0%)	1	(5.6%)
Unconventional	0	(0%)	0	(0%)
Anti-control	19	(82.6%)	15	(83.3%)
Total Lines	811		744	
Pro-control	95	(11.7%)	90	(12.1%)
Conventional	0	(0%)	2	(.3%)
Unconventional	0	(0%)	0	(0%)
Anti-control	716	(88.3%)	654	(87.9%)

Purchased Space: The concern among local pro-gun anti-control activists that not only local but national general media were covering the "assault-weapon" issue in an extremely biased fashion that did not present much relevant information to the public reached the point that donations were solicited from the members of several local gun clubs to *purchase* space for an anti-control statement in the sports pages of *Evening-Private* (March 15) and both the daily (March 15) and Sunday (March 12) editions of *Morning & Sunday-Chain*. This purchased statement warned sportsmen that the media were not telling the public about the draconian features of "assault-weapon" legislation being proposed at state as well as federal levels, and noted that as worded such measures would even cover a very popular .22-caliber semi-automatic rifle. The

121-line piece ended with a plea for "sportsmen, hunters, and gun owners" to unite in active opposition to "assault-weapon" controls.

A more ordinary purchased piece relevant to this issue appeared in both local newspapers on May 2. Publicity and the prospect of strict controls on the acquisition of semi-automatic military-style firearms increased interest in them, which in turn sent their prices skyrocketing. Taking advantage of this situation in fine capitalist style, a Fairfield, Illinois gun shop ran a 6-line advertisement headed, "Attention Gun Collectors: Last chance to own an assault type pistol," complete with an illustration of an M-11 9mm pistol and listing a $399.00 price tag in the Evansville newspapers. *Evening-Private* mentioned the shop in an unconventional locally-written article the next day, noting that the gun's price had increased $150.00 since the push for controls began, and *Morning & Sunday-Chain* was taken to task via a May 13 letter to the editor for carrying the advertisement. That letter drew a May 30 letter defending the advertisement.

Origins: The preceding description of news-service, syndicated-column, and other coverage of the "assault-weapon" issue in the newspapers of Evansville, Indiana demonstrates just how much local newspapers are dependent on media outlets based in large urban areas for the news, commentary, and entertainmemt they present to their readers. And this description also demonstrates that the news, commentary, and entertainment provided by these urban outlets has been heavily permeated by perspectives on the "reality" of "assault weapons" and their control that correspond with those of the pro-controllers ranging all the way from the pro-gun to the anti-gun varities. In fact, if it had not been for local input, particularly from the grassroots through letters to the editors, guest columns, and purchased statements, the pro-gun anti-control perspective on the "reality" of "assault weapons" would have received negligible public exposure through these newspapers during the first six months during which such weapons became a national issue — January 18, 1989 through July 17, 1989.

Both newspapers presented their readers with considerably more items blatantly supportive of "assault-weapon" legislation than they did items blatantly opposed to such legislation — 44 to 27 for *Morning & Sunday-Chain* and 37 to 19 for *Evening-Private*. Since many of these pro-control items were cartoons or comic strips that did not add to the line count, the line counts for these categories in both newspapers were considerably closer — 2291 to 1508 for *Morning & Sunday-Chain* and 1383 to 1069 for *Evening-Private*. But this is only the tip of the media-bias iceberg from the perspective of the pro-gun anti-controllers. To bring the rest of the iceberg into view, local grassroots input must be subtracted from these item and line count totals as I have done in Table 8.

216.

Table 8: Total Item and Line Counts Minus Grassroots Input

	Morning & Sunday-Chain		Evening-Private	
Total Items	67		60	
Pro-control	40	(59.7%)	35	(58.3%)
Conventional	17	(25.4%)	15	(25%)
Unconventional	7	(10.4%)	8	(13.3%)
Anti-control	3	(4.5%)	2	(3.3%)
Total Lines	3710		3026	
Pro-control	2196	(59.2%)	1293	(42.7%)
Conventional	927	(25%)	1029	(34%)
Unconventional	368	(9.9%)	416	(13.7%)
Anti-control	219	(5.9%)	288	(9.5%)

But there is even more to the bias iceberg, since those items labeled "conventional" helped to perpetuate the pro-control perspective on the "reality" of "assault weapons" by reporting and commenting on such weapons in terms of assumptions concerning them, their use, and opposition to their regulation associated with that perspective — the blurring of the distinction between full- and semi-automatics, the unquestioned acceptance of claims that *semi automatic* "assault weapons" are the "weapons of choice" of drug lords, the unquestioned acceptance of "sporting-use" criteria for judging whether or not civilians should be allowed to own semi-automatics, and so forth. Therefore, if pro-control and conventional non-grassroots item and line counts are combined on the one hand, and unconventional and anti-control non-grassroots item and line counts are combined on the other hand, the bias iceberg is almost revealed in its entirety, as can be seen in Table 9.

Table 9: Combined Non-Grassroots Item and Line Counts

	Morning & Sunday-Chain		Evening-Private	
Total Items	67		60	
Pro-control/Conventional	57	(85.1%)	50	(83.3%)
Unconventional/Anti-control	10	(14.9%)	10	(16.7%)
Total Lines	3710		3026	
Pro-control/Conventional	3123	(84.2%)	2322	(76.7%)
Unconventional/Anti-control	587	(15.8%)	704	(23.3%)

But there are still other dimensions to this bias issue. From the tables presented above, it can be seen that over the six months following the California schoolyard shooting, readers of the local newspapers were subjected to a heavy and continuous barrage of news reports, commentaries, cartoons, and so forth, either blatantly supportive of "assault-weapon" regulation or taking the assumptions of that position for granted (see Appendix). On the other hand, published reader response to these journalistic pieces were heavily opposed to "assault-weapon" regulation, as can be seen from the item and line counts of letters to the editors, guest-columns by local residents, and purchased statements presented in Table 10.

Table 10: Combined Grassroots Item and Line Counts

	Morning & Sunday-Chain		Evening-Private	
Total Items	28		20	
Pro-control/Conventional	4	(14.3%)	3	(15%)
Unconventional/Anti-control	24	(85.7%)	17	(85%)
Total Lines	1384		873	
Pro-control/Conventional	95	(6.9%)	92	(10.5%)
Unconventional/Anti-control	1289	(93.1%)	781	(89.5%)

But even though the grassroots input constituted from half to approaching three quarters of the combined unconventional/anti-control content of both newspapers as measured by either item or line counts, the combined unconventional/anti-control content of each of these newspapers measured either way ranged only from 33.8 to 38.1 percent of their total "assault-weapon" contents. In other words, though without grassroots input both newspapers would have contained considerably less unconventional/anti-control material, even with grassroots input such content lagged considerably behind the pro-control/conventional content of both newspapers. Receiving little assistance from newsmen, columnists, cartoonists, and so forth, a number of pro-gun anti-controllers (including me) tried to defend their position on "assault weapons" against the heavy and constant attack on that position mounted by a considerable majority of the professional media folk reporting or commenting on these weapons through these newspapers. But the latter held several advantages.

If a major columnist like Art Buchwald writes five anti-"assault-weapon" columns in six months, he is in step with most other major columnists, political cartoonists, etc., and even with the assumptions informing the major print and electronic media news treatments of these guns. Consequently, readers who know nothing about the other side of the issue and who were horrified by the California shooting might be inclined to agree with him even if they are not completely trusting of the media. If over the same period of time an ordinary citizen writes five letters to the editor defending the civilian possession of "assault weapons," he/she may achieve minor folk-hero status among his/her fellow pro-gun anti-controllers, but he/she risks being dismissed as a single-issue crank out of step with all but other single-issue cranks. Consequently, even the most committed pro-gun anti-control letter writers are likely to ration their responses to items blatantly supportive of gun controls or conventionally reporting on such measures. Since many pro-gun anti-controllers seem to feel that they are not informed and/or articulate enough to tangle with the professional word workers, letter writing is left to the few who are confident enough to take on this task but who feel that they must ration their responses. And while new letter writers occasionally join the ranks of the committed, others become disgusted and drop out when they see that their careful explanations of, for example, the differences between full- and semi-automatics or their critiques of the "sporting-use" criteria for the civilian possession of "assault weapons" have failed to stem the tide of pro-control/conventional items that continue to ignore such things. Other pro-gun anti-controllers have given up writing letters after editors have refused to publish several of their offerings. As a result of all this, many challengeable pro-control/conventional items go unchallenged even by letters to the editor. And the letters that are written may be dismissed in some circles because they fly in the face of the conventional wisdom transmitted through the media in general. I have drawn on my own personal experience as a letter writer and on the experiences of friends and acquaintances for this final comment on the nature and impact of media pro control bias.

TOWARD AN EXPLANATION

When pro-gun anti-controllers charge the general media with pro-gun-control bias, they have in mind the sorts of things that I have attempted to document and even to quantify in the preceding pages. They are exasperated by news reports permeated by the unexamined claims and assumptions of the pro-controllers. They are enraged by the incessant abuse heaped upon them, their interests, and their organizations by the vast majority of editorial writers, columnists, cartoonists, and comic artists who take stands on gun ownership and have easy access to the public through the media. And they are frustrated by their own lack of comparable access to the public through these same media, and by their inability to draw their antagonists into meaningful and sustained public debate. As Balof has noted in Chapter 12, "there is no national debate over gun ownership." But why would the newspapers of Evansville, Indiana, which is located in the heart of an area where guns are very popular and attempts to regulate their possession tend to be greeted with suspicion, be so permeated by pro-control sentiments that often reach the anti-gun level? Not being privy to behind-the-scenes decision-making at either newspaper, I can only offer a few sociologically-informed suggestions.

To a certain extent, the pro-control orientation of these newspapers, if not the anti-gun sentiments often to be found in them, surely reflects the position on guns taken by their owners and/or editors. During a telephone conversation, the editorial-page editor of *Morning & Sunday-Chain* told me that Scripps Howard editorial policy is supportive of gun controls, but that he welcomed opposing viewpoints. And in response to several letters from me pointing out the pro-control orientation of his newspaper, the editor of *Evening-Private* wrote the following in a late 1988 letter to me: "I believe there should be some controls on guns purchased, and I would absolutely, unconditionally oppose the general confiscation of guns. I believe that is the view of the majority of Americans." He subscribes, in other words, to what I have referred to as the pro-gun pro-control position. At the time of these contacts, both local newspapers had stopped publishing my gun-issue letters after having published almost everything that I had sent them over a period of approximately seven years, and I had sent them item and line counts critiquing their coverage of the attempt to establish a national seven-day waiting period for handgun purchases. *Morning & Sunday-Chain's* editorial-page editor called me after the California shooting to tell me that he anticipated many gun-control commentaries and that not only would my letters on the subject be welcome but that I could do a guest column for his newspaper. He was quite friendly, but the explanation he offered for not having published my last three letters applied to only one of them. I had written that I suspected that his newspaper's editorials were not written by persons employed by the newspaper. Since they are written by Scripps Howard employees in Washington, I was wrong, but he hesitated to exclude my comment for fear that the exclusion would be taken for censorship. No explanation was given for the rejection of the other letters. The tone of the letter from *Evening-Private's* editor was exasperated, my letters were referred to as "diatribes," and I was accused of believing that only my opinions are "relevant and fair and right." He had written a similar letter to me approximately two years previously, but he did publish the letter that had prompted this second written response to me.

But regardless of the views of their editors, as can be seen from Tables 2, 4, and 5, the very few news pieces and commentaries and the single political cartoon actually produced by local employees of these newspapers who have easy access to the grassroots, were not out of balance in favor of "assault-weapon" legislation. The vast majority of pro-control/conventional items and lines that put both of these newspapers out of balance on that side of the "assault-weapon" controversy came from the news services and syndicates upon which these newspapers are so dependent, and these organizations are based in large urban centers. As members of local elites of the sort discussed by Hawely in Chapter 9, the local editors have a vested interest in promoting trust in government and maintaining a civic order that can draw businesses to the community and keep them there. Consequently, even if these editors are pro-gun, they may see no harm in allowing the government and its police forces to regulate the civilian possession of guns in the hope that such regulations will help to promote and maintain a more orderly community, nationally as well as locally. Yet these editors do seem to be willing to publish professionally-done items presenting the other side of the gun issue. As the very anti-handgun editorial-page editor of the old *Evening-Chain* once told me, his newspaper simply did not receive any anti-gun-control items. And it is relevant to note here that of the four syndicated items opposed to "assault-weapon" legislation that were covered by this study, *only one of them was written by a professional columnist.*

When the issue is gun control, why do news items and commentaries critically examining or rejecting the pro-control position so rarely get to these local newspapers through the major national news services and syndicates? As the treatment that the "assault-weapon" issue and other gun-control efforts have received from the major media as well as the local newspapers indicates, it would appear that the answer to this question is that there are very few major newspersons, editorial writers, syndicated columnists, cartoonists, or comic artists able or willing to critically examine gun-control proposals, let alone take a public stand against them. Why?

During 1979 and 1980, Lichter, Rothman, and Lichter systematically studied 238 randomly-selected reporters, columnists, department heads, bureau chiefs, editors, and executives from the *New York Times*, the *Washington Post*, the *Wall Street Journal*, *Time*, *Newsweek*, and *U.S. News and World Report*, and correspondents, anchors, producers, film editors, and news executives from *CBS, NBC, ABC*, and *PBS* — the "media elite." They reached the following conclusions:

The demographics are clear. The media elite are a homogeneous and cosmopolitan group, who were raised at some distance from the social and cultural traditions of small-town middle America. Drawn mainly from big cities in the northeast and north central states, their parents tended to be well off, highly educated members of the upper middle class. Most have moved away from any religious heritage, and very few are regular churchgoers. In short, the typical leading journalist is the very model of the modern eastern urbanite.

The dominant perspective of this group is equally apparent. Today's leading journalists are politically liberal and alienated from traditional norms and institutions. Most place themselves to the left of center and regularly vote the Democratic ticket. Yet theirs is not the New Deal liberalism of the underprivileged, but the contemporary social liberalism of the urban sophisticate. They favor a strong welfare state within a capitalist framework. They differ most from the general public, however, on the divisive social issues that have emerged in the 1960s   abortion, gay rights, affirmative action, et cetera. Many are alienated from the "system" and quite critical of America's world role. They would like to strip traditional powerbrokers of their influence and empower black leaders, consumer groups, intellectuals, and . . . the media.[37]

Gun control is one of the divisive social issues covered by the blanket "et cetera" in the previous quote. In fact, it was one of the issues that a columnist Lichter, et. al. quote, Joseph Kraft, criticized his colleagues for writing "off as disconnected single issues."[38] If Lichter, et. al. are right, the typical member of the media elite has not lived

[37] S. Robert Lichtyer, Stanley Rothman, and Linda S. Lichter, *The Media Elite* (Bethesda Maryland: Adler & Adler, Publishers, inc., 1986), p. 294.

[38] Ibid., 33-34.

a life or acquired a political outlook that could be expected to have provided him/her with even minimal familiarity with firearms and the wide-ranging variety of traditionally-accepted uses to which various types are regularly put, or with any appreciation at all for the libertarian concerns of the defenders of the individual-rights interpretation of the Second Amendment.

But even most of those individuals with other than typical backgrounds who have achieved media-elite status may absorb the appropriate political perspectives once immersed in the cosmopolitan journalistic culture, as *Policy Review* managing editor Dinesh D'Souza has noted in his own publication concerning well-known TV journalists hailing from the nation's heartland.

No matter where he comes from, however, the aspiring TV journalist typically adopts a left-liberal world view as he picks up the tools of his trade. There is nothing conspiratorial in this. To get their stories on the air, TV journalists have to embrace the culture of network news, either consciously or unconsciously. It is only natural that an ambitious, social climbing reporter from the heartland who wants to please his colleagues and his superiors will absorb their ideas of what makes a good story, of what is considered responsible journalism. And since the culture of television journalism is liberal, it is hardly surprising that reporters get their idea of what is news — ultimately the most ideological question in journalism — from a whole range of left-liberal assumptions, inclinations, and expectations.[39]

When such shifts in perspectives occur, those who experience them are likely to view them in terms of maturation or intellectual growth rather than in terms of old ideologies being replaced by new ideologies, as D'Souza illustrates through a few revealing comments from the likes of TV's Sam Donaldson and Tom Brokaw.[40] The old assumptions are viewed not simply as different but as unenlightened. They have been examined and found wanting. The new assumptions go unexamined.

For the most part, therefore, it seems that members of the adversarial, cosmopolitan media elite responsible for keeping the public informed about such controversies as the one surrounding the widespread civilian ownership of guns in this country may be completely out of touch with, and even antagonistic toward, the world of guns that is part of a traditional bedrock America which they have either never known or known and rejected. That the world of guns is so alien to the media elite is reflected in their confusion over such a simple matter as the distinction between full-automatics, the civilian possession of which has been federally regulated since 1934, and semi-automatics that have been commonly used by civilians since the turn of the century. And the media elite's antagonism toward the world of guns is

---

[39] Diesh D'Souza, "Mr. Donaldson Goes to Washington: Politics and Social Climbing in the TV Newsroom," *Policy Review* (Summer, 1986), 24.

[40] Ibid., 24-25. For a sociological discussion of such tranformations, see Peter L. Berger, *Invitation to Sociology: A Humanistic Perspective* (Garden City, New York: Anchor Books, 1963), Ch. 3.

reflected in their reluctance to treat the inhabitants of that world as "authorized knowers" who can explain guns and the legitimate uses to which they are regularly put to that part of the public that is not familiar with them.[41] In fact, the major media regularly define these inhabitants and their organizations, particularly the NRA, as deviants not to be trusted, while they bestow "authorized-knower" status on the gun-control advocates who demonstrate little familiarity with guns or a desire to confuse the gun issue. For example, in a November 4, 1985 column in the old *Morning-Local*, well-known syndicated columnist Jack Anderson, who often berates the NRA, referred to Handgun Control, Inc. as a "public interest group."

Indeed, Canadian criminologists Ericson, Baranek, and Chan argue that marking off deviance in accordance with the expectations associated with the dominant ideologies is a defining feature of journalism in complex modern societies caught up in the ongoing battle between various class, ethnic, regional, and other factions over what is or is not acceptable behavior.[42] From this social-constructionist perspective, news is not simply reflecting reality or gathering facts but interpreting reality and telling stories. And this interpretation and story telling is a product of ongoing communication between journalists and influential sources or sources that journalists have come to consider credible.

This situation leaves the vast majority of citizens as mere spectators to the processes of deviance designation and control represented in the news. Moreover, it is extremely difficult for anyone outside the deviance-defining elite to penetrate its inner circle and sustain competing or alternative accounts.

The cultural and social organization of news work narrows the news aperture, so that the news is ideological or "partial" knowledge in two senses. First, it is partial because it gives preferred readings to the ideological messages of particular source organizations, either by omitting altogether the ideological messages of other organizations that have something to say on the matter or by relegating them a less significant status. News represents particular interests, allowing accounts of justification, excuse, and apology to selected individuals, organizations, and institutions. Journalists' "words are also deeds," enacting a view of the world partial to particular sources and their versions of reality

Second, this same methodology also makes news partial knowledge in the sense that it is "a procedure not to know." The very act of discovering and construing events in the world in journalistic terms blinds the journalist and consumers of his product to other ways of seeing. The result is not the whole truth but truth reduced to the genre capacities of the newspaper or broadcast-news item.[43]

[41] Richard V. Ericson, Patricia M. Baraneck, and Janet B. L. Chan, *Visualizing Deviance: A Study of News Organization* (Toronto: University of Toronto Press, 1987), pp 17-18.

[42] Ibid., Chapters 1 & 2.

[43] Ibid., 9.

Ericson, et. al. could have used the gun issue to illustrate these general news-creation processes. As Kates and Varzos have noted in Chapter 8, in some circles gun enthusiasts are considered to be psychiatrically suspect, and this view of them is reflected in a number of the columns, cartoons, and comic strips that I have cited in this study. Such sentiments are often projected through the offhand comments of newspersons as well. For example, I once heard a well-known TV journalist covering a shooting perpetrated by an emotionally-disturbed individual ask the person she was interviewing why the killer's interest in guns had not led his acquaintances to question his emotional stability. And of course, the NRA is routinely depicted as a rogue organization irresponsibly using its alleged great wealth to subvert democratic processes and the will of the American people — this in spite of the fact that pro-controllers receive millions of dollars worth of publicity for their position free of charge through the general media.[44]

Of course, unconventional and anti-control items are occasionally presented to the public through the general media, and some of these items are even produced by professional journalists.[45] However, such items are mere tokens that do not foster sustained debates, and they typically make no lasting impression on the ongoing general-media treatment of guns and their control and the conventional media wisdom that informs these treatments. Many pro-gun anti-controllers are convinced that this conventional media wisdom on guns is quite deliberately sustained by media folk who know better or easily could know better. They believe, in other words, that what Reed Irvine, the controversial driving force behind Accuracy in Media, has called "the Pinsky Principle" is routinely put to work when guns and gun controls are being covered. Walter Pinsky, a North Carolina Journalist, wrote in the *Columbia Review of Journalism* in 1976: "If my research and journalistic instincts tell me one thing, and my political instincts another . . . I won't fudge it, I won't bend it, but I won't write it."[46]

The Pinsky Principle may indeed help to account for the dearth of unconventional and anti-control items issuing forth from major-media outlets. Certainly, apparent media fakery of the sort exposed by Colonel Fackler does much to undermine faith in journalistic integrity. I myself have seen numerous TV reports on "assault weapons" showing full-automatics that are already federally regulated being fired while semi-automatics that pro-controllers want to regulate are being discussed. And on March 16, 1989, *CBS'* "48 Hours" showed reporter David Martin either violating a federal law by having a gunsmith convert a semi-automatic version of an AK-47 to

---

[44] David J. Bordua, "Gun Control and Opinion Measurement: Adversary Polling and the Construction of Social Meaning," in Kates (ed.) *Firearms and Violence*, pp. 51-70.

[45] See Allen, "The Mystique of Guns" (very unconcentional); Donald Baer, et al., "Guns," *U.S. News & World Report* (May, 1989) and accompanying articles, 20-28 (somewhat unconventional); and "Rifle Orientation" (editorial) *the Wall Street Journal* (Friday, March 24, 1989), A10 (verging on anti-control).

[46] Cited in Rael Jean Isaac and Erich Isaac *The Coercive Utopians: Social Deception by America's Power Players* (Chicago: Regnery Gateway, 1983), p. 269.

full-automatic, or as the technology branch of the Bureau of Alcohol, Tobacco, and Firearms apparently believes, reporting a fake conversion aimed at demonstrating that such operations can be carried out faster than they can actually be carried out.[47] Yet Ericson et. al. note that fakery of this sort is commonly practiced in newsrooms and is not thought of as intentional deception. Within the newsroom cultures they studied, the term "fake . . . referred to simulation devices, and fictions that would add order, coherence, and unity and thus make their items, segments, and entire newscasts more presentable and plausible."[48] If a reporter and his colleagues already think that they know how powerful an AK-47 is, but the hole in the melon does not dramatically demonstrate that power, why not use a hollow-point slug from a pistol to demonstrate the otherwise non-observable but assumed reality of AK-47 power? If a reporter sees no meaningful difference between full-automatics and semi-automatics, or believes that the latter can be easily converted to the former, why not use footage of the rapid-fire full-automatic to impress viewers with the capabilities of such weapons? In other words, having learned to see things a certain way through their interaction with colleagues and trusted sources, reporters have difficulty seeing them other ways and may resort to fakery to help news consumers to see things as reporters are convinced they really are.

While the studies and commentaries mentioned above did not examine general-media treatment of the gun issue, they all in various ways paint pictures of media culture and/or processes that shed light on what is commonly known as media bias. In shedding this light, they help to explain the major-media pro-gun control coverage that filters down to local areas more accepting of guns.

SUMMARY AND CONCLUSION

Gun control is a controversial issue in the United States, and controversies by definition have more than one side. Actually, there are at least three identifiable positions on gun control, pro-gun anti-control, pro-gun pro-control, and anti-gun pro-control, but the latter two positions share something that sets them apart from the first position — a trust in government and its police powers. How are the citizens of a nation dedicated to democratic principles to know which position to support and which to reject? Theoretically, a free press attempts to keep them fully informed by presenting them with the "facts" that various opposing factions consider to be relevant and with the arguments that the opposing factions put forth. Presumably, the citizen who knows nothing about the gun issue but who wants to become informed about it can acquire a basic familiarity with the views of the various opposing factions through his/her newspapers, TV news programs, and so forth — presumably. As I hope that I have convincingly demonstrated through this study of their treatment of

[47] Larry Pratt, Executive Director of Gun Owners of America, Inc., "CBS' Lie or Felony" (letters) Gun World (September, 1989), 8, 20.

[48] Ericson, et. at., 339.

the "assault-weapon" issue, readers relying on the newspapers of Evansville, Indiana to keep them informed about this gun issue would be far more familiar with the arguments of the pro-controllers, both pro- and anti-gun, than they would be with those of the pro-gun anti-controllers. And they would be even less informed about the pro-gun anti-control position, were it not for the ongoing letter-writing efforts of a few of their fellow readers to counter the steady stream of news stories grounded on the assumptions of the pro-controllers and of editorials, columns, cartoons, and comic strips blatantly supporting the pro-control position. These anti-control letters and guest columns were always defensive and prompted by attacks on the pro-gun anti-control position which has strong support in the Evansville region, by pro-control editorials and so forth, the vast majority of which came to the local newspapers via news-services and syndicates based in large urban centers. But while this grassroots input on "assault weapons" was reactive, it sparked no discernible reaction on the part of the newspapers, it generated no ongoing debate, and it was completely ignored by the faraway producers of pro-control and conventional items. It is this state of affairs that draws charges of media bias from pro-gun anti-controllers. Indeed, what else can it be called?

But how can such a situation exist in the newspapers of a small city located in a very pro-gun region? It can exist because the newsmen, editorial writers, syndicated columnists, political cartoonists, and comic strip artists who take stands on gun controls are, for the most part, products of, recruits to, or immersed in a world far different from the one, similar to those that Stenross, Olmsted, and I have described in Chapters 5, 6, 7, and 1, respectively, that makes guns such an accepted and non-threatening part of the lives of local pro-gun anti-controllers. This at least, is what several recent studies of and commentaries on the major media would suggest, even though none of them have dealt specifically with the gun-issue coverage of these media. The point that these studies make is not that a deliberate and consciously deceitful attempt to push a cosmopolitan world view is being conducted through these media, though Pinsky's comments indicate that such attempts can occur. The point they make is that the news and commentary transmitted to the rest of the nation through these urban outlets are heavily permeated by the unexamined assumptions of the cosmopolitan elites who consider the traditional ways of provincial bedrock America to be outdated and anti-progressive.

But intentionally or unintentionally, the cosmopolitan world view is being pushed relentlessly even through provincial media that are so dependent on cosmopolitan media outlets for their material. Letters to editors have no more discernible impact on the flow of conventional and pro-control items than a BB from an airgun has on the forward motion of a tank. Is it any wonder that people, even gun owners, who know no more about the gun controversy than they absorb through the general media regularly tell pollsters that they support whatever gun legislation is currently being promoted? Consider again Hummel's Chapter 11 offering. Only politically-active pro-gun anti-controllers who have been exposed to alternative gun realities through their own experiences, the gun press, and/or recent scholarly efforts are in a position to resist the reality of guns presented to them through their local newspapers, news magazines, network TV, and so forth. But defeats via referenda of various gun-control efforts thought to have widespread public support on the basis of poll results, such as the one described by Furnish in Chapter 10, seem to indicate that support for gun controls in many areas is still quite soft and easily undermined through exposure to the pro-gun anti-control position.[49] But pro-gun anti-controllers generally have to spend a great deal of money to combat the deviant label applied to them by the general media and to present their alternative view of the reality of guns to the public, while the pro-controllers enjoy public-interest-group status and have their views transmitted through the media free of charge. It remains to be seen how long this uneven battle between the entrenched pro-gun anti-controllers and the influential pro-controllers (pro- and anti-gun) to determine the place of firearms in our society can be waged.

[49] Also see Bordua, "Gun Control and Opinion Measurement."

APPENDIX

In the following pages, a day-by-day listing of "assault-weapon" items carried in each of the Evansville, Indiana newspapers during the period covered by this study — January 18, 1989 through July 17, 1989 — is presented. Grassroots items —letters to the editor, guest columns by local non-journalists, and purchased space —appear in **bold print,** while items done by local employees of these newspapers are *italicized* and news-service and syndicated items are not specially treated. Item and line counts are also provided and classified as Pro-Control (Pro-C), Conventional (Con), Unconventional (Uncon), and Anti-Control (Anti-C).

MORNING & SUNDAY-CHAIN

	Pro-C	Con	Uncon	Anti-C
January				
18 — News, AP		25		
22 — Editorial, Scripps Howard	40			
25 — Column, M. Royko, Chicago Tribune	140			
25 — Cartoon, ?	X			
February				
1 — Cartoon, United Features	X			
5 — Editorial, Scripps Howard	17			
5 — Letter, Evansville				43
5 — Letter, Evansville				32
10 — Letter, Evansville				7
11 — News, AP		32		
13 — Column, R. Cohen, Washington Post	103			
17 — Cartoon, United Features	X			
17 — Letter, Evansville	17			
20 — News, AP		5		
21 — News, New York Times		109		
21 — News, New York Times			51	
21 — Column, Washington summary			16	
22 — Column, A. McFeatters, Scripps Howard	42			
23 — Column, A.M. Rosenthal, New York Times	119			
23 — Letter, Evansville	23			
23 — Local News		66		
27 — Cartoon, United Features	X			
27 — Letter, Evansville				31
March				
6 — Local News		84		
9 — Local Guest Column				135
12 — Purchased				121
14 — News, New York Times		68		
14 — Column, A. McFeatters, Scripps Howard	4			
15 — Purchased				121
15 — News, Scripps Howard		67		
17 — Letter, Mt. Vernon, Indiana				52
17 — Local News			78	
18 — News, Wire Reports		112		

228.

EVENING-PRIVATE

	Pro-C	Con	Uncon	Anti-C
January				
21 — Canned Editorial	44			
24 — Cartoon, Copley News Service	X			
February				
1 — Cartoon, NEA	X			
2 — Column, G. McNatt, Baltimore Sun	96			
4 — Letter, Evansville				59
4 — Letter, Evansville				46
7 — Column, A. Buchwald, Los Angeles Times	71			
8 — News, UPI		79		
11 — Letter, Evansville				6
13 — Column, L. Grizzard, Atlanta Constitution	4			
17 — Letter, Evansville	30			
18 — Cartoon, NEA	X			
20 — Column, S. Grady, Knight-Ridder	96			
27 — Column, L. Grizzard, Atlanta Constitution	56			
March				
1 — Canned Editorial	51			
6 — Column, A. Buchwald, Los Angeles Times	68			
6 — Cartoon, NEA	X			
6 — Cartoon, NEA	X			
11 — Letter, Evansville				64
11 — Letter, Evansville				82
14 — News, UPI		31		
15 — News, Washington Post		133		
15 — Purchased				121
16 — News, UPI		57		
17 — Local Column			106	
18 — News, UPI		81		
20 — Local News			99	
20 — Column, S. Grady, Knight-Ridder	94			
21 — Column, A. Buchwald, Los Angeles Times	76			
23 — Column, G. Will, Washington Post	110			
25 — Column, S. Grady, Knight-Ridder	11			
25 — Letter, Evansville				84
25 — Letter, Evansville				52

MORNING & SUNDAY-CHAIN

	Pro-C	Con	Uncon	Anti-C
March				
19 — Local News			*63*	
19 — Editorial, Scripps Howard	43			
20 — Cartoon, United Features	X			
21 — Column, A. McFeatters, Scripps Howard	86			
23 — Letter, Newburgh, Indiana				44
24 — Column, M. Royko, Chicago Tribune	160			
25 — News, AP		33		
26 — Cartoon, United Features	X			
27 — Column, L. Larsen, Scripps Howard	87			
April				
3 — News, New York Times			106	
3 — Column, Los Angeles Times	9			
3 — Cartoon, United Features	X			
4 — Letter, Huntingburg, Indiana				42
4 — Column, A. McFeatters	4			
6 — Local Guest Column				190
9 — Column, R. Cohen, Washington Post	145			
17 — Letter, Evansville				13
18 — Column, R. Cohen, Washington Post	6			
20 — Letter, Evansville				47
24 — Comic Strip	X			
25 — Comic Strip	X			
25 — Column, J. Kilpatrick, Universal Press				123
25 — Letter, Evansville				36
26 — Column, R. Cohen, Washington Post	7			
27 — Comic Strip	X			
27 — Letter, Buckskin, Indiana				36
28 — Comic Strip	X			
30 — Column, A.H. Malcolm, New York Times	539			
May				
2 — Advertisement				6
5 — Column, P.C. Roberts, Scripps Howard				96
7 — Comic Strip	X			
7 — Column, L. Branham, Scripps Howard	107			
7 — Local Column	*101*			
10 — Column, J. Anderson, United Features	73			

EVENING-PRIVATE

	Pro-C	Con	Uncon	Anti-C
March				
31 — Comic Strip	X			
April				
4 — Column, A. Buchwald, Los Angeles Times	64			
6 — News, AP		36		
10 — Column, T. Clancy, Washington Post			153	
10 — Column, D. Shoemaker, Knight-Ridder	62			
10 — Column, L. Grizzard, Atlanta Constitution	77			
12 — News, AP		72		
14 — Letter, Evansville				37
15 — Cartoon, Copley News Service	X			
20 — Column, H. Johnson, Washington Post		1		
20 — News, Knight-Ridder		221		
21 — Column, L. Grizzard, Atlanta Constitution	8			
22 — Letter, Evansville		2		
22 — Cartoon, NEA	X			
24 — Cartoon, NEA	X			
25 — Column, C. Page, Chicago Tribune		1		
29 — Letter, Orleans, Indiana				70
May				
2 — Advertisement				6
2 — Cartoon, Copley News Service	X			
3 — *Local News*			77	
4 — Column, R. D'Angelo, Hartford Courant				135
5 — Letter, Wadesville, Indiana				25
11 — News, Los Angeles Times			5	
15 — News, AP		109		
15 — Column, Washington Post	13			
18 — Column, S. Grady, Knight-Ridder	97			
19 — Column, L. Grizzard, Atlanta Constitution	3			
25 — News, Washington			28	
27 — Column, L. Grizzard, Atlanta Constitution	72			
27 — Letter, New Harmony, Indiana				41
27 — Letter, Evansville				33
June				
1 — Comic Strip	X			
5 — Comic Strip	X			

MORNING & SUNDAY-CHAIN

	Pro-C	Con	Uncon	Anti-C
May				
12 — News, AP		44		
13 — Letter, Evansville	14			
14 — Letter, Evansville				88
14 — Letter, Boonville, Indiana				24
14 — Comic Strip	X			
16 — News, AP		38		
18 — Letter, Boonville, Indiana				41
20 — Comic Strip	X			
21 — Column, M. Royko, Chicago Tribune	43			
23 — Letter, Sturgis, Kentucky				20
25 — Comic Strip	X			
25 — News ?		13		
30 — Letter, Evansville				23
June				
1 — Letter, Carmi, Illinois				69
5 — Letter, New Harmony, Indiana				35
7 — *Cartoon, Local*				X
13 — Letter, Boonville, Indiana	41			
18 — News, AP		4		
18 — News, AP		139		
18 — Column, T. Teepen, Cox News Service	111			
26 — Column, R. Cohen, Washington Post	92			
July				
8 — News, Scripps Howard		76		
10 — Comic Strip			X	
12 — News, AP			54	
12 — Letter, Evansville				33
15 — Column, M. Royko, Chicago Tribune	114			
15 — Column, L. Branham, Scripps Howard	4			
17 — News, AP		12		
Total Item Count	44	17	7	27
	(46.3%)	(17.9%)	(7.4%)	(28.4%)
Total Line Count	2291	927	368	1508
	(45%)	(18.2%)	(7.2%)	(29.6%)

EVENING-PRIVATE

	Pro-C	Con	Uncon	Anti-C
June				
5 — Column, J. Katz, Washington Post			5	
6 — Column, A. Buchwald, Los Angeles Times	65			
15 — News, AP		21		
16 — News, AP			82	
17 — Letter, Newburg, Indiana	60			
17 — Canned Editorial	20			
21 — News, AP		46		
24 — Letter, Evansville				27
July				
7 — News, AP		51		
8 — News, Baltimore Sun		88		
12 — News, Washington			14	
14 — Canned Editorial	35			
15 — Letter, Evansville				6
15 — Letter, Henderson, Kentucky				22
Total Item Count	37	16	8	19
	(46.3%)	(20%)	(10%)	(23.8%)
Total Line Count	1383	1029	416	1069
	(35.5%)	(26.4%)	(10.7%)	(27.4%)

233.

pro-gun anti-controllers who have been exposed to alternative gun realities through their own experiences, the gun press, and pro-gun voluntary efforts are in a position to resist the reality of guns presented to them through their local newspapers, news magazines, network TV, and so forth. But defeats via referenda of various gun-control efforts thought to have widespread public support on the basis of poll results, such as the one described by Furnish in Chapter 10, seem to indicate that support for gun controls in many areas is still quite soft and easily undermined through exposure to the pro-gun anti-control position. But pro-gun anti-controllers generally have to spend a great deal of money to combat the deviant label applied to them by the general media and to present their alternative view of the reality of guns to the public, while the pro-controllers enjoy public-interest-group status and have their views transmitted through the media free of charge. It remains to be seen how long this uneven battle between the entrenched pro-gun anti-controllers and the influential pro-controllers (pro- and anti-gun) to determine the place of firearms in our society can be waged.

About the Authors

Eugene Balof is head of the Department of Communications and Theatre at the University of North Alabama in Florence. He received his BA in political science from Augustana College and holds a Ph.D. from the University of Missouri. Dr. Balof teaches courses in communications and media. He has also consulted for a variety of organizations and individuals in government and business.

Brendan F.J. Furnish is Professor of Sociology and chair of the Sociology Department at Westmont College in Santa Barbara, CA. He holds degrees from California State University, San Francisco (B.A., M.A.), and the University of Southern California (Ph.D.). Dr. Furnish has taught at Westmont College for 21 years. He came to sociology from a background in physics and electronics and has published books and articles on a variety of different areas of sociology. He is presently completing a book (with Dwight H. Small) on "the ethics of armed self-defense."

F. Frederick Hawley, a native of Louisiana, received his doctorate in Criminology from Florida State University. His research and publication interests include folk crime (e.g. cockfighting), sociology of law, violence and the study of the media/crime issue relationship. In 1989 he contributed the principal article on guns in the South to the authoritative *Encyclopedia of Southern Culture.* He is continuing his decade-long review and examination of the Southern Violence Construct.
Presently, Dr. Hawley is Professor of Criminal Justice and chairman of the Department of Social Sciences at Louisiana State University in Shreveport.

Richard Hummel is a Professor of Sociology at Eastern Illinois University where he has taught since 1969. He received his Ph.D. from Indiana University in 1976.
Professor Hummel is researching the issue of public opinion regarding firearms issues and the factors which affect public perceptions of the nature of firearms and their uses. He is also conducting ongoing research into the history, social psychology, and social conflicts surrounding "blood sports" (hunting and fishing). He took an academic sabbatical in 1987 to engage in participant observation of the various types of sport hunting adventures marketed to the American sport hunter. His arduous research took him to Scotland (two times), Canada, Idaho (two times), Texas and Africa (Zimbabwe). The results of those researches are being compiled into a planned forthcoming book on the blood sports.

Don B. Kates, Jr. has been a civil rights activist in the South and has also been an associate professor of law at St. Louis University. Mr. Kates attended Reed College and is a graduate of Yale Law School. Currently a civil liberties attorney in San Francisco, he does much work on gun-ownership rights, is a Second Amendment scholar, and is a nationally-recognized authority on these subjects.
Mr. Kates is the editor of *Restricting Handguns: The Liberal Skeptics Speak Out, Firearms and Violence: Issues of Public Policy,* and special gun-control

issues of such journals as *Law & Policy Quarterly* and *Law and Contemporary Problems*. He has not only edited these collections but contributed to them, and his numerous articles have appeared in a variety of publications — scholarly, legal, and professional journals; popular, outdoor, and firearms magazines; and newspapers, large and small. Mr. Kates is the author of the entry on the Second Amendment in the *Encyclopedia of the American Constitution*.

David B. Kopel formerly served as an Assistant District Attorney in New York City and is now practicing law in Denver. Mr. Kopel graduated from the University of Michigan Law School, where he served on the *Michigan Law Review*. He earned his Bachelor of Arts in history from Brown University. Mr. Kopel's thesis, *The Highbrow in American Politics: Arthur M. Schlesinger Jr. and the Role of the Intellectual in History* was awarded the National Historical Society Prize.

The Cato Institute published Mr. Kopel's Policy Analysis, *Trust the People: The Case Against Gun Control* in July 1988. His op-ed articles on subjects including the right to bear arms, world hunger, civil liberties, the environment, and animal rights have appeared in the *Wall Street Journal, the Baltimore Sun, the Rocky Mountain News, the Houston Post, the Chicago Tribune*, and elsewhere.

Mr. Kopel is presently a Special Consultant for Firearms Policy for the National Association of Chiefs of Police.

Edward F. Leddy is currently teaching in the Criminal Justice Program at Tarleton State University in Stephenville, Texas. After receiving his bachelor's degree from Manhattan College, he worked for many years as a New York State parole officer in the South Bronx before completing his Ph.D. at Fordham University.

Professor Leddy is the author of *Magnum Force Lobby: The National Rifle Association Fights Gun Control*, an analysis of the National Rifle Association and its role in the gun controversy, and is editor of the *Journal on Firearms and Public Policy*.

A. D. Olmsted is Associate Professor of Sociology at the University of Calgary. He received his B.A. and M.A. degrees in sociology from the University of Saskatchewan and his Ph.D. from the University of Washington.

Professor Olmsted's areas of interest are social psychology, community, human ecology, gun ownership, and collectors and collecting. "Morally Controversial Leisure: The Social World of Gun Collectors," his recent article in *Symbolic Interaction*, is based on insights drawn from these various areas of interest.

John R. Salter, Jr. is Professor and chair of the Department of American Indian Studies at the University of North Dakota, Grand Forks. He is a sociologist and community organizer who did much trade union organizing in the 1950s; was deeply involved in the Southern Civil Rights Movement in the 1960s; and directed large-scale community justice organizing in Chicago and Rochester, NY, in the 1970s. Prof. Salter has taught at, among other places, Tougaloo College (sociology), Coe College (sociology), and the University of Iowa (graduate program in Urban & Regional Planning).

He is the author of *Jackson, Mississippi: An American Chronicle of Struggle & Schism;* and many articles on civil rights, civil liberties, and social justice

—including "Reflections on the Klan and Poor People," and "Reflections on Ralph Chaplin, the Wobblies, and Organizing in the Save the World Business — Then and Now." He was awarded the 1989 Martin Luther King, Jr. Award by the North Dakota State Martin Luther King, Jr. Commission and Gov. George Sinner.

Barbara Stenross is lecturer, Department of Sociology, and academic adviser, College of Arts and Sciences, The University of North Carolina at Chapel Hill. She received her B.A. from Wittenberg University, her M.A. from Duke University, and her Ph.D. from Indiana University, Bloomington.

Her research interests include work, leisure, and material culture. Her most recent publication is "The Highs and Lows of Emotional Labor: Detectives' Encounters with Criminals and Victims," *Journal of Contemporary Ethnography* 17, January 1989 (with Sherryl Kleinman). An article examining how gun enthusiasts create dignifying accounts to deal with outsiders' negative definitions is forthcoming in Clinton Sanders (ed.), *Marginal Conventions: Popular Culture, Mass Media, and Social Deviance* (Bowling Green State University: The Popular Press).

William R. Tonso is Professor of Sociology at the University of Evansville, IN, where he has taught a wide variety of courses since 1969 but has specialized in the areas of social deviance and ethnic and minority group relations. He received his Ph.D. in sociology from Southern Illinois University-Carbondale, and his B.S. in industrial education and M.S. in business administration (personnel management) from the same institution.

Professor Tonso became interested in the gun issue during the late 1950s, and his sociological interest in the subject began to develop in the late 1960s. He is the author of *Gun and Society: The Social and Existential Roots of the American Attachment to Firearms,* and a contributor to *Firearms and Violence: Issues of Public Policy,* edited by Don B. Kates, Jr. His shorter gun-issue pieces have appeared in several scholarly and professional journals; popular, outdoor, and firearms magazines; and a number of local, major, and national newspapers. Dr. Tonso has also presented papers on the gun issue at scholarly meetings and at a Congressional symposium.

Nicole Varzos, M.A., is a doctoral student in clinical psychology at the Professional School of Psychology located in San Francisco. She has, for the past four years, served as a Staff Research Associate for the University of California, Davis, Medical Center in the Departments of Physical Medicine and Rehabilitation and Psychiatry.

Her research has centered on testing and assessment of adolescents with spina bifida, children and adults with neuromuscular diseases and young victims of sexual abuse. Ms. Varzos has authored and co-authored various abstracts and articles for the *Archives of Physical Medicine and Rehabilitation* and *Developmental Medicine and Child Neurology.* She is currently on staff with the Roseville Community Hospital as case manager for the Teenage Pregnancy and Parenting Program.

Roy Wortman is Professor of History at Kenyon College. He received his Ph.D. in History at Ohio State University. Dr. Wortman offers coursework in United States social, labor and cultural history.

The author of *From Syndicalism to Trade Unionism,* he has also written articles on labor and ethnic history and served as humanities advisor for the Ohio Farmers Union in the American Farm Project, an endeavor designed to bring the humanities to non-traditional farm audiences. Additionally, he worked in the field of labor education with local unions and was involved in other adult education projects for community service. His current research is on agricultural protest in the United States since the New Deal. He has a special interest in civil liberties issues, especially in the area of Second Amendment constitutional matters.